D0122209

Agricultural and Rural Development in Indonesia

Also of Interest

Indonesia, Donald W. Fryer and James C. Jackson

Indonesia's Oil, Sevinc Carlson

Rice in the Tropics: A Guide to Development of National Programs, Robert F. Chandler, Jr.

Irrigated Rice Production Systems: Design Procedures, Jaw-Kai Wang and Ross E. Hagan

Administering Agricultural Development in Asia: A Comparative Analysis of Four National Programs, Richard W. Gable and J. Fred Springer

Food, Politics, and Agricultural Development: Case Studies in the Public Policy of Rural Modernization, edited by Raymond F. Hopkins, Donald J. Puchala, and Ross B. Talbot

Appropriate Technology for Development: A Discussion and Case Histories, edited by Donald D. Evans and Laurie Nogg Adler

Agricultural Credit for Small Farm Development: Policies and Practices, David D. Bathrick

Bangladesh: The Test Case for Development, Just Faaland and John Richard Parkinson

Agriculture in the Third World: A Spatial Analysis, W. B. Morgan

Managing Pastures and Cattle Under Coconuts, Donald L. Plucknett

Small Farm Development: Understanding and Improving Farming Systems in the Humid Tropics, Richard R. Harwood

Plantation Agriculture, Second Revised Edition, P. P. Courtenay

Underdevelopment and Agrarian Structure in Pakistan, Mahmood Hason Khan

Green Revolution? edited by B. H. Farmer

The Agrarian Structure of Bangladesh: An Impediment to Development, F. Tomasson Jannuzi and James T. Peach

Westview Special Studies in
Social, Political, and Economic Development

Agricultural and Rural Development
in Indonesia
edited by Gary E. Hansen

This book provides a broad, interdisciplinary overview of the major facets of Indonesia's contemporary agricultural and rural development, while exploring the macro
and micro factors that account for uneven development
patterns. In assessing the rate and distribution of
economic growth within the rural sector of the Indonesian
archipelago, the authors analyze trends in employment
generation, income distribution, and smallholder agricultural production. They specifically examine policy dimensions of agricultural production, the Green Revolution,
the effects of migration, and resource management of fisheries and forests. Emphasis is placed on the island of
Java as the most-studied area of Indonesia.

Dr. Gary E. Hansen is research associate at the East-
West Center's Resource Systems Institute in Honolulu.
From July 1978 to August 1979 he was team leader for an
AID-funded project with the government of Indonesia to
design a short- and long-term national training strategy
in regional planning and management.

Agricultural and Rural Development in Indonesia

edited by Gary E. Hansen

Westview Press / Boulder, Colorado

Chapter 2, by C. Peter Timmer, is drawn from a longer essay entitled "The Political Economy of Rice in Indonesia," which appeared in *Food Research Institute Studies*, Vol. XIV, No. 3, 1975.

Portions of Chapter 3, by Anne Booth, appeared under the title "Ipeda--Indonesia's Land Tax," in *Bulletin of Indonesian Economic Studies*, Vol. X, No. 1, March 1974.

Chapter 4, by Dibyo Prabowo and Sajogyo, appeared in the book *Changes in Rice Farming in Selected Areas of Asia*, published by the International Rice Research Institute in 1975.

Portions of Chapter 7, by Dwight King and Peter Weldon, appeared as an article under the title "Income Distribution and Levels of Living in Java, 1963-1970," in *Economic Development and Cultural Change*, 25:4 (July 1977):699-712. Reprinted by permission of the University of Chicago Press.

Portions of Chapter 13, by Anne Stoler, have appeared under the title "Garden Use and Household Economy in Rural Java," *Bulletin of Indonesian Economic Studies*, Vol. XIV, No. 2, July 1978.

Portions of Chapter 15, by William Collier, have appeared in *Income, Employment and Food Systems in Javanese Coastal Villages*, by William Collier, Harjadi Hadikoesworo, and Suwardi Saropie, published by Ohio University Center for International Studies, Southeast Asia Series, No. 44, 1977.

Westview Special Studies in Social, Political, and Economic Development

Published in 1981 in the United States of America by
Westview Press, Inc.
5500 Central Avenue
Boulder, Colorado 80301
Frederick A. Praeger, Publisher

Library of Congress Catalog Card Number: 80-24414
ISBN: 0-86531-124-2

Composition for this book was provided by the editor
Printed and bound in the United States of America

Contents

The Contributors

Achmad T. Birowo is Chief of the Bureau of Planning in
the Ministry of Agriculture and Director of the Agro
Economic Survey. He is also chairman of the Agricultural
Economic Society of Southeast Asia and former chairman
of the Indonesian Society of Agricultural Economists.

Anne Booth is an economist and is currently a Research
Fellow in the Department of Economics, Research School of
Pacific Studies, at Australia National University. She
was also on the faculty for several years at the Univer-
sity of Singapore. She conducted extensive field work in
Indonesia on land taxation in 1972-1973 and returned to
Indonesia in 1975 to work with the National Planning Pro-
gramme in Jakarta.

William L. Collier is an agricultural economist and since
1968 he has been an Associate of the Agricultural Development Council assigned to the Agro Economic Survey and
the Bogor Agricultural University.

Paul Deuster is an economist and faculty member in the
Department of Economics at Ohio University. He was in
Indonesia in 1968-1969 and 1972-1973 to conduct extensive
field research. He has made a number of return visits to
Indonesia and Malaysia in undertaking assignments on
problems of rural and agricultural development.

Wade Edmundson is a geographer and is currently on the
faculty at the University of New England in Armidale, New
South Wales. He undertook research in Indonesia in 1970-
1971 and has since returned to Indonesia on repeated
visits in conducting studies on the relation between
energy intake and human metabolic efficiency.

Gary E. Hansen is a research associate at the Resource
Systems Institute, East-West Center. His first assign-
ment in Indonesia was as a Ford Foundation staff member

from 1963 to 1965. He was a Fulbright Scholar in Indonesia from 1969 to 1970 and has made repeated visits to
Indonesia to undertake assignments relating to rural and
agricultural development.

Arthur J. Hanson is an ecologist who recently completed a
five-year stay in Indonesia, working with the Ford Foundation. He was affiliated with the Bogor Agricultural
University and assisted in the establishment of resource
and environmental activities there and in other universities. At present he is the Director of the Institute
for Environmental Studies at Dalhousie University, Hali-
fax, Nova Scotia.

Dwight King is on the faculty in the Department of Political Science at Northern Illinois University. From
1972 to 1975 he resided in Indonesia where he conducted
research and acted as a consultant to the Central Bureau
of Statistics in Jakarta.

Timothy Mahoney is an anthropologist and is currently on
the staff of the Agency for International Development.
He spent 1975-1976 in Indonesia conducting research on
rural development.

Willem Meijer is a faculty member in the Department of
Botany at the University of Kentucky. He was a botanist
at the Botanical Garden in Bogor from 1951 to 1954, and
served as a forest botanist in Sabah from 1959 to 1968.
He also served on the Faculty of Agriculture at Andalas
University in West Sumatra from 1955 to 1958.

Roger Montgomery is currently serving as an agricultural
economist on the staff of the International Maize and
Wheat Research Center in New Delhi. From 1976 to 1979
he was on the Ford Foundation staff teaching at the Bogor
Agricultural University and working on the analysis of
agricultural census data at the Central Bureau of Statistics in Jakarta. He also spent 1971-1972 in Indonesia
undertaking research on trade and labor absorption in
rural Java.

Dibyo Prabowo is an economist and a member of the Faculty
of Economics at Gadjah Mada University.

Sajogyo is a rural sociologist and a member of the faculty at the Bogor Agricultural University. He is a former
director of the Agro Economic Survey and is currently
Director of the Institute of Rural Sociological Research.

Alden Speare, Jr., is a member of the faculty in the Department of Sociology at Brown University. From 1974 to

1976 he worked as a Population Council staff associate assigned to the Population Studies Center of LEKNAS, LIPI in Jakarta.

Anne L. Stoler is currently a Fulbright Fellow in Indonesia. She is working on a social history of Javanese plantation workers in North Sumatra. From 1972-1973, she carried out field research in rural Central Java on the relationship between economic stratification, household production strategies, and the position of women.

C. Peter Timmer is a faculty member in the School of Public Health, Harvard University. He served as an economic advisor to the Indonesian National Planning Agency from 1970 to 1972. He has made repeated return visits to Indonesia in undertaking various assignments relating to food and agricultural policy.

Peter Weldon is a sociologist and served on the staff of the Ford Foundation in Jakarta from 1973 to 1978. He was involved in a national Indonesia social science training program and served as a lecturer and consultant on a number of research projects. He is currently a staff member of the Ford Foundation in Bangkok, Thailand.

Benjamin White is an anthropologist and since 1975 he has been assigned by the Agricultural Development Council to the Agro Economic Survey in Bogor to undertake a long-term study of rural change relating to production systems, employment and rural institutions. He also undertook research in rural Java in 1972-1973. He currently has a Research Fellowship at the Institute of Social Studies, The Hague.

Preface

Surprisingly little is known about the underlying
economic and social features which characterize the diverse and variegated patterns of agricultural production
in the Indonesian archipelago. For the most part, sufficient funds and manpower have not been available within
institutions of higher learning and government research
units in Indonesia to undertake sustained and systematic
research in examining the composition of ecological,
social, and economic relationships which structure the
process of resource use and allocation within the rural
economy. This lack of data generation applies equally
well from both the macro and micro perspective. Thus,
very little research has been undertaken on policy and
program assessments relating to agricultural and rural
development, and only a limited number of base-line
studies are available which explore and monitor economic
and social change at the farm and village level. In
recent years a more concerted effort is being made to
extend greater financial and institutional support for
socio-economic research within the rural sector but sufficient numbers of skilled manpower are still lacking in
managing this task. The social and agricultural sciences
will continue to require substantial support in order to
build a larger skill and knowledge base in these professions and to assure that the research function is accord-
ed its proper role in addressing the larger problem of
rural change and agricultural growth.

As the process of research on policy and more basic
structural problems of development in the rural sector
acquire greater momentum and depth, it is important that
studies and research findings be made available for wider
circulation in order to foster further discussion and
examination of basic substantive and methodological issues. This book is dedicated to this purpose. It is
hoped that it will contribute to a greater understanding
of major problem areas in rural and agricultural development in Indonesia and that it will also illuminate areas

where future research might be undertaken in acquiring a
more balanced and holistic view of rural and village dynamics. In this context, the essays in this book will
likely foster the asking of more questions than they will
serve to offer answers. If this is the case, then the
purpose of the book has been accomplished. Too little is
known to provide highly reliable generalizations on the
character and direction of rural and agricultural change
in Indonesia, but enough is known to generate some new
courses of inquiry.

The essays in this book do not cover all aspects of
the agricultural continuum in Indonesia. There are no
essays which focus upon the plantation sector or upon
swidden agriculture. There is also a bias towards
coverage of Java, largely because most research on agricultural and rural development has taken place in this
area. Nonetheless, a word of caution is warranted in
noting that the material on Java should not be viewed as
representative of social and economic conditions in this
densely populated island. Despite its small size, the
character of rural society in Java is much more hetero-
geneous than what is revealed in a cursory review of the
aggregate data. This diversity is known to most who have
explored Java's countryside, but the range of variation
is much less understood.

Much appreciation is owed to Theodore Smith, President of the Agricultural Development Council, and to Tom
Kessinger, Representative of the Ford Foundation in Indonesia, for the financial assistance provided by their
offices in supporting the publication of the book. In
addition, particular thanks are in order to Karl Jackson
for his continuous encouragement and support during the
preparation of the volume.

Gary E. Hansen

Agricultural and Rural
Development in Indonesia

1
Agricultural and Rural Development: An Overview

Achmad T. Birowo and Gary E. Hansen

Spread over an expanse of nearly three thousand miles along the equator, the nation of Indonesia, with its three thousand islands, provides a diverse range of topographical and climatic conditions for the growing of a wide variety of agricultural crops. While monsoons are a dominant meteorological feature within this great archipelago, significant variations can be found in rainfall patterns, with the level of precipitation showing a gradual, but marked decline in moving towards the southern and eastern parts of the island chain. Thus, many areas in Kalimantan and Sumatra receive a higher rainfall than is the case in Java, whereas much drier conditions can be found in the eastern Nusa Tenggara islands. The benefits of a relatively stable monsoon pattern are further enhanced by the varied terrain of most of the islands, which allows for the cultivation of both highland and lowland agricultural crops. While detailed soil and land use surveys have yet to be undertaken, in most areas of Indonesia it appears that topographical conditions can be classified into three major terrain patterns: (1) mountainous land (mainly lithosols and andosols) which account for approximately 66 percent of Indonesia's total land area, (2) level or undulating to hilly land (mainly red-yellow podzolics, ferralsols, red-brown mediterranean soils, and regosols), which account for 32 percent of total land area, and (3) swampy lands (mainly organic soils and alluvials) which accounts for 27 percent of total land area. Much of Sulawesi (69 percent of its total land area) and Kalimantan (41 percent of its total land area) fall within the first category, whereas Nusa Tenggara scores very high (59 percent) in the second category. The three terrain types can be found in roughly equal proportion in Java (including Bali and Madura) and Sumatra.

The absence of soil maps makes it difficult to accurately assess the extent to which Indonesia's variegated topography could be made available for suitable agricul-

tural purposes. Current estimates suggest that a sizeable proportion, perhaps up to 80 percent, of the level
to hilly areas, might be a potential agricultural resource,
whereas a much smaller portion (10 to 20 percent) of the
swampy and mountainous land would be available for cultivation. These estimates would suggest that from a total
land area of approximately 200 million hectares, roughly
60 million hectares would be suitable for agricultural
use. From this potential base figure approximately 16
million hectares are already under cultivation, with
another 24 million hectares set aside for forestry reserves and concessions. It therefore appears that a remaining 20 million hectares could be brought under agricultural cultivation, with most of this potential being
confined to the islands of Sumatra, Kalimantan, and Sulawesi.

While most of Indonesia's current and future investments within the agricultural sector will be confined to
the major islands of Kalimantan, Sulawesi, Sumatra, and
Java, which together account for roughly 70 percent of
Indonesia's land area, Java, with only 6 percent of the
total land mass, still assumes a dominant role in the accounting for a very high proportion of the country's total agricultural production. Thus, among the major field
crops, Java accounts for 75 percent of Indonesia's total
corn production, 60 percent of its sweet potatoes, 80
percent of its cassava, 90 percent of its soybeans, all
of its total sugar output, and finally, for approximately
50 percent of total rice production. These figures reflect a major difference in modes of land utilization between Java and the outer islands, with almost 70 percent
or more of Java being cultivated year round, and only
about 4 to 6 percent of total land area currently being
used for agricultural purposes in the outer islands. The
agricultural pattern in the outer islands is still based
upon more extensive dry-land or swidden cultivation techniques, whereas on Java, irrigated and rainfed wet rice
cultivation has emerged as the dominant agricultural pattern.

Swidden agriculture involves the clearing of forested areas, with the land being subjected to a cycle of
intermittent cultivation interspersed with much longer
fallow periods when the soil is allowed to recover its
natural fertility. The cropping regimen in a particular
swidden plot is usually quite diverse and can involve the
intercropping of more than a dozen of such cultigens as
dry rice, cassava, gourds, maize, yams and a wide range
of other vegetables and fruits. Hudson points out in his
study of agricultural practices in Kalimantan that swidden culture involves both commercial and subsistence features.

In almost all areas where it is practiced, the
swidden horticultural system serves as only one
strand in a multiplex socio-economic system that
has both subsistence and cash components. The
subsistence component involves not only the products of horticulture, but of fishing, hunting,
and the gathering of such commodities as rubber,
rattan, and timber, but could probably be expanded to include other cultigens suited to non-
alluvial soils of the region. The multiple
strands of the subsistence and cash components
form an integrated but loose mesh to create a
fabric that is flexible enough to adjust fairly
easily to cover a wide variety of conditions.
Depending on the climatic, social, economic,
and political conditions obtaining at any given
time, it is possible for the swidden to place
greater emphasis on one or another strand in
the system without rending the fabric.[1]

Early in this century many swidden farmers began to adopt
a more commercial orientation in the smallholding cultivation of rubber, a tree which can be grown and maintained with minimal care and tapped when the market is
favored by relative high export prices.

The dynamics of swidden agriculture, in the outer islands, contrast sharply with the intensive double and multiple cropping patterns associated with small farm wet-
rice culture in Java. The typical Javanese farmer must
operate within the narrow confines of having access to
only a few miniscule plots, for which he must press the
soil into continuous service, following a cropping pattern which varies according to whether the land is an
irrigated (sawah) wet-rice parcel, or whether an unirrigated tegalan plot. Many farmers will have both kinds of
parcels under cultivation, in addition to a house garden
for the growing of fruits and vegetables. Approximately
half of all smallholder cultivated land in Java falls
within the category of sawah land, with the remaining half
being mostly unirrigated land along with some coastal
ponds.

More than 40 percent of the total sawah land in Java
is serviced by modern irrigation facilities, enabling farmers to plant rice crops in both the wet and dry seasons,
whereas the remaining sawah land is dependent upon more
elementary village and rain-fed systems, which frequently
allow for only a wet season rice crop, followed by the
planting of soybeans, maize, or other secondary crops in
the dry season. Corn, the second largest user of land,
along with cassava, soybeans, groundnuts, and sweet potatoes, accounts for the dominant crop selection in tegalan
areas.

While the plantation sector constitutes an important component within the agricultural economy, in all the major islands, peasant smallholder production still remains as the dominant organizational mode for the production of approximately two-thirds of total rubber production, for practically all copra and coffee production, and for all of the production of rice and other secondary food crops. On Java, approximately 5.4 million hectares are under smallholder cultivation, as opposed to 676,000 hectares under estate control, whereas in Sumatra 3.8 million hectares is under smallholder production with 1.3 million hectares being under estate control. In Sulawesi and Kalimantan the plantation sector accounts for less than 10 percent of total land under cultivation.

While in the past half century the outer islands have continued to assume a larger role in the total agricultural economy, the island of Java still occupies a position of critical importance in the structure of agricultural development. Historically, Java has held a comparative advantage by virtue of its highly fertile volcanically enriched soils, and in the precolonial and colonial eras there evolved a relatively intensive and elaborate agro-economic system in the cultivation of its generous resource endowment. It was in Java that the great Hinduized kingdoms took root, basing their power and complex administrative hierarchies upon the taxes generated from a rice intensive agricultural economy. In the subsequent period of protracted colonial rule, Java assumed a pivotal role as the cornerstone of the Dutch imperial empire, with its agricultural products commanding a position of major importance in the markets of world trade. From beginning to end, the major vector of colonial policy was centered in Java, where sizeable investments were made in the development of a transport, irrigation, and administrative network designed to enhance the production of export crops. In the early years of colonial rule, Java's agricultural produce was extracted by means of forced deliveries from the smallholder producer, but in later years, particularly with the advent of the so-called "Liberal Policy" in the 1870s, the plantation system began to emerge as the major institutional mode of growing and exporting agricultural products, with many Javanese peasants now functioning as full or part-time wage labor in these commercial enterprises.

The preeminent role of Java in Indonesia's agricultural economy is in some measure reflected in the rapid growth of population on this small island. Within a one century period, from 1870 to 1973, Java's population grew from a total of 16.2 million to 80,077 million.[2] The principal factors which gave rise to this rapid increase are the subject of considerable scholarly analysis, but at the very least, this growth in numbers is indicative of the immensely favorable climatological and geological

conditions for the cultivation of irrigated rice in the
island's rich alluvial basins, and the attendant responsiveness of Javanese social structure in readily absorbing higher levels of labor inputs in the more intensive
care and cultivation of its rice fields. Nevertheless,
beginning with the turn of this century, when most available agricultural land in Java was already under cultivation, the pressures generated from a rapidly decreasing
land/man ratio began to place considerable stress upon
the island's resource endowment. With most of the lowland agricultural areas already under intensive farming,
many peasants began to move to higher elevations in order
to cultivate the hillsides and mountain slopes within the
hinterland. By World War II, these practices had resulted in the elimination of Java's arable forest land,
and during the past 30 years the denuding of forest land
for agricultural cropping has increased, particularly in
East and Central Java, where erosion and attendant problems in flooding and the silting up of low-land irrigation networks has become quite extensive. The rapid
diminution in additional and suitable agricultural land
for outward expansion on Java has been accompanied by a
simultaneous "inward" expansion in the form of increasing
fragmentation of existing farm land, and a decline in
average farm size. According to the 1973 Agricultural
Census, approximately 47 percent of all land in Java is
under cultivation and most of this land is under smallholder use, with an average farm size of .64 compared to
1.34 hectares for Sumatra, 2.71 for Kalimantan, and 1.38
for Sulawesi.[3] Whereas, approximately 58 percent of all
farm holdings in Java are less than 0.5 hectares, the
figure is only 25 to 30 percent for the outer islands.

In general, the aggregate data, when compared to
other developing countries, reveals that Indonesia does
not suffer from a high level of tenancy or of conditions
where a minority of farmers hold a large percentage of
the agricultural land. For Indonesia as a whole, 74.8
percent of all farms are entirely owner operated, and
even in Java 73.5 percent of all farms are fully owner
operated.[4] Montgomery and Sugito note that only 83,700
farms, from a national total of 14 million farms, are ten
hectares or more in size, and that these holdings are
concentrated in the outer islands where tree crops and
shifting cultivation constitute the dominant cropping
patterns.[5] In Java itself, farms below 0.5 hectares account for 63 percent of total area under cultivation.

While the aggregate census data indicates that Indonesia does not suffer from high levels of inequality in
landholdings, it seems very likely that these quantitative
indicators are understating important differences in both
relative and absolute measures of rural welfare, particularly in Java where, in starting from a remarkably low
base figure of .64 in average size of farm holding, any

standing above or below this average can mean the difference between near impoverishment or relative economic security. When the category of landless households is
added in, a group which numbers at least two million
households, most of which are located in Java, it becomes
apparent that even minor differences in the possession or
control of land can account for major variations in economic welfare. The existence of these differences assumes a somewhat greater reality when viewed in the context of Sajogyo's calculations that, based upon a poverty
line of a per capita annual income equivalent of 240 kg
of rice, 57 percent of Java's rural inhabitants are
having to sustain themselves at a level below this minimum standard.[6] The privations associated with such per-
vasive conditions of poverty are no doubt reflected in
Indonesia's high rate of infant mortality and the widespread incidence of such nutritional deficiencies as protein and calorie malnutrition, and nutritional anemia.
More important is the fact that the poverty line calculation is an indicator of higher levels of relative inequality than is conveyed in the aggregate census data.
These disparities in rural welfare are more fully revealed in micro level qualitative data where numerous
case studies indicate that in many villages in Java, 40-
60 percent of the peasant households are landless or near
landless, that many smallholder households have simply
lost control over their land by virtue of their indebtedness to money lenders, and that a high proportion of village land is frequently under the control of large landholders. In brief, it appears that many small farmers
have simply been transformed into sharecroppers and are
cultivating their land at the cost of having to give over
a sizeable portion of the harvest to creditors. Large
numbers of landless peasants are involved in similar
arrangements, where credit indebtedness entails repayment
through the provision of labor at very low returns.

With a sizeable proportion of Java's rural households having little or no access to agricultural land,
many peasant families must seek employment in a diverse
range of income producing activities, some involving
agricultural wage labor, but with a large proportion of
their labor involving off-farm activities in petty trade,
construction, animal husbandry, handicrafts, fishing, and
other related activities. As observed by White, "occupational multiplicity" becomes a survival strategy for
these households, with the younger members of a family
performing household chores in order to relieve the older
children and the male and female adults to assume some
role in the labor market.[7] Given their lack of capital
and savings, and an environment where higher wage employment is quite scarce, these households frequently have no
choice but to accept work involving very low levels of
labor productivity and low returns for labor. Thus, in

many areas of Java, the concept of unemployment is less applicable than is a situation where members of low income households are having to work long hours in a wide range of endeavors in order to meet their minimum welfare needs. This condition stands in contrast to medium and larger landholding households, where by virtue of having access to capital assets (land), and their attendant income producing activities, adult household members are able to be much more selective in engaging in activities which yield much higher returns to labor than would be the case for members of landless and near landless households. These differences in labor allocation patterns reveal, in great measure, the dire implications of having little or no access to agricultural land. Heads of such households and many of their dependents operate at the edge of poverty where the constant quest for employment, no matter how low the productivity or marginal returns to labor, represent an unavoidable imperative in the struggle for survival.

The problem of poverty and declining welfare levels within the rural sector, particularly and most primarily on Java, has been magnified by the inability of the agricultural economy, and more explicitly, the food crop sector, to grow at a rate equal to the needs of feeding a large and growing population. Early in the 1950s, rice imports were used to fill the gap generated by shortfalls in domestic rice production, and dependency upon external food markets has continued to grow in the past two decades, with Indonesia now annually importing around 1.5 million tons of rice, a figure which constitutes approximately 10 percent of total national rice consumption. For numerous reasons, per hectare yields in the food sector still remain relatively low, and whereas more land has been brought under cultivation in the outer islands, high transport costs serve to impede the flow of crops from surplus to food deficit areas. In this sense, Indonesia has yet to achieve a truly unified economy with respect to enabling production in the agricultural sector to reach a higher level of output and integration in the regional and national flow of goods and services from producer to consumer.

II

The growing problems of food shortage, poverty and underemployment in Indonesia, and the need for formulating a public sector effort of considerable scope in addressing these issues, has been an issue of long standing concern at the national policy level. In 1952, the government inaugurated the Kasimo plan with the intent of achieving self-sufficiency in rice production by 1956. Increased emphasis was placed upon the distribution of fertilizer and improved seeds, and funds were made available for irrigation rehabilitation. Most of these activities were concentrated on Java where growth in rice production during the initial phase of the plan was considerable, although it is not clear whether many of these gains could be attributed to the campaign itself or simply to the recovery of an economy long neglected during the Japanese occupation and the ensuing struggle for independence. Nevertheless, the goals of the Kasimo plan were not fulfilled and the entire effort was terminated in 1955, when major floods damaged a large proportion of the rice crop.

From the mid 1950s through 1960, rice production in Java grew by only a small margin, although in the outer islands more substantial gains were recorded as new land was opened to cultivation. The government was therefore impelled to allocate its scarce foreign exchange for large imports of rice in meeting growing consumer demand. In an effort to reduce this import burden another rice production campaign was launched in 1959, and again fertilizer, improved seeds, and credit were distributed primarily in Java in an effort to increase the output of Indonesia's principal food crop. This campaign, known as the "Padi Centra Program," met with little success, as major administrative shortcomings were encountered in its management, and only negligible gains were achieved in boosting production. In large measure, the extension service lacked sufficient manpower and training to adequately support a campaign of such scope and magnitude. In addition, major problems were encountered in collecting credit repayments from those farmers participating in the program. This condition reflected the fact that agricultural credit was given out on excessively easy terms, with the government expecting repayment in kind in the form of rice to reprovision its own stocks. In general, most farmers objected to this policy, for the government frequently collected the repayment in rice at an assessed value well below the current market price. Thus, many farmers simply neglected to repay the credit, and the government was forced to write-off a substantial loss in financing the program.

In 1962, the Padi Centra Program was terminated and for the first time in Indonesia's history, annual rice imports moved beyond the one million ton mark. With the country facing serious balance of payment problems and rice imports accounting for a larger proportion of its foreign currency expenditures, investment in the agricultural sector began to greatly subside as rampant inflation and instability within the larger political arena served to seriously constrain government action in support of agricultural development. Rural roads and irrigation networks fell into a serious state of disrepair, and a condition of general institutional inertia came to prevail over the rural sector as most government agencies lacked the necessary funds to provide even the most basic administrative services within the rural economy.

The long years of political and economic instability in the post-independence period came to a rapid demise when the "New Order" regime under the leadership of President Soeharto, assumed the reins of power in 1966. The emergence of a new regime also brought with it a renewed and more concerted emphasis upon halting the economy's downward economic spiral, checking inflation, and reviving productive output in both the agricultural and industrial sectors. Advances in this direction were made with unanticipated rapidity, and by the late 1960s, inflation had been brought under control and the government was able to expand its time horizon and adopt a more long term approach in economic planning. Thus, in 1969, the regime launched its first five year plan (Repelita I) with agriculture as the focal point in its effort to generate some forward movement in economic development.

With the agricultural sector constituting the primary investment priority, government policy objectives made it very clear that most of its resources would be devoted to expanding and stabilizing the production of Indonesia's faltering rice economy. The major goal of the five year plan was simply stated as one of achieving self-sufficiency in rice production, an effort which would entail an approximate 50 percent increase in domestic output. The optimism which underlay this ambitious goal was, in great measure, founded upon the premise that Indonesia's recent acquisition of the new high yielding rice varieties or "miracle seeds" would generate a "Green Revolution," and thereby a major production breakthrough in achieving the long sought after goal of ending the country's dependence upon imports in meeting its annual deficit in domestic rice production.[8] It was also recognized that the rice economy had long been deprived of essential production inputs, particularly fertilizer and credit, and it was expected that immediate and high rates of return could be achieved with the provision of these inputs, along with attendant investments in irrigation and market infrastructure.

Translating the goals of the first five year plan into actual administrative action involved a substantial effort in infrastructure rehabilitation, agricultural extension, and the distribution of fertilizer, seeds, pesticides, and credit. Many of these activities were incorporated in the Bimas campaign, a national effort which involved the provision of the necessary inputs (credit, seeds, fertilizer, etc.) needed in cultivating the new high yielding varieties.[9] Most of the Bimas activities have been centered on Java, and at its high point in 1974-75, a large proportion of the island's low-land rice growing areas were covered by this program.

Although the intent of the Bimas campaign has been
to achieve a high adoption rate for the high yielding
varieties, and while many farmers have some experience
with the new varieties, in many instances a large proportion of the farming population are still using more conventional seed varieties.[10] Nevertheless, sizeable gains
were recorded in the Bimas program during the first five
year plan, with rice production increasing at an average
annual rate of 4.6 percent from 1969 to 1974. In part,
this growth can be attributed to an increase in the number of total hectares under cultivation, but major advances were also sustained in increasing average per
hectare yield from 1.26 tons in 1968 to 1.80 in 1974.
This latter achievement in raising productivity can only
be partially explained by reference to the use of the new
rice technology, as many farmers are not planting the
high yielding varieties. Rather, it appears that in some
measure, yield increases have occurred in response to the
increased availability and application of fertilizer.
Thus, in 1968, total urea consumption in Indonesia was
205,000 metric tons, a figure which increased to 669,000
tons in 1973.

While the government's Bimas campaign yielded some
impressive results in the period of the first five year
plan, and although major efforts have been made to sustain this momentum in the second five year plan (Repelita
II), current evidence indicates that rice production did
not continue to increase by a similar margin in the mid
1970s, and that a leveling-off has occurred during the
past several years with respect to total output. Thus,
current estimates indicate that total rice production remained relatively constant from 1974 through 1976, with
fertilizer consumption also leveling-off during this
period. This standstill has also been reflected in a decline in the rate of participation within the Bimas campaign. The Bimas effort peaked in the wet season of
1974/1975, when the area of coverage included nearly 2.2
million hectares of rice land and over 2.6 million farms.
In the years thereafter there followed a measurable decline in the area covered and an even more substantial
decrease in the number of farmers enrolled as recipients
of Bimas inputs.

A great many factors must be featured in trying to
account for this decline in the upward movement of the
production curve. Serious problems are beginning to
emerge with respect to the repayment of Bimas credit, as a
large number of farmers have fallen into arrears on loan
repayment. In part, the growing incidence of credit default can be attributed to a laxity in collection efforts, but the declining repayment rate also reflects a
more complex set of problems which relate to the environmental and institutional factors which condition the performance of the new high yielding varieties. More ex-

plicitly, for the past several years, the high yielding
varieties in Java have been subject to increased pest infestation, with severe losses being sustained through the
spread of new biotypes of the brown plant hopper. Many
farmers have simply been unable to harvest a full crop in
the Bimas program, and no doubt this accounts in part for
the increasing default rate in credit repayment. Although the retail price for pesticides is under heavy
government subsidy, major institutional shortcomings have
been encountered in assuring that appropriate formulations and spraying equipment are readily available in
support of crop protection measures. The government
sponsored BUUD agricultural cooperatives are responsible
for providing this service to farmers, but these organizations are without the logistical capacity to effectively
undertake this task and the extension service has not
been able to generate much farmer support for pesticide
application in crop protection.[11]

A similar set of institutional problems can be identified with respect to marketing in accounting for the
slowdown in the government's rice production program.
Beginning in the late 1960s, the government introduced a
rice price support program to assure that rice prices
would not fall below a predetermined level designed to
provide rice farmers with adequate production incentives.
The BUUD cooperatives were assigned the primary role at
the village level in administering this price protection
policy, and they were mandated to receive government
credits to purchase rice from the local market when the
price fell below the floor. In practice however, the
cooperatives have not performed well in this undertaking.
It appears that many are purchasing rice at a price less
than the established floor price in order to increase
their profit margins, and a great many of these organizations have failed to repay government purchasing credits
and have therefore been disqualified from acquiring further funds to engage in such market purchases. As a consequence of these deficiencies, in many cases, local level
farm prices have fallen below the floor, and it appears
that this has served to somewhat dampen interest in continuing to cultivate the more cost- and risk-intensive
high-yielding varieties.

Finally, another risk factor which has served to reduce farmer interest in the high yielding varieties relates to the lack of adequate irrigation facilities. Beginning in the late 1960s, the government initiated a
substantial irrigation rehabilitation program, but a number of obstacles have been encountered in this effort,
particularly in Java, where delays in the completion of
these projects have served to reduce the potential contribution of the BIMAS effort in attaining higher yields.
Some of these shortcomings can be attributed to the fact
that the expenditures for irrigation rehabilitation in

the first construction phase were allocated on the premise that central government funds would only be used in
the repair of primary and secondary canals, with local
governmental units being charged with the task of undertaking the reconstruction of tertiary and drainage channels. In practice however, the latter expectation has
frequently failed to materialize, with many local government organs being unable to mobilize the technical skills
and funds to undertake this task. With these constraints
in view, a change of policy occurred with the initiation
of the second five year plan and provision was made for
partial central government funding in the construction
of tertiary canals. It is still unclear, however,
whether these measures will foster greater local level
initiative in the repair of tertiary structures, and
thereby enable the government to regain a higher return
on its investments in primary and secondary canals.

The above shortcomings have served to impede government efforts in the attainment of self-sufficiency in
rice production. From 1972 through 1975, annual rice imports averaged around 1.2 million tons, and in 1976/77,
total imports reached 1.5 million tons. During this time
wheat imports also increased from over 500,000 tons in
the early 1970s, to approximately 1.0 million tons in
1976/77. It appears that a large proportion of total
wheat imports has served as a substitute for rice consumption.

The declining rate of growth in rice production must
be viewed with further concern when assessed in the context of growth rates for other major non-rice food crops.
Over the past decade, total corn production has been in
decline and only minor gains have been recorded in the
production of cassava, soybeans, and peanuts. While
yields per hectare for these crops have frequently increased, they still remain low in comparison to yield potential. In an effort to increase the production of rice
substitutes, in 1972-73, soybeans, corn, peanuts, and
cassava were entered in the Bimas program and separate
input packages were made available to farmers engaged in
the cultivation of these crops. In spite of this policy
change, the area of Bimas coverage for such secondary
crops has been quite marginal, and in general, the performance of the secondary food crop sector has not been encouraging.

While the problem of increasing domestic food output
has continued to occupy a position of high priority in
government policy-making, the issue of rural welfare, and
more explicitly of employment and income generation for
the rural poor has come to assume a much larger role in
the agenda for action in rural development. The urgent
need for widening the parameters of agricultural development policy, in accommodating a more specified concern for
employment and income generation, rapidly assumed promi-

nence when it became clear that the Bimas program was having little visible impact in improving the welfare of lower income households. Thus, where there have been increased labor inputs in the cultivation of the high-yielding rice varieties, these gains have often been offset by such labor saving practices as the more frequent use of the sickle in place of the traditional ani ani blade in the cutting of the rice stalk, and the apparently more generalized practice of reducing labor inputs in the harvesting process through the use of the tebesan system.[12] Thus, it appears that the Bimas effort has contributed little to alleviating the conditions of poverty ·for landless labor. A similar assessment can likely be offered with respect to the small and marginal farmer. The uncertainties and risks associated with the use of the high-yielding rice technology have served to greatly constrain the rate of adoption within this sector of the farming population.

Much greater concern was devoted to income and employment issues when, in April 1974, the government launched the second five year plan. Again, the major emphasis was placed upon rice production, with the goal of self-sufficiency still occupying a central role in the allocation of planning priorities. At the same time, however, greater emphasis was placed upon expanding those development activities relating to employment generation for small farmers and landless labor. In particular, funding for medium- and small-scale labor-absorbing public works programs was substantially enlarged. In general, these funds were distributed among three distinct programs; the Kabupaten Program, Padat Karya, and the Subsidy Desa program. Each of the programs shares common goals, but at the same time each operates within a distinct administrative framework which manifests its own peculiar set of contributions and problems in fulfilling mandated goals.

The Kabupaten Program was initiated in 1970, and probably constituted one of the more innovative approaches introduced by the government in fostering greater local initiative in the financing of public works projects. This program involves the provision of a central government allocation to each kabupaten or district, the amount of the grant being determined by a set rupiah sum multiplied by the number of inhabitants within the kabupaten; a formula which obviously favors the more labor surplus districts located in Java. Medium-scale public works projects (roads, bridges, irrigation canals, etc.) are financed with these funds, and project selection and design is undertaken by the kabupaten government with particular emphasis being placed upon labor-intensive construction methods. An added feature of the Kabupaten Program is the incorporation of an incentive element, whereby the central government provides additional

project funds for those districts who perform well in the
collection of local taxes; a strategy which has served to
greatly improve district level performance in meeting
their collection targets.

While the Kabupaten Program continues to account for
a large proportion of district level expenditures in infrastructure improvement, it seems that the actual contribution of these projects in generating more rural employment is somewhat less than was envisaged in the
original program formulation. By the end of the first
five year plan, the Kabupaten Program was generating employment for around a half million laborers. In many
cases, however, construction is undertaken by urban based
contractors who frequently recruit their own work force
from urban rather than rural areas. Aside from this factor, a number of other obstacles continue to constrain
project performance at the local level. Project design
capabilities still remain relatively limited at the kabupaten level and this has constituted a major bottleneck
in engineering more elaborate infrastructure projects.
Finally, improvements need to be made in performing
proper and routine maintenance functions in order to sustain the longevity of completed projects.

A second program, commonly referred to as "Padat
Karya," is also designed to support the construction of
rural infrastructure in the generation of more employment
opportunities in the rural sector. An important and
basic difference exists between the Kabupaten and Padat
Karya program, in that the latter is administered by the
sub-district (katjamatan), the unit of government which
stands between kabupaten and the village. Because it
represents the last rung in the government's administrative hierarchy and is thereby able to engage most directly in the coordination of village and inter-village development activities, many view the sub-district as a
kind of natural development unit, and with increasing frequency government development programs are being designed
with the sub-district occupying a more important administrative role in their execution. Thus, the operational
boundaries of the government's multipurpose cooperative
program (BUUD) have largely been defined in terms of the
sub-district unit, and the Padat Karya program represents
a similar move in bringing the locus of development activity into closer proximity with the intended beneficiaries. For this reason, a closer examination of the Padat
Karya effort is warranted, not only for what it reveals
about the nature of the program itself, but also for what
it might illuminate with respect to the more general capacity of the sub-district in undertaking rural development projects.

The Padat Karya effort started with a modest financial base in 1969, and initially only involved several
hundred sub-districts, but in 1976 plans were undertaken

to greatly increase its budget with the intent of involving more than one thousand sub-districts in the program. The goal of Padat Karya activities has remained
the same, however, and that is to (1) provide short-term
employment for the rural poor during the slack agricultural season and (2) involve these laborers in the construction of those small-scale infrastructure projects
which will yield more long-term gains in productivity and
income generation within the rural sector. Most of these
small-scale projects involve some kind of earth-work in
road, drainage, and irrigation construction. The sub-
district is the primary administrative agent, as current
policy rules out the participation of private contractors, and the central government has tended to confine
the program to those sub-districts, mostly on Java, with
a high proportion of the work force being unemployed
landless labor. In this context, government regulations
stipulate that most of the program expenditures must be
paid out as wages, a condition designed to foster the use
of high labor inputs in the construction process.

A review of sub-district performance in the administration of the Padat Karya effort reveals that a number
of obstacles have been encountered in achieving the intended purpose of this rural development program. A
major deficiency has been evident in the lack of long-
term cost-benefit projections in project selection.
Thus, projects have frequently been selected which generate short-term yields, i.e. immediate employment, but
provide only marginal long-term gains in productivity and
added employment. Where project selection has been
undertaken with a projection of long-term benefits, these
gains have frequently been lost because of substandard
practices in construction and maintenance. Many of these
problems can be attributed to the fact that sub-district
staff frequently lack the skills and time required in
making the technical assessments for appropriate project
selection and design. Shortcomings have also been encountered in project phasing, with construction being initiated at the peak of seasonal labor demand rather than
at the low point in the agricultural cycle.

The above problems are recognized as being major im-
pediments in program administration, and actions are being taken to enhance the capacities of local administrative units in the performance of these developmental
roles. In many instances, however, these improvements
will also need to be accompanied by reforms needed in the
higher levels of the bureaucratic hierarchy where delays
and constraints in the allocation of project monies frequently prevents local officials from being able to initiate or complete their projects on schedule. This lack
of prompt and appropriate center to periphery responses
is further illuminated in the frequent inability of government organs to provide the kinds of follow-up action

and back-up support in assuring that local project managers are able to perform their designated tasks. These
discontinuities in administrative practice are not merely
found in such programs as the Padat Karya effort, but are
manifest in many of those development activities where
the national bureaucracy is seeking to engage local government units in specific project actions. The problem
is acute at both ends of the organizational hierarchy,
with both subdistrict and central government units need-
ing to increase the number and technical competence of
their personnel in order that the former can effectively
undertake local level project administration, and the
latter can monitor these activities and respond when
their services are required.

A third major program which falls within the scope
of the government's attempt to improve welfare levels
within the rural sector concerns the Subsidi Desa program, an effort which entails the provision of an annual
central government grant to each village within Indonesia. The Subsidi Desa operation was initiated in 1969,
with each village receiving a 100,000 rupiah grant, and
over the years this amount has been increased, with present funding having reached an annual level of 350,000
rupiah per village. The intent of these allocations is
to mobilize greater local-level participation within the
development process. Each village is expected to submit
a project proposal to the central government and stipula-
ted within the program mandate is the condition that the
subsidy funds can only be used in the construction of
infrastructure projects. Government regulations further
specify that the funds can only be used in the purchase
of construction materials not available in the local village. Since locally available materials and all labor
requirements must be donated by the village, the process
of constructing these projects would appear to have little direct impact in generating much employment and income. Once completed, however, many of these projects
would likely add to the productivity of land and labor.
In actual practice, however, it is frequently the case
that the village lacks the necessary skills to undertake
proper project design and construction, and while local
government units are expected to assist in this process,
such services are often not available when needed. It is
therefore unclear as to whether the operative duration of
some of the projects is sufficient to allow for their
making a longer-term contribution to village welfare.

The above three programs are designed with the ex-
plicit intent of generating employment-intensive projects
in the public works sector. A fourth program which falls
somewhat outside this category but at the same time prom-
ises to make a major contribution in income and employment for lower income groups, is the Penghijauan and
Reboisasi Program, an effort which entails the rehabili-

tation of the many areas suffering from severe soil erosion in upland Java. Soil deterioration in these upland areas is widespread, with nearly 80 percent of all <u>kabupaten</u> having areas where erosion is in progress. In some upper-slope gradients, erosion has reached a point where once cultivated land has been abandoned because of a serious decline in soil fertility. The government has come to recognize the seriousness of this problem and in 1975, the Penghijauan and Reboisasi program was launched with the dual purpose of introducing a reforestation effort for upper-slope areas and initiating a terracing program in low-gradient slopes for the cultivation of more appropriate soil-conserving cropping regimens. These rehabilitative measures demand sizeable labor inputs in planting, terracing, and maintenance, and with current funding being relatively substantial, the entire effort should begin to generate many additional employment opportunities for those engaging in the rehabilitation process itself, and in the anticipated increase in labor-inputs resulting from the rising productivity of the restored land.

The aggregate impact of the above programs and other similarly related government induced development efforts upon the generation of additional employment in the rural sector is difficult to assess with any precision, and little evaluative information is available to determine whether such efforts as the Kabupaten Program or the Padat Karya effort are yielding levels of job-creation equal to their estimated potential. In terms of potential impact, it would appear that on Java alone, the island which has received the bulk of the government's financial resources in rural development, current rates of program funding for employment oriented programs could be providing between 1.5 and 2.0 million man years of labor. Actual levels of achievement are likely to be lower than this total, given the various administrative constraints which continue to impede program performance. Nevertheless, assuming that these obstacles will gradually be overcome, given the magnitude of the underemployment problem in Java, and the growing number of young adults entering the labor force, these programs are not likely to effectuate major changes in the absorptive capacity of the rural labor market.

Understandably, the government's employment strategies in the first and second five year plan were not designed to soak up the vast numbers of rural Java's underemployed, and it would be unrealistic to expect that a public works effort could or should assume the entire burden of such an undertaking. Clearly, the problem of underemployment, equity, and income generation for lower income groups in Java can only be addressed by a broader range of policies and programs, and the government will need to face this challenge more directly as it begins to

chart the future course of development actions for the
third and fourth year plans. In this context, a longer
range response would seem to call for a more diversified
but complementary set of strategies in raising productivity and levels of employment and income in the rural
sector. An emphasis upon agricultural diversification,
rural industry, and resettlement in the outer islands
will obviously constitute some of the important elements
in this approach to rural development. The remaining or
outstanding question which must now be addressed with
some additional elaboration concerns those conditions
which will determine whether government goals and inten-
tions can be translated into actual practice in transforming the rural sector into a more dynamic element of
the national economy.

III

An attempt in seeking to identify those factors
which will account for relative levels of effectiveness
in goal achievement and program performance with respect
to future rural development efforts, would seem to warrant
a more generalized response in suggesting that Indonesia
is likely approaching the threshold of a new era, a future in which increases in rice production and other food
crops will depend upon the assemblage and orchestration
of a new set of policy and institutional arrangements, and
the modification, if not abandonment of approaches which
worked in the past but which now have less relevance for
the future. More explicitly, many of the production
gains achieved in the rice sector during the late 1960s
and early 1970s, can be attributed to a quantitative leap
ahead in the infusion of agricultural inputs in the production mainstream. In many instances, increases in per
hectare yield were simply achieved because the smallholder rice sector had operated under conditions of input
scarcity and economic instability during much of the
1950s and 1960s. Substantial rates of return could be
expected in the New Order era when much of the smallholder sector, particularly on Java, was able to gain access to a more stable and adequate supply of production
inputs. These advances have been made, however, within
an environment where only minor adjustments were undertaken within the larger institutional environment, and it
is precisely at this point where the character of development policy will need to make a shift from a primarily
quantitative, to a more qualitative restructuring and expansion of organizational capacity and manpower resources
within the rural sector. Perpetuating a policy of simply
providing more inputs, more roads, and more irrigation
canals, without a concomitant modification in existing institutional structures, will likely yield marginal and

diminishing returns. This is not to suggest that more
inputs and infrastructure improvements are not needed,
but it is to stress that a point is being reached where a
continued reliance upon physical inputs must be comple-
mented with the introduction of new organizational capacities in order to maximize the full potential of existing government programs as they impinge upon the process
of growth and change in the rural sector.

A major area in need of basic institutional innovation concerns the problem of water management for smallholder irrigation. For nearly a decade, major investments
have been made in rehabilitating the many primary and
secondary canals which cut across the lowland rice growing areas in Java. The contribution to agricultural output from these rehabilitation efforts has been seriously
constrained, however, by a lack of those local organizational capacities needed in properly regulating and distributing water at the sub-district and village level.[13]
The problem is particularly acute in Java, where gravity
flow networks prevail and where the flow from secondary
canals to individual holdings must be regulated in accordance with some advanced projection of water availability,
and then distributed in accordance with estimates of actual needs at the farm level. The proper performance of
these planning and administrative functions necessitates
a relatively high level of sustained organizational activity at the village and sub-district level, where decisions on the timing and quantity of irrigation discharge
must be calculated on the basis of variable cropping
regimens and related demands for water at different intervals in the growing cycle. Overlaying this concern is
the need to assure that individual holdings receive a
fair share in the allocation process, particularly for
those plots more distantly located from the tertiary outlets. Similarly, where more than one village unit inter-
sects with an irrigation canal, measures need to be undertaken to secure their cooperation in a water management
system which reflects a concern for both equity and productivity. The complexities of this task are further
magnified where, as in Java, a multitude of small farmers
must act in concert in order to attain adequate irrigation services, and where under periodic conditions of severe water shortage, decisions on irrigation allocation
can have a profound impact in sustaining or decreasing
agricultural output and farm income.

Most of the local administrative tasks associated
with water management, particularly in the regulation and
maintenance of the tertiary canals, have been entrusted
to village government and the local irrigation service,
and for many reasons, these instrumentalities have been
unable to effectively coordinate the allocation of irrigation services to individual fields. A major shortcoming can be found in the manner with which authority is

exercised at the sub-section level, where a government official administers the amount of irrigation discharge for
release to the tertiary outlets. In his designated area,
the sub-section official usually controls irrigation delivery from those secondary canals which intersect several contiguous sub-districts, and his decisions on the
volume and timing of water allocation are based upon information on water availability from district officials,
matched with his own estimates of irrigation needs at the
farm level. The latter information is presumably gathered by his various assistants at the village level.
Once the actual decision is made by the sub-section head
on the volume and timing of irrigation discharge to the
secondary and tertiary channels, responsibility for the
actual distribution of water to individual holdings is
entrusted to the village itself, with an identified village official usually assuming the task of regulating and
monitoring the flow of water to the farm plots. Serious
deficiencies can be found in this system of water management, particularly at the lower end of the hierarchy,
where water demands at the local level must be calculated
in terms of projected cropping patterns and then for-
warded to the sub-section officials. The assistants of
the sub-section head, along with the village irrigation
official, are expected to gather this data, but neither
are generally equipped with the necessary skills to adequately perform this task. Their schooling and expertise
is minimal, and they are frequently prone to error in the
measurement of local irrigation needs.

Aside from certain shortcomings in skill levels, a
more basic structural deficiency can be found in the organization of lower level accountability and authority as
they relate to the distribution of irrigation services.
Thus, the sub-section head occupies a key decision-making
position in the allocation of water resources, but faces
few pressures from either above or below to assure that
this role is conducted in a responsible and impartial
manner. A similar set of problems are encountered at the
level of the lowest administrative unit, where the village irrigation officer functions as a subordinate under
the authority of the village headman and his senior
staff. In neither instance, is the sub-section official
or the village irrigation officer operating in an environment where they can be held fully accountable for assuring an adequate and timely distribution of water.
Rather, both levels of decision-making are highly vulnerable to outside pressures, particularly from those local
elites, who by virtue of their relative influence and
power, can provide numerous inducements in acquiring special consideration in the distribution of water resources.

The problem of accountability and its manifestation
in the efficient and equitable management of irrigation

services is currently being addressed through the introduction of a number of institutional innovations designed
to strengthen farmer participation in local-level water
organizations and to make the local decision-making apparatus more broadly responsive to smallholder needs.
Nevertheless, much more effort will need to be devoted to
these institutional requirements before most farmers can
enjoy the full benefits of irrigation. Until such a condition is achieved, the rate of adoption and the yield
performance of the high-yielding varieties will continue
to remain at a level well below their full potential.

The difficult organizational problems associated
with water management in the lowland areas have their
counterpart representation in the upland areas of Java,
where major institutional questions still remain to be
resolved in administering the government's rehabilitation
programs for land eroded areas. Again, questions of accountability loom large in the effort to assure that measures designed to restore eroded land are accepted and
supported by the local populace. Unless local residents
view it in their interests to cooperate in the adoption
of new land-restoring cropping schemes, it is unlikely
that the government will be able to make much sustained
progress in soil conservation for the upland areas. Securing grass-roots support for these rehabilitation measures will entail some form of local organizational response, and the emergence of mechanisms of collective
action which enable villages to assume responsibility for
assuring that new cultivation practices are consistently
applied in the terraced and reforested project areas.
Eliciting this kind of cooperation will require a relatively sophisticated administrative operation in mobilizing popular participation, and in providing the many extension and back-up services needed to adequately support
this soil conservation effort.

Aside from the various organizational issues associated with water management and soil conservation, a related set of institutional issues can also be discerned
with respect to the distribution of production inputs
within the smallholder food sector. Thus, whereas the
level of fertilizer consumption has greatly increased
during the past decade, the per hectare rate of application still remains relatively low, and major efforts will
need to be made in order to sustain gains in fertilizer
use and to absorb the increasing output of Indonesia's
rapidly growing capacity in domestic fertilizer production. Enhancing the levels of smallholder fertilizer
consumption will, in great measure, depend upon the adoption of certain fundamental policy and institutional reforms in streamlining the existing distribution and marketing network within the rural sector. The BUUD
agricultural cooperatives have been given major responsibility for the marketing of production inputs in the

smallholder sector but their performance of this role has
been constrained by a lack of local-level storage facilities and by shortcomings in their own management practices. Many retail outlets are not easily accessible to
consumers, and the quality of the fertilizer is frequently
sub-standard due to poor handling and storage. Most of
these problems are recognized and the government's recent
decision to improve the profit margin for local distribution and to provide a larger role for private traders in
retail distribution constitutes a major advance in addressing these obstacles. Nevertheless, rigidities in
administration still remain, and major attention will
need to be devoted to the development of improved management and marketing capacities in order to generate increased fertilizer use. A similar set of problems can be
found in the provision of pest management services. The
growing problem of pest damage within the rice sector,
particularly in Java, can in part be attributed to shortcomings in the organization of intermediary and local-
level services in pest management. Current market incentives for pesticide distribution are relatively weak, and
appropriate pesticide formulations and sprayers are frequently unavailable or late in delivery to infested
areas.

The various issues which underly the organization of
agricultural services in Java, whether they be in the
area of water management, erosion control, or in the extension and adoption of new cropping systems, will need
to be addressed with some immediacy in order to regain
momentum in raising levels of smallholder productivity
in the lowland rice sawah areas, and to improve low
levels of agricultural performance in the upland areas.
In this context, much more emphasis will need to be placed
upon increasing the quantity and quality of manpower
available for involvement in all of the many and variegated facets of local level project development and administration. As a result of the government's increased
budget surplus from oil revenues, during the past four
years there has been at least a two to threefold increase
in local level project funding, and in many sub-districts,
the increase has been from three to fivefold in total
program funding. These increases have not been matched
by equivalent improvements in local-level administrative
capacity, and thus serious shortcomings have been encountered in assuring that projects are properly designed and
implemented. These deficiencies are more visible at the
sub-district (katjamatan) level, where an undermanned and
poorly equipped sub-district staff are expected to direct
and monitor an array of development projects, which in total annual funding, frequently exceed 100 million rupiahs.
These shortcomings in management are also accompanied by
shortages in technical personnel within the line agencies. Much more attention is being devoted to strength-

ening the technical services, but this alone will not suffice in enhancing the process of technology diffusion down to the farm level. A greater number of para-technical manpower will need to be trained in order to assure that services are properly transmitted and utilized at the local-level.

The need for strengthening manpower capacities within the rural sector will assume further importance as the government seeks to tailor and elaborate existing development programs to meet local needs. Thus, substantial work will need to be undertaken in refining the Bimas packages in meeting location-specific input requirements under conditions of soil and environmental variability. Soil surveys will need to be conducted in existing and new production areas, followed by the introduction of fertilizer trials to determine rates of appropriate application. The extension service will need to administer the various field trials and demonstration plots associated with this effort, and their upgrading will be needed to adequately perform these roles.

The need for improving organizational and manpower capacities within the rural sector emerges as an even more critical priority in the agenda of development action when viewed in the context of anticipated population growth during the next two decades, and the attendant demands this will place upon domestic resources in generating adequate food supplies and employment for a rapidly expanding labor force. Current projections on Indonesia's population in the year 2000 range from 175 million to 260 million, and assuming that actual growth will fall somewhere between these extremes, it is likely that Indonesia will enter the twenty-first century with around 220-240 million inhabitants. A growth rate of this magnitude will place enormous demands upon the agricultural sector. Using an estimated annual population growth rate of 2.35 percent and a total income growth rate of 7.5 percent, Mears projects for the year 1985, a range of variation for domestic demand of rice from a high of 26.4 million to a low of 22.8 million tons.[14] He suggests that even under the best of conditions, i.e., an annual growth rate of 5 percent in rice production, total output would only reach 23.8 tons by 1985.

The above estimates would seem to suggest that shortfalls in domestic rice production will persist for at least the medium term, and that Indonesia will need to continue to import rice in meeting its own consumption needs. The question arises, however, as to whether the gap between domestic production and consumption will grow in relative proportions or whether Indonesia will be able to gradually reduce its dependence upon imports. Many of the environmental and institutional problems associated with the current leveling-off in rice production will not be amenable to rapid improvement in the short-run, and

therefore, other measures will need to be pursued to increase the availability of food in meeting growing consumer demand. In this context, it is increasingly recognized that much greater emphasis will need to be placed
upon expanding the domestic production of non-rice food
crops in order to bring more balance and diversity in the
existing range of food sources and to reduce a growing
dependence upon rice imports. In large measure, the negative income elasticities of demand for these crops and
the decrease over the past decade in relative price differences between rice and secondary food crops, has served
to constrain the growth in additional demand for non-rice
food consumption. Thus, in order to provide more production incentives in the cultivation of secondary food
crops, increased attention will need to be placed upon the
introduction of improved seeds and cultivation practices
as a cost-saving measure in reducing prices. It is likely that this effort will need to be accompanied by a rise
in rice prices in order to secure the substitution of
these foods for rice in consumer expenditure.

During the first two five year plans very little research was devoted to the development of new cropping
systems, particularly for secondary non-rice food crops
in upland rainfed areas. Rather, the target sector for
many of the government's recent agricultural development
programs has been concentrated in the lowland irrigated
sawah of Java, the latter being areas where it was expected that more immediate and larger incremental gains
could be achieved in boosting total rice production.
With current evidence indicating that lowland rice yields
are beginning to level-off, much greater attention will
need to be placed upon enhancing the productivity of new
and existing upland cropping regimens.

The need for allocating more resources for upland
farm development emerges as an important policy issue,
given the increased emphasis upon equity goals in the
third five year plan (1979-1984), and the even greater
concern for generating more income and employment within
the rural sector. While equity considerations in the
spatial distribution (lowland vs upland) of program benefits will assume a more prominent role in the design of
rural development strategies, considerably more attention
will need to be devoted to addressing the problem of
equity in the distribution of benefits within income and
stratification categories at the village level. In this
context, the question emerges of what can be done to improve the welfare of small farmers and landless labor in
the small but densely populated island of Java. This
problem will need to be addressed with the adoption of
some entirely new approaches in meeting basic employment
and income requirements for this large segment of the
rural populace. For the short- and medium-term, much
greater emphasis could be placed upon rural industriali-

zation and enhancing the forward and backward linkages
between agriculture and the non-agricultural sectors.
Similarly, new methods can be devised in making market
and institutional services more accessible to small farmers and landless labor.

From a longer term perspective, an issue of considerable importance arises concerning the prospects of sustaining measurable progress in raising welfare levels on
Java, given its large and growing population and the
enormous investments which will be needed to generate
further economic growth within the confines of the island's existing resource base. Even under the best of
conditions, the growth process in Java will be a slow and
arduous process. The question therefore arises as to
whether other more inviting alternatives might be sought
in accelerating social and economic improvements in the
rural sector. In this context, the larger question immediately comes to the fore as to whether greater long-
term gains could be achieved in providing more opportunities for employment and income growth in the outer islands. It has long been the vision of Indonesian policy
makers that the outer islands would assume a greater role
in absorbing a high proportion of Java's surplus labor.
Government sponsored transmigration schemes were implemented throughout the 1950s and 1960s, and both of the
Repelita I and II plans have allocated a sizeable volume
of funds in support of such resettlement schemes. The
results of these efforts have had little if any impact in
checking population growth in Java. Only 416,471 transmigrants were moved in the 1951-1968 period, and 182,414
persons in the period of the first five year plan.[15]

The logistics of opening and sustaining a larger
resettlement program, with the intent of greatly increasing the number of transmigrants, is currently beyond the
government's administrative capacity. In addition, much
still needs to be done in surveying soil conditions in
potential resettlement areas in order to arrive at cropping regimens which are compatible with existing ecological conditions. It would appear therefore, that for the
near future, Java-to-outer island transmigration will not
increase much beyond its present rate, and that at least
for the duration of the third five year plan, government
programs will need to be directed at undertaking the
necessary site surveys, infrastructure construction,
cropping trials, and other supporting activities which
will enable future resettlement areas to link into a larger markets and commercial networks. Greater attention can
then be focussed upon making the transmigration programs
a more integral component of the regional planning process in order to properly secure the settlements in a
larger matrix of social, economic, and administrative
services. In this context, the goals of the current five
year plan (Repelita II) constitute a basic shift in em-

phasis, with less attention being devoted to transmigration as a means of simply easing Java's population problem, and with more consideration being given to incorporating the resettlement programs into a larger effort in outer island regional development. Assuming that the government can move ahead in achieving these ends in Repelita III, the groundwork should then be established in the mid-1980s for a larger volume of both government sponsored and spontaneous Java-to-outer island migration. More importantly, however, if properly administered, this transmigration effort should facilitate the making of a more integrated national economy, with the increased movement of labor, goods, and services assuming their proper role in enhancing prosperity throughout the Indonesian archipelago.

NOTES

1. A. B. Hudson, "Swidden Systems and Agricultural Development: A Case From Kalimantan" (Paper presented at the Conference on Indonesian Agricultural Development, Madison, Wisconsin, July 1974), p. 2.
2. Biro Pusat Statistik, Statistik Indonesia 1974/75 (Jakarta: BPS, 1975), p. 23.
3. Roger Montgomery and Toto Sugito, "Changes in the Structure of Farms and Farming in Indonesia between Censuses (1963-1973) and Initial Insights on the Issue of Inequality and Near Landlessness" (Jakarta: Central Bureau of Statistics, 1976), p. 3, and Biro Pusat Statistik, Sensus Pertanian 1973, Jilid I (Jakarta: BPS, 1976), pp. 1-53.
4. Montgomery and Sugito, "Changes in the Structure of Farms and Farming," p. 32.
5. Ibid., p. 27.
6. Sajogyo, Ringkasan Hasil Evaluasi Projek UPGK: Usaha Perbaikan Gizi Keluarga (Bogor: Lembaga Penelitian Sosiologi Pedesaan, 1974), p. 73.
7. See chapter eight by Benjamin White in this volume for further discussion on the concept of occupational multiplicity.
8. The new high yielding rice varieties refer to the varieties developed in the mid-1960s at the International Rice Research Institute, Los Banos, The Philippines. These varieties became available in Indonesia in 1967-1968.
9. The word Bimas is an acronym and stands for "Bimbingan Massal," or "Mass Guidance" program. Beginning in the mid-1960s, most of the government's rice intensification programs have been referred to by this name.
10. In this case, conventional varieties refer to the commonly used traditional or local varieties, and also to those improved varieties which have been developed in Indonesia through breeding work with local varieties.
11. The BUUD cooperative movement is a government sponsored campaign and involves establishing multipurpose agricultural

cooperatives throughout Indonesia. The program was initiated in 1971, and the number of BUUD cooperatives has rapidly grown, with their number now totalling well over 3000. The cooperatives are engaged in the retailing of agricultural inputs, and the provision of rice milling services. They are also mandated to serve as buying agents in the purchase of rice in support of the government's price protection policy.

12. See chapter nine by William Collier in this volume for further comment on the practice of tebesan.

13. The following analysis relies heavily on Anne Booth's excellent survey of problems in irrigation management in "Irrigation in Indonesia (Part I and II)," Bulletin of Indonesian Economic Studies 13, no. 1 (March 1977), and 13, no. 2 (July 1977).

14. Leon Mears, "Indonesia's Food Problems, Pelita II/III" (Paper prepared for SEADAG seminar on Indonesian Development and U.S. Response, Reston, Virginia, May 14-15, 1976).

15. Suratman and Patrick Guinness, "The Changing Focus of Transmigration," Bulletin of Indonesian Economic Studies 13, no. 2 (July 1977): 83 and 87.

Part I

Policy Dimensions

Introduction

Much of the recent literature and discourse in development economics is concerned with exploring the various policy implications of moving the rural sector to a more paramount position in the hierarchy of development priorities. In large measure, this emphasis reflects a more generally held notion that urban based industrialization strategies have generated few linkages with the rural sector. Agriculture remains undercapitalized and government policies reflect an urban bias in turning the terms of trade against the rural sector. Thus, in many third world countries, urban-rural disparities become more pronounced with many small farming and landless households experiencing little or no rise in welfare levels.

The following two essays address a number of important policy issues with respect to government interaction within the smallholder agriculture sector. In the first selection an assessment is undertaken of the various elements which constitute the political economy of policy-making towards the rice economy. It is contended that the primary motive of public policy has been to regulate trade and market factors in such a way as to depress rice prices. In varying degrees, the self-perceived effectiveness, if not legitimacy of government authority, is directly related to its capacity in satisfying consumer demand for Indonesia's major food crop. This is particularly the case for the urban sector where mass discontent fomented by rising rice prices could constitute a potential challenge to established authority. The concern of policy-makers in maintaining low rice prices is further anchored in the persistence of government efforts to control inflation and in the recognized importance of maintaining a ceiling on rice prices in achieving this goal. Finally, it is Timmer's view that this relatively conservative approach towards the rice economy is reflective of a more general lack of confidence in the supply elasticities of the smallholder producer and the efficiencies

31

of the existing system of rice marketing.

The impact of the above policy orientations has frequently resulted in a repetitious and self-defeating process of bureaucratic intervention in regulating the rice economy. In general, the rice farmer has seldom been given the incentive and terms of trade which would serve to induce higher productivity. Finally, in its effort to depress rice prices, the government has been unable to use pricing policy as an instrument in attaining its larger goal of reaching self-sufficiency in rice production.

The second essay focuses upon another important facet of the policy mix in its examination of agricultural taxation. Land taxation has long been an integral feature of rural administration in Indonesia, but it is only in the last decade that the government has sought to use agricultural taxation as a means of supporting its larger development effort. Tax assessments have been increased several-fold and various administrative inducements are being employed to improve collection rates. In general, the performance of the rural bureaucracy in administrating agricultural taxation has been relatively uneven. Because of incomplete records on land ownership in the outer islands, tax collection has been much less effective in these areas than is the case for Java (as well as for Bali and Madura) where land registration procedures and the practice of taxation constitutes a long-standing feature of rural administration.

It is noted by Booth, that given the high incidence of informal taxation within the agricultural sector and the lack of up-to-date data on crop yields, production costs, and farmgate prices, it is difficult to judge whether the agricultural tax is appropriately calibrated in securing a fair and equitable return upon farm income. In the absence of such information, the government has tended to rely upon the periodic issuance of across-the-board increases in agricultural taxes, a condition which likely produces a regressive impact in its affect upon lower income farm households. Indeed, because of the enormous administrative tasks involved in properly assessing and administering an agricultural tax in the small farm sector, and the low income levels of many of these farmers, a strong case can be made for suggesting that marginal landholding households should be exempted from the tax.

2
The Formation of
Indonesian Rice Policy:
A Historical Perspective

C. Peter Timmer

Rice policy is conditioned not only by technical, economic, and social factors, but also by its own history as well. Three centuries of rice policy, and especially the past three decades, set a frame of mind for the ruling elite about what was important from rice policy and how it was to be achieved. Many of Indonesia's present rice problems have their roots well into the past. An historical analysis, therefore, is essential in understanding how the current objectives of rice policy and constraints on policymakers interact to yield policies and implementation.

I

Rice policy has been a function of rice prices for the entire recorded history of the Indonesian archipelago. Sunan Amangkurat I (1645-1677), prohibited the export of rice from Java in 1655, in response to a severe drought that sent rice prices up by 300 percent.[1] For the next two centuries rice prices were very unstable around a steeply rising trend, and in 1847, the first recorded imports of rice appeared in Java from Saigon. Basic Dutch policy was to minimize controls, subject to broadly satisfactory welfare levels for producers and consumers, although the latter generally fared better. In 1863, for instance, the import duty on rice was annulled following a bad harvest. Efforts were made to increase production to keep rice prices low, and when prices fell drastically in the 1880s, as part of the worldwide overproduction of cereals, the Dutch response was to require that all government needs be supplied from domestic supplies. In 1911, poor crops and the approaching world war sent rice prices up again, and again exports were prohibited. A long period of declining rice prices started in 1930, due to Asian overproduction and the world monetary crisis. Other food prices fell in step with rice prices, farmers found they were unable to pay their taxes, and it appeared that the limit to the functioning of the free market had been met.

In March 1933, the colonial government decided
to intervene. It put an end to the free import
of rice and restricted it by a system of licen-
ses. This meant more than merely a checking of
free importation; it signified the intention to
work toward a system of self-supply with regard
to rice. Javanese rice, which until then had
been offered chiefly in local markets, had to
find its way to all the Outer Provinces. In the
few rice-surplus areas of these provinces, such
as Bali, Lombok and South Celebes, an inter-
insular rice trade had to be started . . . .
Care had to be taken to insure a stable price so
as not to raise the cost of living in the rice-
consuming districts. In short, no failure of
crops and no record harvest in a single terri-
tory of the vast archipelago could ever be allowed to become the occasion of a just reproach
that the Government had neglected the obligations which it had undertaken to be responsible
for a steady and regular supply of rice . . . .

The peculiar character of both the raw material
and the final product of the rice hulling mills
made it inadmissible to allow a free growth of
these plants. Danger was seen in the withdrawal
of too much rice from the producer-consumers in
some areas and the increase of the share of the
Java mills in the paddy crops, sold in five years,
from 12 to 21.5 percent. Therefore, in 1940,
the provisions of the regulations under the industrial ordinance were applied to rice hulling
mills with a capacity of 2-1/2 H.P. or more. In
addition, the mills were organized and their
sales centralized, on condition that they keep
to the paddy purchase and rice selling prices
fixed by government directive. To compensate
for this restriction of liberty, the Government
declared its readiness to take over any unsale-
able rice surplus at the official price.[2]

A specialized government agency was clearly needed
to implement this revolutionary degree of interference in
the functionings of the rice market. It was established
in April 1939, as the Sticting Het Voedingsmiddelenfonds,
or VMF. Its finance for imports was gained from the
Javasche Bank with government guarantee; finance for purchase of domestic rice was arranged with private banks.
Looking back with a thirty-year perspective, this action,

and others like them, reveal how thoroughly Dutch policies
of the 1930s laid the path for what was to follow. The
physical apparatus in the form of rice mills, transportation, and communication networks, and the like, and the
legal and institutional apparatus in the form of the VMF
and regulations, carefully organizing all aspects of trade
in rice, were put in place. In addition, and perhaps most
importantly, a philosophy was established. It argued
that rice was too important to be left alone, and direct
intervention in the marketplace, frequently with trade
barriers, price ceilings and floors, and an ultimate reliance on cheap foreign imports to maintain stability,
was the proper government response. Whether an efficient
Dutch civil service adequately implemented these policies
is a question without a full answer. Whether an inex-
perienced and underpaid Indonesian civil service could
implement similar policies drawn from this inherited
philosophy is a question with all too final an answer, as
the history of the first two decades of the new Republic
shows.

After the chaos of the war years and the fight for
full independence, rice policy settled into the old Dutch
pattern. The VMF was renamed BAMA (Jajasan Bahan
Makanan, or Foundation for Food) in 1950, but its activities were unchanged. In 1952, this became the JUBM
(Jajasan Urusan Bahan Makanan, or Foundation for Food Affairs), again with little changed activities. Continuing
inflation, in 1950 and 1951, did bring a new policy that
was a glimpse of the future: rice rations distributed in
kind to civil servants and the military (and their families) to protect their real income. With this policy the
government rice agency was no longer interested solely in
avoiding high rice prices during scarcity and low prices
during surpluses. It now had fixed distribution commitments, month in and month out, commitments that had to be
honored. A government that cannot pay its civil servants
and army will fall, and thus, the first claim on foreign
exchange for imports and on the rupiah budget for domestic purposes went to rice. The move to making partial
salary payments in rice, while perfectly understandable
and indeed laudable on welfare grounds, clearly served
over time to politicize further a commodity that historically was already nearly beyond the control of normal
market forces.

Perpetual shortages of foreign exchange to buy foreign rice frequently caused the government to turn hopefully to the countryside for increased output. Early attempts, e.g., the Kasimo welfare plan announced in 1952,
were undertaken with the intention of achieving self-
sufficiency in rice by 1956. These plans were never
adequately staffed or funded, but still, rice prices were
stable from 1952 to 1954, and plans were made to eliminate imports in 1955, on the basis of the promising

trends. Nevertheless, yields on Java in 1955 were lower
than in the previous years, and imports were continued
for the next few years on a large scale: an average of
770,000 tons per year from 1956 to 1958, compared with
only 225,000 tons from 1953 to 1955. Despite these imports, however, rice prices more than doubled from early
1957 to late 1958, as part of the inflation created by
budget deficits, and the "feeling of ease," now badly
shaken, was not to return for a decade.

   With sources of foreign exchange drying up under the
banner of Sukarno's Guided Democracy (and economy), the
government turned to the farmer for help, and an ambitious three-year program for self-sufficiency was announced in 1959. Again, however, the program failed, and
imports were larger in 1962 and 1963, than in 1958 or
1959--over a million tons in each of the latter years,
and rice production was lower in 1969 than in 1960.

   The politization of rice reached full bore under
Sukarno. It was, in the words of "Guided Democracy"
rhetoric, "the main food of the people whose distribution
and spreading in the guided economy was not allowed to be
made an object of trade or of speculation."[3] As the domestic economy deteriorated under the brunt of exploding
government deficits, spiraling inflation, and negative
investment, the rice economy crumbled as well. To pick
the worst years, rice production dropped by 13.6 percent
on Java from 1960 to 1964.

   If it is true that marketing is "the very glue that
holds the economy together," then the economy in the mid-
sixties was quite literally coming unglued. Typically,
the highest retail rice price in provincial capitals in
Indonesia would be four times the level of the lowest retail price. The entire economy, rice marketing an important and special example, was unable to perform the very
basic tasks of marketing--matching seasonal and regional
price differences to the costs of storage and transportation. "At fault were all the factors common to under-
developed market economies--shortage of credit, lack of
communication and information, inadequate marketing facilities (especially on the outer islands)--and these were
accentuated in Indonesia by the rapid inflation and deteriorating infrastructure."[4] Nevertheless, the government's penchant for intervention made matters far worse.
For example, rice mills could operate only for the government. In addition, despite attempts of the central
government to regain control of regional rice price and
movement policy from regional administrators, authority
and proper communications were lacking, and most regional
administrators protected their own local interests before
thinking of Jakarta. Since the national government was
unlikely to be of much help in times of shortage, most
regional administrators simply prohibited the export of
rice from their regions, no matter how low prices fell.

Rice trade was easily taxed, especially at military
checkpoints, and it probably provided the bulk of finance
for surplus and deficit regions alike. "Rice policy,
such as it was, emphasized consumer interests and local
revenue generation. It is no wonder that production suffered and prices were unstable."[5]

II

The abortive coup attempt late in 1965 seemed the
climax of a nightmare, except the unreality of the previous half decade turned out to be real. The year ended
with 1,000 to 1 revaluation of the rupiah, and by March
of 1966, when leadership was transferred to the triumvi-
rate of General Suharto, Adam Malik, and the Sultan of
Yogyakarta, an evaluation showed no rice in the warehouses
of the food agency (then called BPUP), no foreign exchange in the treasury, and an inflation rate of 600 percent per year.
Although rice prices increased more than three-fold
during the year, the country did survive, and by early
1967, General Suharto emerged sufficiently powerful to set
the country on a course of stabilization. With the military emergency over, the BPUP, now called KOLOGNAS, was
disbanded and replaced with BULOG, the presently functioning Food Logistics Agency, directly under the control
of the President. Despite the new government's resolve
to keep rice prices low, and a fairly successful domestic
purchase program that brought in over 500,000 tons of
milled rice in the face of obvious administrative and financing difficulties, limited supplies in the world export market, due to strong competition from China, Japan,
and the Philippines, meant that there was not enough rice
available to meet demands. A severe food shortage
gripped Indonesia when the dry season rice crop turned
out sub-average, and from the harvest low at the end of
May 1967 rice prices doubled by the end of October, and
redoubled by mid-January 1968.
The hard-learned lessons of 1967 had immediate returns in 1968. The government was determined to pay farmers an incentive price for their surplus rice, based on
the Rumus Tani (farmer's formula), which recommends that
the price of milled rice and urea ought to be about the
same for the farmer. Complementary to this incentive was
a major effort to extend and improve the BIMAS (mass guidance) rice intensification program. While the regular
BIMAS program went forward as usual, in 1968, shortages
of fertilizer supplies and domestic credit led the government to try another approach as well, BIMAS Gotong
Rojong (BGR, or "mutual self-help program"). In this
case, the government contracted with several foreign companies (CIBA, Geigy, AHT, Hoescht, Mitsubishi) to provide

rice areas with fertilizer and pesticides to increase
yields. However, by early 1970, it became apparent that
the BIMAS Gotong Rojong effort was suffering from some
serious shortcomings and the program was terminated in
June 1970.

In the 1970s, the evolution of Indonesia's rice
policy was intimately related to the government's larger
effort in development planning. Although the First New
Order Five-Year Development Plan (Repelita I) was drafted
in 1968, and inaugurated April 1, 1969, it is a document
of the seventies. It was formulated on a premise of stability, which came to full fruition in the 1970-1972
period, and it was built around rice.

> It was inevitable that rice, because of its
> paramount importance in the national economy,
> would be called upon to play a dual role . .
> . . Since rice production and processing were
> the chief source of livelihood for about half
> the Indonesian population, production would
> have to increase if there was to be any wide-
> spread increase in per capita incomes. And
> . . . . because of the new high-yielding rice
> varieties (partly developed from Indonesian
> rice strains), Indonesia's comparative advan-
> tage, at least in the short run, lay in agri-
> culture. The most lucrative import substitu-
> ting investments were likely to be in rice
> production. Self-sufficiency in the basic
> foodstuff became the leading priority of
> Repelita.[6]

The plan fortunately did not spell out program details. The failure of BIMAS Gotong Rojong and the BULOG
domestic purchase program in 1969 required major changes
if self-sufficiency was to be achieved, and major changes
in both areas were soon forthcoming. When BGR was sud-
denly discarded in mid-1970, it was replaced by a more
incentive-oriented "perfected BIMAS" organized around
"village units." The program stressed getting profitable
inputs, subsidized credit, and information out to the
farmers and letting them decide whether and how much to
participate. Fertilizer distribution was partially
turned over to the private market, with a charge to sell
for no higher than the ceiling price of Rp 26.6 per kg
for both urea and tri-sodium phosphate (TSP). The price
required a subsidy to distributors of Rp 7-8 per kg (in
1971), which was covered from the Development Budget.

A second innovation in rice policy was to implement
an effective floor price for stalk paddy. With a national fertilizer price ceiling established, it was possible to establish a national floor price for rice. Although the floor price was stated as Rp 13.2 per kg for

stalk paddy in the village, it was implemented by BULOG
by paying Rp 36 per kg at rice mills. With the introduction of a floor price taken on behalf of the farmer, the
government felt it could likewise commit itself to a na-
tionwide ceiling price for rice: medium quality rice in
urban markets was not to sell for more than Rp 50 per kg.
This permitted an expected spread of between Rp 8 to Rp
10 per kg between the seasonal low price and the seasonal
high price. Although this margin was very narrow in
terms of prevailing interest rates, the private trade did
seem to find it profitable to carry stocks in 1970 and
1971.

By mid-1972, the new rice programs looked like major
success stories. Rice production was exceeding the high
targets set in Repelita, BULOG was so successful it took
over handling responsibilities for wheat flour and sugar, and the National Planning Agency (BAPPENAS) and the
Ministry of Finance were trying to find sources of revenue to take the place of food aid counterpart funds,
which seemed about to disappear. Unfortunately, however,
the generally good weather from 1968 to 1971 ran dry. In
addition, BULOG moved too fast to improve its buying
standards in order to reduce storage losses and ended up
buying very little rice in 1972. In a repeat of 1969
(and 1967), the dry season crop was poor, BULOG stocks ran
out, and the government reverted to emergency imports as
the solution. More than a million tons of very expensive
rice poured into Indonesia from mid-1972 to mid-1973. A
year earlier it had seemed that no imports at all might
be needed.

III

With the above historical overview of Indonesian
rice policy in perspective, some attention is warranted
in evaluating the impact of these policies, particularly
with reference to the post-1970 period. In this context,
an attempt will be made to assess Indonesia's rice policies from three different perspectives: (1) the impact
of policy upon the larger rice economy, (2) the efficiency of rice policy in achieving its overall objectives,
and (3) the welfare impact of policy upon populations
within the rural and urban sectors.

Concerning the first assessment, it is very easy to
lose sight of the real economy when talking about policy,
and it is especially easy to lose sight of trends in rice
production and consumption when rice policy is so heavily
oriented toward price stability. A proximate evaluation
is made merely by looking at rice prices, but clearly the
production and consumption interactions that determine
rice prices are the important variables in the long run.

   Under the influence of generally good weather, much
improved availability of inputs under the BIMAS program,
and profitable prices for output, rice production rose
dramatically between 1967 and 1971, from 9.05 million
tons of milled rice to 12.77 million tons, an increase of
41 percent. This should be compared with the mere 3 percent increase from 1960 to 1967.

   Even more remarkable is that net supplies available
for consumption increased more rapidly than production
during this period because of increased imports. The recovery in per capita consumption levels was especially
dramatic, with levels from 1969 forward exceeding any
previous level in Indonesia's history. Clearly, the rice
policy was successful in these gross terms--increased
production and increased consumption. The increased consumption, especially, reflected higher per capita incomes
as the deterioration of the economy was repaired, new investment started to flow, and stability seemed assured.
The pronounced preference of the great majority of Indonesia's population for rice as the basic foodstuff, when
it can afford it, was emphatically demonstrated in the
1967 to 1971 period.

   However, the 32 percent increase in per capita consumption of rice during the 1967-1971 period did not stem
entirely from increased incomes. While urban rice prices
were being carefully stabilized below the Rp 50 per kg
ceiling throughout Indonesia (for part of this time this
ceiling price was higher than the world market price),
the prices of other commodities, both the directly competing foodstuffs such as maize, cassava, sweet potatoes,
soybeans, and peanuts, and other nonfood items in the
average consumer's budget, were still increasing. Especially over the four years from early 1968, to the end of
1971, rice became a significantly cheaper food, and further substitution into rice was made as a result of this
development.

   But even in 1971, the impact of the lower real price
of rice on incentives for the farmer was an issue. It
was pointed out that continued subsidies on inputs, especially fertilizer, would leave the farmer's benefit/cost
calculations unchanged:

     But it is total real income that the farmer
     is ultimately after, not a benefit/cost ratio,
     and here the cost-reducing technology is cru-
     cial. Even lower prices can lead to higher
     profits if the average costs of production
     fall fast enough. And this is the ultimate
     promise of the miracle seeds. If this stra-
     tegy could be successfully implemented, it
     would provide progressively cheaper rice as
     agriculture's contribution to development.
     Achieving this agriculture-to-other-sectors

transfer seems to be a critical factor in
achieving self-sustaining economic progress.
Whether it is too soon for Indonesia's rice
sector to play this role is not yet known. . .[7]

The answer did emerge as production in both 1972, and
1973, declined from the 1971 peak. Bad weather is obviously a major factor in this, and yet it does not to-
tally explain why fertilizer applications stagnated at
1971 levels as well. In this, the progressively lower
real prices to farmers almost certainly play a role: incentive prices work so long as they are incentives.

Any discussion of efficiency of rice policy, the
second perspective of policy analysis, must be impres-
sionistic at best. Still, a number of issues emerge from
the previous discussion that bear directly on how well
policies have worked, and whether alternatives might have
been feasible and desirable. The need for offering a
higher level of price incentives raises a much larger
comparative issue. Even in 1970, when the evidence seems
to show that farmers were receiving an incentive price
relative to earlier years, Indonesian farmers received
among the lowest prices for their rice, relative to the
price they paid for fertilizer; only Burma and Thailand
were lower. Assuming a response to fertilizer similar to
that of other Southeast Asian countries, and price-respon-
sive farmers, the question emerges as to why self-
sufficiency was not achieved by paying somewhat higher
rice prices--prices that would still be only average for
that part of the world. A different set of rather technical constraints seems to have prevented this strategy,
apart from its obvious conflict with the objective of
maintaining low prices for the cities, and the weaker conflict with price stability (stability at somewhat higher
prices is still stability). Self-sufficiency could not
be achieved (in 1970 and 1971) by moving up the short-run
supply curve, because of the interaction of an internal
and an external constraint. The external constraint was
the availability of very low-priced rice in Southeast
Asia. Quotations out of Singapore, Rangoon, and Bangkok
ranged as low as US $75 per ton, which compared with the
ex-mill floor price of about US $95 per ton at the pre-
vailing exchange rate. Even though all rice imports were
handled by BULOG on government account, this cheap rice
served as an effective constraint on how high prices
could be within Indonesia. It has been said that "God
intended Indonesia for free trade." Thousands of miles
of unsupervised coastline, and customs officials who are
frequently willing to look the other way for a price,
gives rise to a condition where the smuggling potential
is so great that the internal price of rice cannot be
much higher, after allowing for transportation and risks,
than the prevailing prices for low-quality rice in

nearby markets.

The more narrow internal constraint preventing higher prices to farmers is administrative. BULOG, after serious problems in 1969 in implementing a rather vague incentive price program, was in no position in 1970 or even 1971, to defend a floor price higher than the already indicated Rp 13.2 per kg for dry stalk paddy (or Rp 36 per kg of milled rice at the mill). Complaints were heard during these two years of prices below the floor, and although the evidence on average prices for stalk paddy shows a dramatic improvement over 1969, there clearly were specific instances in most of the surplus areas where prices were too low. For BULOG to be able to defend a truly incentive price for farmers, in view of the historical experience, will require considerable further administrative and financial upgrading.

If welfare, the third perspective of policy analysis, could be measured simply by how much rice is consumed per capita, the judgement would be relatively straightforward. Indonesians are consuming more rice than ever before. But this simple measure, while appealing and not without some merit, misses at least two major aspects of welfare, even within the narrow context of the food input to the total welfare function. First, Indonesians consume other foods than rice, and second, not unrelated, an average consumption figure masks a tremendously wide variation in individual consumption levels. Thus, while rice consumption increased at an annual rate of 5.5 percent over the 1968 to 1971 period, the other major carbohydrate sources fell sharply behind. Maize consumption dropped by over 10 percent per year, cassava by more than 7 percent, and sweet potatoes by 5 percent. The protein sources fared slightly better, with the decline in peanut consumption being somewhat offset by an increase in soybean intake. The startling figures, however, are the decline, by almost one percent per year, in the total dry weight intake, and the 7.7 percent decline in food intake excluding rice.

How, in the face of rapidly rising per capita incomes--estimated at 5 percent per year for the period--could calorie consumption decline on average from what were already among the world's lowest levels? Bad statistics may be part of the answer, but additional evidence suggests an alternative scenario. The critical element is what happened to rural incomes during this period. The evidence indicates that not only did average paddy prices decline by about 30 percent, but also the prices of non-food items rose by 38.3 percent, for a total adverse move in the terms of trade of more than 60 percent. The incentive price policy, implemented in 1970, reversed this trend, with farmers regaining about 20-25 percent, or about a third of their loss from 1968. However, in 1971 their position began to erode again, with

real farm prices clearly lower in 1971 than in 1968, as
the 20 percent increase in production was not enough to
prevent a fairly serious decline in real incomes of rice
farmers. Since rural incomes, especially on Java, are so
heavily influenced by incomes from rice farming, the conclusion must be that rural incomes probably declined in
the 1968-1971 period, despite an apparent 5 percent per
year increase in per capita incomes for the Indonesian
population as a whole.

A decline in farm income could happen only if there
was a fairly dramatic shift in income distribution away
from the rural sector and toward the urban (and manufacturing, mining, and oil) sector. With this happening, it
is possible to reconcile declining calorie consumption in
the face of rising incomes. In fact, the lower two-
thirds of the population probably had decreasing real incomes during this period. The inescapable conclusion,
therefore, if the statistics are approximately correct,
is that a minority of basically urban consumers were considerably better off during this period but that a good
part of the improvement was at the expense of the rural,
especially farm, population.

NOTES

1. Badan Urusan Logistik, Seperempat Abad Bergulat Dengan
Butir-butir Beras (Djakarta: BULOG, 1971), p. 10.
2. Julius H. Boeke, The Evolution of the Netherlands Indies
Economy (New York: Institute of Pacific Relations, 1946),
pp. 112-115.
3. Seperempat Abad Bergulat Dengan Butir-butir Beras, p. 48.
4. Saleh Affif and C. Peter Timmer, "Rice Policy in Indonesia,"
Food Research Institute Studies in Agricultural Economics, Trade and
Development 11, no. 1 (1972): 135.
5. Ibid., p. 135.
6. Ibid., p. 136.
7. Ibid., p. 152.

3
The Role of Agricultural Taxation

Anne Booth

In many countries of the Asian continent the advent of the new agricultural technologies and the potential they appeared to bring for dramatic increases in farm incomes naturally gave rise to considerable interest in the question of agricultural taxation. The need was felt for a form of taxation that was sufficiently elastic with respect to increasing revenues to tap a proportion of the increment in income accruing to rural producers. In countries such as India a considerable body of literature accumulated on the deficiencies of the system of agricultural taxation and the need for reform. The various types of taxation inherited from colonial times, notably the land tax, had been allowed to fall into disuse, either because they were seen as hated legacies of the colonial era, or because of the power of agricultural producers in central and regional government, or simply because the administrative system was unable to continue to assess and collect taxes as the colonial power had done. Numerous writers in the Indian case endeavoured, with some degree of success, to prove that the tax burden on the agricultural sector was disproportionately light and farmers were paying considerably less in tax than their urban counterparts earning the same income. The Indian debate culminated in 1972 in the publication of the Report on the Taxation of Agricultural Income and Wealth, prepared by a committee under the chairmanship of Professor K. N. Raj, which advocated the implementation of an Agricultural Holdings Tax, assessed progressively on potential income from agricultural land.[1]

The Indonesian experience in the post-war era offers some interesting parallels and contrasts with that of the countries of the Indian sub-continent. Like them, Indonesia (or to be more precise Java, Bali, South Sulawesi, and Lombok) inherited from colonial times a system of land taxation based on a detailed cadastre of all agricultural land. However, in the post-1966 era the Indonesian government has been making a determined effort to

44

revive land taxation as a source of revenue and, more importantly, to use the revenues as a means of promoting regional development initiative in the selection and carrying out of local development projects.

This paper attempts to assess the current scope and future potential for agricultural taxation in the Indonesian context. The analysis begins with an historical introduction to the problems of agricultural taxation in Indonesia, paying particular attention to the development of land revenue (<u>landrente</u>) during Dutch times. This leads to a discussion of the current administration of land taxation, paying particular attention to techniques of assessment, collection, and use of funds. The question is then addressed of other forms of taxation, including levies in labour and kind, on the agricultural sector. Finally, an attempt is made to evaluate the role of agricultural taxation in Indonesia in the coming decades.

I

As long as settled government has existed in Java, levies of one sort or another have been imposed on the peasantry. With the consolidation of the power of the East India Company in the course of the seventeenth century, a system of forced deliveries from the local rulers to the foreign power was instituted. As Day, Furnivall, and Selosoemardjan have pointed out, demands from the nobility were compounded by those of tax farmers, and the burden on the cultivators was often such as to leave them with only the barest means of subsistence.[2] Pressures for change were mounting by the end of the eighteenth century, but the first steps towards reforming the revenue system in Java were undertaken by Sir Stamford Raffles who headed the British occupation of the island during the Napoleonic Wars. Raffles and his assistants were much influenced by their Indian experience, especially the attempts being made in the Madras region to settle land rights (and therefore tax obligations), not with landlords or local nobility but with the individual cultivators. The abuses inherent in the indirect system were to be removed by setting a fixed amount of payment on each cultivator and collecting it through a government bureaucracy specially set up for the purpose. The fault with Raffles' plan lay in the fact that a basic requirement for individual settlement was a detailed land cadastre, and this did not exist in Java. It was Raffles' sanguine expectation that the basic data on land area, ownership, land type, and land yields required for a cadastre, could be obtained from village chiefs. As most village chiefs had no accurate notion of these data and no way of determining them, the figures handed into the

revenue authorities were largely fictitious. Assessments
were made in a rough and ready fashion, and the system in
practice proved to be as inequitable and unjust as the
old one.
     The returning Dutch abandoned all attempts at indi-
vidual assessment and from 1820 to 1872 collected revenues by a system of bargaining with village chiefs.
Pressures for a reform of the system again mounted towards the end of the century, but it was not until the
early years of the present century that attempts were
made to prepare detailed individual assessments based on
careful measurement and classification of each plot. In
the first three decades of the twentieth century all
agricultural land in Java, Bali, Lombok, and Southern
Sulawesi was classified in this way. The land surveying
and assessment was done for each kawedanan on a rotating
system so that all land was reclassified and new tariffs
drawn up every ten years.
     By the time the Japanese army assumed control over
the islands in 1942, the land tax in Java, Bali, Lombok,
and South Sulawesi had reached a considerable degree of
sophistication in its assessment and collection. Following World War II and the winning of its independence, the
Indonesian government faced the task of introducing a new
set of tax measures. It would have been easy to continue
levying the tax, as the bulk of the extremely detailed
data on land type, land area, crop yields, etc., had survived into the independence period. There also existed a
number of indigenous officials trained by the Dutch in
administering the tax. Nevertheless, the tax was indel-
ibly associated in the minds of the rural people with the
colonial regime. Thus, a compromise was reached to abolish the land tax as such and replace it with an agricultural income tax. Nevertheless, while the old tax office
now became the Office of Land Registration and Land Income Tax, as one observer of the rural Javanese scene in
the early 1950s has pointed out, local officials understood little about the new tax and in most cases simply
went on collecting the land tax based on pre-war assessments (but multiplied by a factor to account for the difference in value between the old guilder and the new
rupiah).[3] The revenues, however, seem to have been small
in amount and it is extremely unclear where they went.
The bulk were probably swallowed up by salaries of local
officials and by administrative costs.
     The generally unsatisfactory working of the new tax
law was recognized by a measure passed in 1959, which re-
vived the concept of land taxation in the pajak hasil
bumi or tax on land yields. This tax was to differ in
two important respects from landrente. First, the tax
was to be levied at a rate of 5 percent of the annual
"net value" of land (instead of the landrente ad valorem
rate of 8 to 20 percent) and second, it was to be used

principally as a source of revenue for the kabupaten
governments to spend on rural development projects. With
the adoption of this new law there was still little progress in the collection of the tax in the 1959-65 period,
largely due to the considerable unrest in rural areas of
Java and Bali and the opposition to the tax on the part
of the powerful Communist-backed Barisan Tani Indonesia.
In November 1965 the name pajak hasil bumi was changed to
Iuran Pembangunan Daerah or Ipeda. The change in name
signalled a new attitude on the part of the central government toward the problem of taxing land, as the measure
represented an attempt to replace the "negative" connota-
tion attached to the phrase pajak hasil bumi (with its
echoes, for the farmers at least, of the old colonial
landrente) with the more "positive" idea of pembangunan
daerah or regional development. Presumably, the farmer
was not now paying a tax (pajak) so much as making a contribution (iuran) to regional, by implication to his own,
development. Indeed, officials in the Ipeda Directorate
now seem rather reluctant to consider Ipeda as a tax at
all and attach significance to the fact that it is under
the jurisdiction of the Directorate-General of Finance
within the Ministry of Finance and not the Directorate-
General of Taxation. The change of the name in 1965 was
also accompanied by a major reorganization of the scope
and administration of the tax. Assessment was divided
into five sectors: rural, urban, estates, mining, and
forestry. Estates, mining, and forestry enterprises had
not before been assessed for land tax, whereas the urban
tax became an extention of the verponding or land tax
levied on urban landowners who were Dutch nationals.

The current administration of the Ipeda tax is under
the control of the Ipeda Directorate within the Ministry
of Finance. The Ipeda Directorate, together with the
Minister and other senior officials in the Finance Ministry and the National Planning Agency, set the annual budget target, whereas the task of compiling the assessment
books for each village, which list the taxpayers by name
together with their individual assessment, falls to the
regional Ipeda officials. These officials are central
government employees posted to the regions; there is
usually one Ipeda Regional Office to each former residen-
cy in Java. It is important to stress that the local
government officials at province, kabupaten, and village
level have no control over the assessment of Ipeda; this
is done by the Ipeda Directorate and the Ipeda Regional
Office down to the individual assessment of each taxpayer in each sector. The local administration assists
in the collection, and the determination over the use of
funds is principally the responsibility of the kabupaten.

II

With the above historical perspective on the evolution of the land tax in Indonesia, some attention is warranted in examining current variations in assessment rates and techniques on both a regional and sectoral basis. An analysis of overall Ipeda assessments in each of the five sectors (rural, urban, estates, mining, and forestry) in the 1969-1974 period reveals that overall rates have increased threefold and realized revenues have almost quadrupled, although these increases have not been uniform for all sectors. Thus, the share of the rural sector in both assessment and realized revenues has declined while the other sectors (except mining) have all increased their proportion of the total. In addition, there has been a particularly large increase between 1973 and 1974 in both urban and estates sector assessment, although the increase in assessment was not accompanied by a correspondingly large increase in realized revenues. Regional comparisons indicate that both assessment and revenues in Java, as a proportion of the total, have declined from 1969 to 1974. The only exception to this trend is in the urban sector, where assessed and realized revenue have increased with reference to the national total. In the estates sector a particular effort has been made to increase revenues from North Sumatra, while in forestry, Kalimantan accounts for the bulk of the revenue. Finally, the mining sector revenues have been dominated by the oil rich provinces of South Sumatra and Riau, although revenues have also expanded in D. I. Aceh, East Kalimantan, and Southeast Sulawesi. In summary, while attempts have been made in recent years to expand revenues in the urban, forestry, and mining sectors, the Ipeda tax remains predominantly a tax on agricultural land, with particular emphasis on smallholder agriculture. Indeed, in 1974, 44 percent of total revenues were still coming from smallholder agricultural land in Java, undoubtedly the poorest sector of all. The equity aspects of this will be discussed later in the paper.

Assessment techniques both within and between sectors vary considerably for the Ipeda tax. In practice, in the rural sector in Java, Bali, Lombok, and Southern Sulawesi, the basis of assessment is still the data on land area and land class dating from Dutch times. In 1959, when the pajak hasil bumi was established, a new tariff was set simply by multiplying the old tariff by 28, the latter figure being derived as follows:

$$\frac{0.05}{0.12} \times \frac{Rp\ 200}{Rp\ 3} = 28$$

This formula was intended to take into account the fact

that the new tax was to be calculated on a basis of 5 percent of net yield (while landrente was between 8 and 20 percent) and that the price of padi in 1959 was Rp 200 per quintal compared with Rp 3 at the time of the last assessment. Between 1960 and 1965 the assessments were not altered despite progressively worsening inflation, whereas in 1966 the new Ipeda Directorate decreed that the assessments in new rupiah should be 60 percent of those in old rupiah (implying a six-hundred-fold increase in tariff in terms of old money).

In the post-1966 era, assessments in the rural sector have increased steadily. In 1967 there was a four-fold increase in individual assessments in the rural sector, and in the period from 1968-1971, increases were applied by the various Ipeda Regional Offices in Java on a varying basis, though on average there was a threefold increase during the period 1968-1971. In 1972 assessments were raised again by 10 percent everywhere in Indonesia, while in 1973 tariffs were raised 20 percent in Java and between 30 and 50 percent in parts of Sumatra. The ostensible reason for these increases was the rise in the price of padi (although such data as are available on rural market padi prices suggest that these rose rather less over the period than Ipeda assessments). Actually, the need to increase assessments arose from the increase in the overall target imposed from Jakarta and published in the national budget. The target in the 1973/74 budget was Rp 18.5 billion, an increase of over 50 percent from the previous year's target of Rp 12 billion. The 1974/75 target was given as Rp 24 billion, while for 1975/76 it was increased to Rp 31.7 billion. Each of these annual increases necessitated in turn an increase in individual assessment by sector.

In almost all the provinces outside the "old areas," assessment in the rural sector is hampered by lack of adequate data on land area, class, and ownership. No detailed measurement or classification of land was carried out under the Dutch in Sumatra, Kalimantan, or the rest of Sulawesi or the eastern islands of Sumba, Flores, and Timor. Thus, the data on land area and class, yields per hectare and tariffs assembled for Java were not available to guide the Ipeda Directorate in these areas in the task of assessing each cultivator. The only alternative, given the constraints of finance and manpower facing the Directorate, was to obtain the information necessary for personal assessment by requiring each landowner to fill in a form stating his landholdings by area and type of land and crop grown. Where areas were not known and could not be accurately estimated, cultivators were asked for details on numbers of trees planted (for crops such as coffee, rubber, coconuts, cloves, etc.) or, in the case of sawah, the amount of seed sown. Not surprisingly, this procedure has led to gross under-assessment in

all the "new areas." Village heads are often lax in
checking that all farmers in their areas have filed
statements on their landholdings, and because these regions lack any historical tradition of land taxation,
farmers are far less willing to comply with the new regulations than in Java. It is significant that Ipeda assessment in Sumatra approaches that of Java only in those
areas of south and central Lampung, where the great majority of the farmers are Javanese migrants. In addition, the proportion of taxpayers to total population is
much higher in the old areas where land measurement and
registration practices have been established for a long
period. Average assessment per taxpayer, however, is
often higher in the "new areas" in Sumatra and Sulawesi
than in Java, despite the much lower tariffs per hectare,
reflecting much larger farm units in the outer islands
compared with Java.

There is still widespread evasion of registration
procedures in the outer islands. For example, while it
would appear that almost all sawah in Java and a substantial proportion in South Sulawesi is being assessed, sawah assessed in Sumatra falls far short of total sawah
estimates by the Department of Agriculture. These latter
are not very accurate either--in the absence of proper
land mapping and measurement, accurate figures are impossible to obtain-- but one can only conclude that the
greater part of sawah in Sumatra is probably not yet
being assessed for Ipeda. The problem for dry land
(small plantations, etc.) in these "new areas" is likely
to be even greater.

In brief, an overview of assessment techniques reveals that while almost everywhere some attempt has been
made to apply the 5 percent of net yield rule, in practice, procedures differ greatly between regions, and over
time. This lack of uniformity can largely be attributed
to an inadequate data base. In the rural sector in particular, a heavy reliance on the old data from pre-war
Dutch assessments in Java, Bali, and Sulawesi, has meant
that assessment procedures in these areas are different
from other parts of the country where landrente was not
levied. Thus, using the data from regional statistics,
there would appear to be little correlation between increases in Ipeda assessment on the one hand and increases
in agricultural output on the other. Looking again at
increases in the value of gross smallholder agricultural
output (food crops valued at current prices) it would appear that any correlation with increases in Ipeda assessment was largely coincidental. At the extreme, agricultural output in West Nusatenggara in 1970-1971 dropped by
20 percent, while Ipeda assessment increased by the same
amount. By and large, however, as a national pattern,
rural sector Ipeda assessments tended to increase at a
steady rate compared with the erratic pattern of in-

creases in value of smallholder output. Nevertheless,
the rate of increase has lagged somewhat behind the increase in smallholder output. Given the fact that the
annual rate of increase in the Ipeda assessment is determined principally by the increase in the central government budget target, it is hardly surprising that the correlation with increases in agricultural output is so
weak.

In summary, current procedures for Ipeda assessment
constitutes a weak mechanism for tapping increments in
agricultural income accruing to the smallholder sector.
This is principally due to the weakness of the data base
on which assessments are calculated and the target system
which necessitates arbitrary across-the-board increases
in individual assessments according to increases in the
budget target rather than any estimate or increase in
value of output. Reform will inevitably be slow, given
the constraints of manpower under which the Directorate
operates. Later in the paper some suggestions are put
forward for changes in assessment procedures, which may
help to make the tax both more elastic with respect to
increases in agricultural incomes and more equitable in
its incidence.

III

The above analysis revealed a wide range of variations with respect to assessment procedures for the Ipeda
tax, and a similar set of circumstances also prevails
concerning the other components of the taxation function,
most notably in the collection and use of the Ipeda tax.
Looking first at collection, inevitably the task of mobilizing small sums of money from a vast number of taxpayers in the rural sector imposes a number of administrative problems. In 1971, there were estimated to be
over twenty-one million taxpayers in the rural sector.
It must be stressed that all landowners must pay Ipeda,
however small the holding. Many of the taxpayers (especially in the densely populated areas of Java) who own
only small house gardens, are paying very small sums, often less than Rp 500 per year. In very poor areas of
Central Java such as Gunung Kidul, over 90 percent of the
taxpayers are paying less than Rp 500 per year, while data
from comparatively more prosperous areas suggest that
about 30 percent of all taxpayers are paying less than
Rp 500.

Despite government efforts in tax collection, a
chronic and sometimes serious problem exists with respect
to the cumulation of arrears on the Ipeda tax. Although
revenue collected increased relative to assessment between 1969 and 1974, total revenues do not usually equal
total assessment in any year for any sector. Uncollected

revenues in any one year are carried over to the following year so that, of total revenues in any year, only a
part will be from the current year's assessment, while the
rest come from arrears of previous years. For example,
from total revenues in 1972 of Rp 14.9 billion, only 58
percent (Rp 8.7 billion) came from the current year's assessment and the rest from arrears. The problem of arrears is obviously a compounding one; if a province or
kabupaten is already in arrears it can concentrate either
on collecting the backlog or on collecting current assessment. There is probably a strong case in those areas
where arrears are comparatively high, for abolishing arrears dating back more than two years and concentrating
on collecting current assessments (the more so as some of
these arrears may well have been paid by the taxpayers
but, owing to tax administration, never properly documented).

The pattern of arrears differs considerably among
provinces and within kabupaten and the reasons for these
great discrepancies, although not immediately apparent,
would seem to relate to the following three factors:
first, the zeal of kabupaten and village officials in
using their kewibawaan (authority) to collect the money
from the taxpayers; second, the ability of the Ipeda
bureaucracy itself to carry out the process of assessment
and delivering the lists of taxpayers to the villages as
early in the year as possible, as well as providing continuing supervision of collection throughout the year;
and third, the ability and willingness of the taxpayers
to pay. Concerning the third factor, it is worth pointing out that there seems to be no strong correlation between "poorness" of an area (defined, for example, in
terms of irrigation facilities) and arrears. For example, in the Malang area of East Java, the kecamatan in the
poor limestone areas in the south were quicker in paying
than several nearer the city in the more prosperous
agricultural areas.

Aside from the problem of collection and arrears,
when seen from the perspective as a revenue source, the
Ipeda tax constitutes the most important fund of development resources for local government agencies. Law 11 of
1959, which regulated the assessment and collection of the
pajak hasil bumi (subsequently Ipeda), also made provisions for the use of the revenues. Article 17 stated
that all yields from the tax were to be deposited with
the second level regions (kabupaten) for financing agricultural development. A subsequent regulation defined
rural development projects for this purpose as including
irrigation infrastructure, roads, bridges, flood control
embankments, seed stations, and the purchase of agricultural inputs such as fertilizer. Ten percent of the
total revenue was to be used for collection fees (as
noted above) but at least 75 percent of the remainder had

to be spent on infrastructure construction and rehabilitation. The regulation further stressed the need for
full accounting of revenues and expenditure in the kabupaten annual budgets. However, later regulations began
to show some weakening of control over use of Ipeda
funds. A 1967 Ministry of Finance regulation stated that
all kabupaten were required to hand over 10 percent of
the Ipeda revenues to the provincial government and, with
a further 10 percent, to purchase shares in the provincial development banks. A 1969 regulation conceded that
if kabupaten income from provincial subsidies and their
own tax sources was insufficient to cover routine expenses, Ipeda funds could be used for this purpose.
Several provincial governments have issued regulations on
the use of Ipeda funds, further elaborating (and sometimes apparently contradicting) those of the central government. In 1970, Central Java abolished the requirement
to deposit both the 10 percent with the province and the
10 percent with the provincial development bank.

In brief, the present situation regarding the use of
Ipeda revenues is very confused. Although a target figure enters the central government budget, and has done so
since 1972/73, the revenues never pass above the kabupaten (apart from the deposits with the province and the
provincial development banks where these are still made).
Responsibility for the use of these funds rests entirely
with the kabupaten, which may either decide to turn a portion of the revenues back to the villages for village
development projects, or use the entire revenues for its
own expenditures. In any case, all kabupaten are required to give a full account of Ipeda (and other) revenues in their annual budgets of revenues and expenditure.
These budgets are the principal financial documents at
the provincial and kabupaten level. They are almost invariably prepared in two parts, routine and development,
listing revenues from subsidies and locally raised
sources, and indicating expenditures on salaries and
wages, routine office expenses and various other categories of development activities. In practice, the con-
tents of the routine and development budgets differ considerably from kabupaten to kabupaten and from province
to province. It is, therefore, impossible to compare total
revenues or expenditures for routine or development purposes in any two kabupaten, since major components may
have been treated differently. However, taken as a
whole, and without paying too much attention to the categories to which expenditures and revenues are assigned,
these budgets give many useful clues to such questions as
the overall importance of Ipeda in total kabupaten revenues, the size of total revenues devoted to development
compared with total Ipeda revenues, and the division of
development funds among various categories within the
development budget.

In a study conducted by the author in 1972/73 of twenty-three kabupaten in Java, Sumatra, and South Sulawesi, it was found that in fourteen kabupaten, planned or targeted revenue from the Ipeda tax exceeded, by a large margin, those targets which had been established for the other two principle sources of kabupaten revenue (provincial subsidies and other kabupaten taxes). While it should be stressed that these estimates are based upon planned, not realized revenues, for those kabupaten where actual collection records for the previous year were available, it appeared that shortfalls compared to planned targets were not large. Another way of looking at the importance of Ipeda revenues in total kabupaten budgets is to make a comparison of Ipeda revenues with kabupaten expenditures on development. Thus, budgets available from thirty-four kabupaten in Java, South Sulawesi, and Sumatra, indicate that their combined (planned) Ipeda revenue in 1972-1973 amounted to Rp 3.3 billion, whereas planned expenditure on "development," as shown in the kabupaten budgets, amounted to Rp 3.1 billion. Of the Rp 3.1 billion spent on development, expenditure on economic infrastructure accounted for Rp 1.1 billion, on social infrastructure Rp 0.52 billion, and on bureaucratic infrastructure Rp 0.66 billion. An amount of Rp 0.27 billion was directly returned to villages to be spent on specified development projects. Overall, a sum equal to 32 percent of the total Ipeda revenues was spent on economic infrastructure, 20 percent on bureaucratic infrastructure, and 15 percent on social infrastructure. It was far from clear from the information given in the budgets where the remaining development revenues went. Given the difficulties described above, in any comparison of kabupaten budgets these estimates must be treated with caution, but they do suggest that only about half of the total Ipeda revenues are being used for economic and social infrastructure.

IV

In the extensive literature that has sprung up in the last two decades on the role of agriculture in economic development, there have been a number of arguments put forward for the necessity and desirability of taxing agriculture. These arguments would seem to fall into four broad categories. Firstly, authors such as Lewis, Nurkse, and Kaldor, argue that some form of taxation on rural producers is essential to induce a growing transfer of agricultural produce to the urban sector as wage goods for the expanding labour force in this sector.[4] Lewis, in his original model stressed the unlikelihood of sufficient food being forthcoming through the market at a price compatible with the maintenance of stable wages in

the urban sector. This is the core of what may be
termed the "surplus extraction" approach to agricultural
taxation. A second argument that has developed in the
literature in favour of land taxation in developing
countries is the favourable effect it may have on encouraging more intensive use of land, and discouraging large
landholdings by assessing the tax at a progressive rate.
This argument has gained wide currency in the Latin
American context, but given the pattern of tiny landholdings and land fragmentation prevailing in much of Java
and many parts of the outer islands, it is probably of
limited relevance to Indonesia.

A third broad argument that has been advanced on the
subject of land taxation is what may be termed the "development from below" argument. This stresses the need
for a land tax (or indeed any tax on the agricultural
sector) to be localized in its operation. Writers such
as Ursula Hicks and Arthur Lewis have argued that farmers
will comply far more happily with tax procedures if they
directly benefit from the use of the funds. Arthur Lewis
argues that,

> Farmers resent paying taxes for which they may
> get no return. However, if the services are
> provided by local authorities under their con-
> trol, to whom the taxes are paid, the farmers
> can see what they are getting for their money
> and are more willing to give voluntary labour
> as well as pay more taxes to meet their own
> needs. Decentralization thus raises taxable
> capacity.[5]

A fourth argument in favour of taxing agricultural land
in developing countries involves the concept of "intersectoral inequity." It is asserted that the agricultural
sector is being more lightly taxed than the non-agricultural sector both in relation to ability to pay and in
relation to benefits received. This argument has gained
wide currency in the literature with respect to the Indian case, although it has also been made in the Indonesian context by Paauw.[6]

It is beyond the scope of this paper to rigorously
evaluate the present system of taxing agriculture in Indonesia in the light of the above criteria. However, an
attempt can be made to briefly delineate some of the
problems and anomalies in the system of agricultural
taxation described above and suggest certain reforms in
the system which would seem both feasible and desirable
in the short run. Taking first the intersectoral inequity argument, the most striking difference between taxation on urban and agricultural incomes in Indonesia is
the very high rates of exemption in the income tax compared with Ipeda. As was pointed out above, Ipeda is

levied on all landholdings, however small, with virtually no exemptions. Whereas recent legislation sharply reduces the burden of income taxation on lower levels of income, both Ipeda and the other imposts on the rural sector are levied on all classes of income.

The tax-free income exemption for the average family (one wage earner supporting a wife and three children) in 1974 was Rp 300,000. Above this income, taxation is reasonably progressive, but below it no tax is paid at all. If presumptive income is computed from one hectare of well-irrigated sawah in 1974 to be about Rp 280,000 (annual yield of ten tons of padi, market price of padi of about Rp 40,000 and a deduction of 30 percent for costs of production), then a farmer would have to own and operate more than one hectare of well-irrigated sawah before his income exceeded the exemption for income tax. In fact, a farmer owning this amount of land anywhere in Java would be paying Ipeda in excess of Rp 7,500. Of course the great majority of farmers in Java do not own one hectare of sawah, and many only own a housegarden. Even farmers owning more than one hectare of sawah will not usually be receiving the full income from it because social obligations may force them to rent or sharecrop out a portion of the land to others. This is usually true of village officials who receive use rights to sawah land in lieu of salary. Pressure of other work usually means that most of this land is, in fact, operated by others, and their income is reduced accordingly.

In brief, it would seem plausible to argue that there is a considerable degree of horizontal inequity between the agricultural and urban sectors in favour of the latter, at least in the lower-income brackets where the bulk of the population is also subject to a number of imposts and levies which are not immediately obvious from official statistics. Also, as Ved P. Ghandi stressed in the study already cited, allowance should be made in comparing tax burdens for the difference in the cost of living between the agricultural and urban sector. Data from the 1969/70 household expenditure survey suggests that this differential is considerable both for Java and the outer islands. Food, housing, education, and other social services all cost more in urban areas, thus reducing the purchasing power of urban incomes compared to rural ones. Account should also be taken of the incidence of public expenditures in comparing intersectoral tax burdens. The relatively higher tax burden on farm incomes must be weighed against subsidies implicit in the Bimas program and the provision of irrigation water at less than cost. Indeed, comparison of fiscal burdens, either intersectoral or interpersonal, is a hazardous statistical exercise in any context and especially so in a country where data is as defective as Indonesia.

If the evidence of intersectoral inequity in fiscal burdens in Indonesia is still somewhat dubious, there is probably a stronger case for arguing that interregional inequities in the tax structure are quite considerable. As was pointed out above, the rate of Ipeda assessment per hectare varies, considerably both within Java and between Java and other parts of the country. Furthermore, the considerable interregional differentials in the pattern of arrears means that effective incidence of the tax again varies considerably between regions, even where assessments are approximately similar. It can be calculated that Ipeda assessment as a proportion of gross value added in the smallholder sector is over twice as high in Java, on average, than in most provinces of Sumatra and Kalimantan. Add to this the fact that arrears tend to be higher in the outer islands than Java, and it would seem plausible to argue that the effective incidence of agricultural taxation in Sumatra and Kalimantan, is considerably less than in Java and Sulawesi. (It must be noted though, that the smallholder cash crop sector, in particular rubber, tobacco, and cloves, is also taxed through the export tax, and this tends to increase the burden on smallholder agriculture in the outer islands relative to Java.)

The second argument that has gained wide currency in the literature is the surplus extraction approach that is implicit in the two sector models of economic development pioneered by Lewis. Against this argument, in the Indonesian case, it can be argued that there is only a weak case for demanding that a tax mechanism be used to extract food supplies from the rural sector when the prices offered to rural producers for their marketed crop is low both by world standards, and in relation to the price of goods they can buy. A considerable literature has evolved in recent years on the question of the price responsiveness of smallholder producers in the agricultural sector, and data from many Asian countries would suggest that farmers' elasticity of supply is positive with respect to price changes. There would thus appear to be a case for at least endeavouring to implement a more favourable price environment for the farmer before relying on taxes to extract food supplies not voluntarily forthcoming through the market.

The two other arguments discussed above for implementing agricultural taxation in an economy such as Indonesia can be analyzed more briefly. As was pointed out in a previous section, there is little evidence that use of Ipeda revenues necessarily reflects the desires and needs of the rural population. The claim that decentralized decision-making may produce results more in accordance with the people's wishes is not very persuasive in a context where political activity is constrained at the village level. Lastly, as was pointed out above, the

argument that land taxation leads to greater land utilization would not appear to be a crucial one anywhere in
land-scarce Java, although it may have some relevance in
parts of the outer islands.

V

With the above arguments in perspective, the issue
must be addressed concerning the future for land taxation and agricultural taxation in general in the Indonesian context. Clearly it would be premature and irre-
sponsible to advocate the outright abolition of the
existing system of land taxation on the grounds of its
manifest defects. As agricultural output continues to
expand and as the importance of revenue from natural resources (oil, timber, and mining) in the government budget diminishes over time, taxation of both agricultural
and non-agricultural incomes must come to play a dominant
role in Indonesian state finance, as it does in developed
countries. It would be ultimately desirable for taxation
on all types of income, regardless of source, to be amalgamated and subjected to the same criteria of assessment.
Professor Raj Krishna identifies two crucial steps necessary to the process of integrating agricultural and non-
agricultural taxation.

> First, all holdings with an acreage which
> yields a net income less than the income tax
> exemption limit on the basis of standard in-
> come coefficients should be exempted from
> the tax . . . . Secondly while the income
> per acre coefficients will be constant for
> all farmers of a certain farm class, the tax
> can be made progressive by size of holding
> according to the income determined--the de-
> gree of progression being similar to that of
> the general income tax.[7]

It will be noted that Raj Krishna stresses that
"standard income coefficients" be used to assess income
from land, i.e., that income be assessed on a presumptive
basis. This indeed was the rationale behind the assessment of landrente in colonial times, described in the
preceding section. Land was classified according to productive capacity and average yields computed for each
type of land from the test plots. The system has the
added advantage of not penalizing incremental effort at
the margin; the tax is levied on presumed rather than
actual income. Because it would seem desirable on both
incentive and administrative grounds to assess agricultural tax on a presumptive basis, the procedure has in
fact been advocated by a number of authorities. It does

not represent full integration with ordinary income tax
because the latter is assessed on an actual basis, but on
the other hand, it avoids having to assess the actual income of millions of smallholder agriculturalists who do
not keep records and to whom the concept of income is
largely alien. This method of assessment of agricultural
income tax has been advocated by the Raj Committee in India and by the Musgrave Commission in Columbia.[8] In Indonesia, in order to adopt a method of assessing agricultural taxation based upon an estimate of presumptive income from land, it would seem that the Ipeda Directorate
in cooperation with other bureaucracies such as the Department of Agriculture, the Land Registration Offices
and the Central Bureau of Statistics, would need to obtain the following data on a regular basis: (1) Up-to-
date data on land areas, land classification, and land
ownership for all cultivated land in Indonesia. (2) Data
on average or standard yields per hectare for all major
crops by region for each class of land. (3) Data on
costs of production for each major land type (taking into
account multiple cropping potential) so that benchmark
percentage deductions can be computed. (4) Data on rural
market prices for all important marketed crops. There
should also be an attempt in each region to note marketing procedures and in particular divergencies between
"farmgate prices" and rural market prices. Where these
seem excessive, there is possibly some distortion operating (such as unofficial levies on the road) which ultimately functions as a tax on the producer.
　　Most of the above data are, in part, at least available, or the machinery exists for obtaining them. The
major constraint as far as the Ipeda Directorate is concerned is lack of manpower for obtaining (1) and collat-
ing the data listed under (2), (3), and (4), which are
available from other sources. Obviously, the Ipeda Directorate alone cannot be expected to undertake unaided the
enormous task of surveying and classifying agricultural
land in the outer islands. There would seem to be a need
for a concerted effort among all government departments
concerned with land use, possibly with external assistance to use modern methods such as aerial photography to
prepare new landmaps for Sumatra, Kalimantan, and Eastern
Indonesia, and to revise existing maps for Java, Bali, and
South Sulawesi. If these data were available, the task
would become much easier in assessing land values that
were an accurate reflection of current production trends.
Data on land classifications could, as a general rule, be
obtained on a ten-year basis, although special exer-
cises would have to be carried out in areas where there
had been dramatic changes in, for example, irrigation
facilities. Up-to-date data on yields for major crops
valued at rural market prices could be used for recalcu-
lating values at two or five year intervals, the

shorter period being more appropriate in periods of rapid
price increase or rapid increase in yields. This would,
in large part, remedy the problem of inelasticity with respect to increasing output and/or rising prices, which has
been the major defect of many land taxes throughout the
world. It would certainly be a more effective means of
introducing elasticity with equity than the arbitrary
across-the-board tariff increases which have been employed by the Ipeda Directorate in the post-1966 period.

It would obviously be desirable if the reformed land
tax were subject to the same degree of exemptions and
progression as the ordinary income tax, and this must be
seen as the long-term goal. However, as was pointed out
above, given the very sweeping exemptions now in force
for the income tax, applying the same exemptions to the
Ipeda taxpayers would effectively mean its abolition in
rural Java. This in turn would deprive most kabupaten of
their major source of internally raised revenue. A more
feasible short-term compromise may be to abolish Ipeda on
all landholdings of less than a certain size and shift
the bulk of the assessment onto the larger landholders.
This, of course, would still be inequitable in the sense
that even the "large" landholders, at least in Java, are
still poor by any absolute standard.

Existing abuses on the use of Ipeda funds could, in
part, be remedied by more stringent earmarking procedures,
which would involve tighter control of the whole kabupaten budgeting process, not just from higher levels of
administration but also from the local representative
councils. There would also seem to be special scope for
expanding village-based projects using at least part of
the village Ipeda assessment. This may provide an incentive for more rapid payment on the part of the taxpayers
(if it were known that the money was to be used for village-based projects) and would also give more opportunities to the village communities to carry out their own
projects (preferably using paid labour). It must be
stressed, however, that few regions anywhere in Indonesia
have at their disposal the means to effectively implement
programs of rural development with finances raised from
their own resources. The most urgent need, therefore, is
for a policy of fiscal decentralization in Indonesia that
specifically caters for providing central government
funds to the various levels of regional government and
rigorously controlling the use of such funds. Funds
would have to be disbursed according to need, taking into
account the ability of each level of government to raise
revenues internally. The very poorest regions would obviously be almost entirely dependent on grants from
above. Given this approach, the crucial need in planning
development expenditures is firstly, to establish what the
minimum needs are, and secondly, to determine, region by
region, where the deficiencies lie. To this end it would

be useful for all provinces, kabupaten within provinces, kecamatan within kabupaten, and villages within kecamatan, to be ranked according to a number of criteria such as population/hectare of cultivated land, irrigated land as a percentage of total cultivated land, total food production (in calorie equivalents) per capita, percentage of rural families owning sawah, percentage of children of school age in school, road mileage in relation to area, etc. It would then be desirable to rank areas according to "need" on the basis of these factors. Funds should be allocated not in a lump sum but disaggregated and earmarked. It is quite possible that a province will be quite well off for roads but very densely populated. The needs of the area would primarily be for increased education, public health (including family planning), and employment opportunities. The poorest of all, the landless and near landless, are probably in need of basic income supplements (in either cash or kind) as well as economic and social services listed above.

The allocation of funds from center to regions depends not only on the development needs of the region concerned but also on its own revenue-raising capacity. This can be determined in a rough fashion by comparing per capita income estimates by province. It is important to stress that in comparing a province's revenue performance with some concept of revenue capacity based on per capita income, all revenues raised including unofficial and village levies mentioned above should be included in the calculation. Too often arguments purporting to show that the agricultural sector is lightly taxed compared to the urban sector fail to fully account for the diversity of taxes and levies imposed on this sector.

In summary, the principal conclusion of this review of agricultural taxation in Indonesia must be that the system is in need of considerable reform if it is to function as an equitable and efficient way of tapping the expected increase in rural incomes in future years. If the overall Ipeda target imposed in the annual budget continues to rise and if funds and manpower are not made available for extension of assessment to the outer islands and for more intensive assessment of urban areas, the Ipeda Directorate will have little option but to continue to increase assessment on the Javanese peasantry. As was pointed out above, there has been encouraging progress during the period 1969-1974 towards lessening the overall burden of Ipeda on the rural sector in general, and particularly on the rural sector in Java. However, the Ipeda, together with the other imposts and levies discussed above, still remains a not inconsiderable burden on the agricultural population and poses considerable problems of intersectoral equity, at least for the lower-income groups.

NOTES

1. Ved P. Gandhi, Tax Burden on Indian Agriculture (Cambridge: Harvard Law School, 1966), and E. T. Mathew, Agricultural Taxation and Economic Development in India (Bombay: Asian Publishing House, 1968). For a critique of the Gandhi-Mathew type approach see in particular Raj Krishna, "Intersectoral Equity and Agricultural Taxation in India," Economic and Political Weekly, Special Number, (August, 1972).

2. C. Day, The Dutch in Java (London: Oxford University Press, 1966); Selosoemardjan, Social Change in Yogyakarta (Ithaca: Cornell University Press, 1962); and J. S. Furnivall, Netherlands India (London: Cambridge University Press, 1944).

3. R. Jay, Javanese Villagers (Boston: Massachusetts Institute of Technology Press, 1969), p. 372 ff.

4. See in particular the widely published article by Nicholas Kaldor, "The Role of Taxation in Economic Development," reprinted in Nicholas Kaldor, Essays in Economic Policy (London: Duckworth, 1964).

5. W. A. Lewis, "Agricultural Taxation in Developing Economies," in Agricultural Development and Economic Growth, Herman Southworth and Bruce Johnston, eds., (Ithaca: Cornell University Press, 1967).

6. For an exposition of this argument in the Indian case see Gandhi, Tax Burden on Indian Agriculture. Douglas Paauw discusses tax burdens in Financing Economic Development: The Indonesian Case (Glencoe: Free Press, 1960).

7. Krishna, "Intersectoral Equity and Agricultural Taxation in India."

8. Government of India, Report of the Committee on Taxation of Agricultural Income and Wealth (New Delhi: Ministry of Finance, 1972), and R. A. Musgrave and S. M. Gillis, eds., Fiscal Reform for Colombia (Cambridge: Harvard Law School International Tax Program, 1972), pp. 139 ff and 387 ff.

Part II

The Green Revolution

Introduction

Beginning in the late 1960s, Indonesia's government embarked upon a widespread campaign in promoting the use of the new high yielding rice varieties (HYVs) among the country's many smallholder cultivators. This campaign, commonly known as the Bimas program, continues as an active component of the government's current development effort, with Java constituting the primary target area, in addition to some locations in the islands of Sumatra and Sulawesi. While a great many problems have been encountered in the administration of the Bimas effort, the program continues to bring a substantial flow of resources to the smallholder sector, and in general, when measured in terms of total aggregate figures, it seems that the HYVs have made a sizeable contribution in increasing rice production. When national production figures are disaggregated, however, it becomes clear that not all segments of the rice producing sector have shared in the benefits of the new rice technology. Thus, at the village and farm level great variations can be found in the rates of adoption, yield levels, net income generated, and the general range of economic benefits engendered by the introduction of the new rice technology. No one single factor can be identified in explaining why such variations occur. In some cases, certain deficiencies can be diagnosed with respect to input and output marketing; in other instances inadequacies are found in infrastructure facilities, whereas in some cases certain socio-economic conditions within the village itself are serving to constrain the impact of the new rice technology.

The following two essays report on research involving case studies of village responses to the Green Revolution and they amply demonstrate the diversity of reactions to the new technology. The first essay examines two villages where the introduction of the HYVs is distinguished by wide differences in their impact upon the village economics. In the first village, located in East

Java, the adoption rate for the HYVs has been quite high, whereas in the second village, located in West Java, the response rate to the new varieties has been much less favorable. In addition, high variability was also discovered in the yield performance of the HYVs in comparison to local varieties. Thus, yield data for the village in East Java indicates that farmers cultivating HYVs were able to achieve marginal gains over those who cultivated local varieties, whereas in the village in West Java, farmers using the local varieties were able, in the majority of cases, to achieve yield levels which exceeded those attained by their neighbors cultivating the HYVs. The study indicates that these differences can be explained by superior irrigation facilities and higher rates of fertilizer application in the former village, whereas in the latter village the HYVs have been subject to serious pest damage. For this reason, many of the farmers in this village have decided to revert back to using traditional and locally improved varieties.

The inability to discern any major production impact in the adoption of the HYVs in the two villages is also reflected in measurements which indicate a lack of significant difference in net income yields between HYVs and local varieties. This data, along with the discovery that the HYVs have not generated a more than marginal increase in labor-use, compels the authors to conclude that the Green Revolution has yet to trigger any major transformation in the economies of the two villages. This rather discouraging assessment stands in contrast to the evidence advanced in the second essay, where the author reports on two village studies undertaken in Sumatra and Sulawesi, where in some instances, the Green Revolution has generated sizeable gains for those farmers who have adopted the new varieties. Thus, the evidence from farmers sampled in one village in West Sumatra indicates that the cultivation of the HYVs involved 99 percent of all rice plantings, a rate of acceptance which has been accompanied by an 85 percent increase in crop yields and an attendant 140 percent rise in net income. For the second village in South Sulawesi, the impact of the new rice technology has been much more limited with the cultivation of the HYVs involving only 20 percent of the total rice plantings. These contrasting levels of adoption are largely attributed to the widespread presence of irrigation facilities in the former village, and the relative absence of such facilities in the latter village.

The changes recorded above generally refer to the more immediate on-farm production and direct income gains generated by the adoption of the Green Revolution technology. In the second essay, however, the author seeks to measure the indirect contributions of production and income increases upon the larger village and local economy.

Thus, the analysis explores the extent to which the Green Revolution has served to generate greater demand for locally produced goods and services. It is generally concluded that because of weak backward and forward linkages within the local economy, the two villages have not been able to capture a great many of the gains and multiplier effects generated by the adoption of the HYVs. Many of these secondary benefits are being absorbed by extra-local systems, whether they be by transfers through agricultural taxation, sharecropping payments to absentee landlords, or demands for goods from urban based manufacturers. The relatively limited local level impact associated with the Green Revolution can be attributed to conditions both internal and external to the village. Thus, traditional patterns of work organization in the village in South Sulawesi have constrained many farm households in moving from two croppings per year to a cycle which could involve nearly three croppings per year. In terms of external factors, it is noted by the author that taxation and rural sector policies are needed which direct the flow of investment towards a more village based development effort.

The following essays clearly demonstrate the wide variability of village and farm level responses to the Green Revolution technology. Adoption rates and production performance seem to be conditioned by a wide range of economic and social factors. In most instances, existing production constraints are amenable to policy intervention. Thus, expansion of irrigation facilities, improvements in pest control, and further investments in research and extension services should open the way to further advances in raising agricultural productivity. The larger question still looms, however, as to whether the benefits which flow from increased farm productivity can be more fully retained within the confines of the rural sector. In great part, this issue can only be addressed by a choice of policy measures which seek to enhance and diversify the capacities of the rural economy in capturing the gains generated by the Green Revolution.

4

Sidoarjo, East Java, and Subang, West Java

Dibyo Prabowo and Sajogyo

The Indonesian government sees adequate domestic rice production as a major policy objective. Population is growing at 2.3 percent per year, per capita rice consumption is increasing, and rice production is not keeping pace. Rice yields have consistently averaged less than 2 t/ha for several decades. For several years the importation of rice has cost Indonesia 5 to 15 percent of her foreign exchange earnings each year. The government has been aware that speedy adoption by farmers of the new rice technology requires funds. Various national efforts have been made to raise rice production. The latest, the so-called Bimas program, is a coordination of extension and credit, and due to this program farmers are using better methods of farming and getting better yields. It is apparent however, that the new rice technology is being accepted more rapidly in some areas than others. To study the reasons for this difference two villages have been examined with high potentials for rice production but with very different experiences in the adoption of modern varieties. The two sample villages are in East and West Java, two of the three major rice growing areas of Java. The East Java village of Sidomulyo has shown a spectacular response to the introduction of modern varieties whereas the West Java village of Cidahu has shown a poor response.

I

Sidomulyo, the "high response" village, is in the large Brantas river delta of East Java. It is only nine meters above sea level, with a dry season of 4.5 to 6 months. The village is forty kilometers south of Surabaya, the provincial capital. Cidahu, the "low response" village, is in the northern coastal plains of West Java. It is 150 kilometers west of Jakarta, the national capital, and it is 90 meters above sea level, on flat and

68

gently sloping terrain, with 3 to 4.5 months of dry season. The rainiest months are December and January. From
the provincial capital, Surabaya, it takes about one hour
to reach Sidomulyo by road. The village is about 1.5
kilometers from Krian town, through which buses pass
regularly. Krian is also on the railroad, but only third
class trains stop there. Local transportation is by
horse cart (becak). Sidomulyo has a road density of ten
kilometers per square kilometer of which six percent is
paved. In the dry climate, dirt roads do not often present a problem for truck-transport. Cidahu is only five
kilometers from its district capital of Subang. Its road
density is four kilometers per square kilometer, of which
27 percent is paved. Sidomulyo has one elementary
school, Cidahu has two. All three are government operated. There is no clinic in either village.

In the 1971 population census, Sidomulyo had 2,137
persons in 453 households. Of its 170 hectares of farmland, half was wet rice land. The rest was used for
trees and vegetables, for other crops, and for the house
sites. Of the wet rice land, one third was rented out
each year for sugar cane production. Population density
on total farmland was 0.08 hectare per capita and on wet
rice land, 0.04 hectare. Cidahu had a population of
3,322 persons in 958 households. Of its 480 hectares of
farmland a little over half was wet rice land and a
fourth was other crops. It had 0.14 hectare of farmland
per person, or 1.8 times more than Sidomulyo.

In both the wet and dry seasons farms in both study
areas usually have enough irrigation water and all sample
farmers were able to double-crop. During the 1972 dry
season a water shortage occurred in Sidomulyo because a
new irrigation system (Karangkates dam) was being developed and water distribution throughout the area was being
controlled in an effort to give all localities equal access to water. For this reason only 70 percent of the
sample farmers in Sidomulyo were able to grow rice during
the 1972 rice dry season. Both study areas are served by
modern canal irrigation facilities drawing water from
the river. Water is under the authority of the Ministry
of Public Works up to the secondary canal, and water
management in the village (tertiary canal) is handled by
village officials (ulu-ulu in Cidahu, kuwowo in Sidomulyo). Each of the fifteen officials in Cidahu is responsible for about 17.5 hectares of rice land. In Sidomulyo, each of the four officials is responsible for 20
hectares of wet rice land in one of the four sub-vil-
lages. Strictly speaking, farmers do not pay for water,
but they pay an assessment in terms of rough rice or
labor service. The amount of each year's contribution
depends on how much work is needed on the repair of
canals, bridges, etc. In Sidomulyo sample farmers made
an average contribution of 25 kilograms in the 1971/72

dry season. In Cidahu farmers contributed 42 kilograms in the 1971/72 wet season and 49 kilograms in the 1972 dry season plus two man-days of labor service each season.

The cropping patterns in both areas are dictated by weather. In Sidomulyo, the wet-season rice crop is grown from December to April, the period of heaviest rainfall and the dry-season crop is grown from May to September. The seasonal variation in rainfall is pronounced, but temperatures vary little. In Sidomulyo, in recent years multiple cropping has been generally adopted. Farmers of Sidomulyo have been obliged however, to rent out a third of their irrigated land each year to the nearby sugar mill in a rotating cycle of eighteen months for the production of sugar cane. The farmers' rice land is thus divided into three parcels. Most plots or parcels are located separately from each other, so all the parcels cannot be cultivated at the same time. Like Sidomulyo, Cidahu also has a reasonably intensive irrigation system, but there is no sugar mill in Cidahu and instead of growing such crops as sugar cane and tobacco, farmers cultivate rice throughout the year. Due to lack of water, a rice-planting intensity of only 100 to 150 percent has been reached. The locally practiced rotation calls for the farmer to leave his land idle during September and October.

Generally speaking farmers in the two villages have limited access to credit. Those who participated in the Bimas program could borrow a fixed amount per hectare to buy modern farm inputs. Loans matured in seven months and interest was 12 percent per year. Farmers in the Bimas program received the necessary agricultural inputs such as fertilizer, pesticides, and insecticides from the government as part of their credit package. For urea fertilizer they were charged Rp 26.60/kg. Urea was available commercially at a price at least 5 percent higher. Farmers outside the program had almost no sources of production credit. In Sidomulyo the paddy bank (lumbung desa) lent paddy mainly for consumption. In Cidahu, fellow farmers, neighbors, and relatives are common sources of credit.

In undertaking the research study, a partial census was made of 150 farm households in each village. This was followed by a sample selection of 75 farmers in Sidomulyo and 77 farmers in Cidahu. These 152 farmers were interviewed in the 1971 dry season, in the 1971/72 wet season, and in the 1972 dry season. Sample households were larger in Sidomulyo than in Cidahu, but farms and the rice area were a little smaller. Nearly all sample farmers were owner-operators. Tenants and part-owners operated on either a share crop or a leasehold system. When share-cropping was practiced, half the crop went to the owner and half to the tenant.

II

Varietal recommendations change overtime, depending
heavily upon the results of rice breeding or evaluation
trials at the Central Research Institute of Agriculture
at Bogor. Before modern varieties were introduced in
Java, several earlier varieties were considered high
yielding. These improved local varieties are commonly
known as bibit unggul nasional (ungnas), and they include
Syntha, Dara, Sigadis, Ramadja and Bengawan. These
varieties were mainly the result of the breeding work
based on Indonesian traditional local varieties that are
medium-responsive to fertilizer and have good flavor.
Farmers in the Bimas program are permitted to plant these
varieties. The more modern varieties, first introduced
in 1967, were known as bibit unggul baru. They included
PB8 (IR8), PB5 (IR5), and C4-63, and their use was required for maximum credit from the program. Modern rice
varieties have spread with encouraging speed from the
point of view of Indonesia as a whole. They covered
190,000 hectares in the total Bimas area in the 1969 dry
season, and 306,000 hectares in the 1970/71 wet season.
By that time the modern varieties accounted for 10 percent of the total rice area in Indonesia, their adoption
occurring mainly through the Bimas program.

In Sidomulyo the first seeds of modern varieties
were obtained in the 1967/68 wet season from the district
extension service. Availability of the seeds was limited, and village heads and some village officials took
the lead in testing the new technology. More general
adoption took place in the 1968 dry season. Under the
Bimas program of that period, 30 out of 75 farmers had
at least a portion of their land planted to IR8 and by
the 1971 dry season and the 1972 dry season, 90 percent
were full adopters (farmers with all land in modern
varieties). It is apparent therefore, that Sidomulyo
sample farmers had confidence in these varieties. Despite a drought in the 1972 dry season, 44 out of 46
rice planters were still full adopters.

Farmers in Cidahu also began adopting the modern
rice varieties in the 1968 dry season. As in Sidomulyo,
the first seeds were obtained from the extension service
and were planted by village leaders. Later, marked
differences in the pattern of adoption occurred. In the
first year of adoption, only three out of the 77 Cidahu
sample farmers used the modern varieties exclusively.
The number of farmers planting all their rice to modern
varieties rose steadily until the 1971/72 wet season.
During the 1971/72 wet season a pest (gall midge) at-
tacked the rice crop and caused especially serious damage
to the modern varieties. Apparently this susceptibility
moved farmers back to local varieties because in the 1972

dry season, the number of full adopters dropped tremendously, from twenty farmers to one. The proportion of farmers planting any modern varieties dropped from 53 percent in the 1971/72 wet season to 17 percent in the following dry season.

A comparison of yield performance between modern and local varieties indicates that in Sidomulyo the modern varieties were as at least moderately higher yielding than local varieties in each of the three crop seasons. The Cidahu local varieties outyielded the modern ones except in the 1971 dry season. The average rice yield was generally lower in Cidahu than in Sidomulyo. There are at least three reasons for this variation. First, in most seasons (except for the special circumstances of the 1972 dry season) Sidomulyo had a better water supply. Second, farmers in this village used more fertilizer, and third, pests have been less destructive in Sidomulyo. In the 1971/72 wet season, an attack of gall midge in Cidahu was considered the worst since 1968. It destroyed 60 to 70 percent of the rice crop. Although Bimas farmers had applied insecticide, four applications of Demicron and Basudin, they got poor results. The farmers also noticed that attacks were much more severe on such modern varieties as PB5 than on local varieties.

Variation in yield from year to year has affected the willingness of a farmer to accept a variety. In Sidomulyo the modern varieties consistently gave high yields. In Cidahu, yields tended to decrease over time and this resulted in a decline in adopters.

A striking increase in use of nitrogen fertilizer seems to have followed the introduction of new varieties in Sidomulyo. In Cidahu the difference was not as consistent or striking, and the general level of fertilizer use was lower. It is difficult to explain why farmers in Sidomulyo continued a higher level of fertilization for modern varieties despite an only slight yield advantage over local varieties, except by pointing to the shorter growth duration of the new varieties. This was important in the extensive cropping system of Sidomulyo, especially because one-third of a farmer's land in any year was rented to the sugar plantation. The recognition of the yield superiority of modern varieties was in comparison with the local varieties such as Merali, Wrijal, and Jawa which averaged only about 2 t/ha. The initial yield advantage of modern varieties has been narrowed considerably, especially comparing their yields with the performance of improved local varieties (Bengawan, Syntha, Dara, Sigadis) with fertilizer.

An examination of related farm practices indicates that in Cidahu, farmers used rotary weeders. In Sidomulyo, hand weeding was common and the labor used for it increased after the introduction of modern varieties. Rotary weeders were not used in Sidomulyo because

straight-row planting was not practiced. Some farmers
tried the rotary weeder, but switched back to hand
weeding. Insecticides were used more in Cidahu because
pests and diseases were considered a more serious danger,
especially to the modern varieties. A third of the sample farmers in Cidahu used sickles to save time and labor
in harvesting, but most still used the ani-ani hand
knife. In Sidomulyo, the sickle was introduced in the
1972 dry season by the village head (lurah). Other
farmers had not begun using it.

Farmers in the survey area obtained credit from both
government sources (Bimas) and from private lending agencies and individuals. Since not all of the sampled farmers were participating in the Bimas program, it was not
possible to obtain data on how farmers outside the program secured credit for farming and other activities. A
new modified Bimas rice intensification scheme began
operations in the area of this study during the 1970/71
wet season and operated throughout the period of the
study. Credit was to come from a government Bank (Bank
Rakyat Indonesia), partly in cash but mostly in the form
of vouchers for such inputs as fertilizer and pesticides,
redeemable either at the village-unit branch or from
farm-input shops in the village. These loans were repay-
able in seven months, i.e. one month after harvest, at 1
percent interest a month (this interest rate is exceptionally low compared with alternative sources of rural
credit). How much was granted depended upon the farmer's
actual credit needs: the farmer got more inputs if he
planted the modern varieties (in "new Bimas") than if he
planted local varieties ("ordinary Bimas").

In the 1971/72 wet season the actual credit granted
under the Bimas program was Rp 13,290/ha in Sidomulyo and
Rp 8,335/ha in Cidahu, which was below the recommended
credit package. Farmers in Sidomulyo received more credit because more of them were planting modern varieties.
They were thus entitled to borrow the "new Bimas" package, which is larger than the "ordinary Bimas" package to
which most of Cidahu's farmers planting local varieties
were limited. Many of the sample farmers in both villages expressed dissatisfaction with the amount of credit
obtained from the Bimas program and would have liked to
borrow more. Repayment of loans in Sidomulyo was 86 percent. The repayment rate in Cidahu was slightly below
50 percent, largely because of serious damage caused by
gall midge in the 1971/72 wet season which reduced rice
yields sharply from the previous season. Seventy of the
152 sampled farmers obtained loans from the Bimas program. Many did not borrow through the Bimas program because they still had outstanding credit from a previous
season and thus were not allowed to participate. Thus,
to finance production and family needs they had to look
for outside help.

Outside the Bimas program, the most common source of credit in Sidomulyo was the paddy bank (<u>lumbung desa</u>). In Cidahu it was neighbors or fellow farmers or relatives. Borrowing was both in money and in kind. Rough rice was borrowed in Sidomulyo, mainly for consumption purposes. In Cidahu loans in kind came from peddlers of cloth, kerosene lamps, etc., who move from village to village. The small size of farms and the large size of households jointly affected the need to borrow for consumption purposes when production fell short of the food demands of the family. Borrowing in kind usually fell short of the food demands of the family. Borrowing in kind usually occurred in the time of scarcity (<u>paceklik</u>). Money loans were much less common. Little money was available for borrowing in the village, and moneylenders in town charged up to 5 to 10 percent a month interest.

III

In examining the contribution of the high yielding varieties to employment generation, it was found in Sidomulyo, that cultivation of modern varieties used 19 man-days/ha more labor than local varieties. This difference related to weeding. Heavy fertilization stimulates weed growth and local varieties, which are less heavily fertilized, required one or two weedings. Modern varieties required two or three weedings. In Cidahu, modern varieties used 16 man-days/ha less labor than local varieties. Pest infestation was high in Cidahu, and plant protection for modern varieties took extra time. But some farmers in Cidahu began to use the sickle for harvesting the modern varieties, while the hand knife continued to be used for harvesting local varieties. This difference in harvesting method reduced the total labor need.

Hired labor accounted for about 70 percent of total labor-use in the sample villages. The majority of Java's small farm operators rely on such hired help and in turn hire themselves out to fellow farmers in their village. Use of labor in Sidomulyo was influenced by the relationship of sugar cane to other crops. When sugar cane was being planted or harvested, labor was in short supply. Laborers hired from as far as 100 kilometers away stayed in the village for two or three months until the work was finished. Farmers in Sidomulyo also liked to work at the sugar mill, because they were paid as much as Rp 200 (about US$0.50) per day. Male laborers in rice production normally received only about Rp 100, plus one meal worth Rp 25 per day, for a seven hour day, and female laborers received only Rp 60, without food for a three to four hour working day.

Philippine data show 70 to 130 man-days of family and hired labor are used on a hectare of rice. Java's farmers in the study areas used roughly twice as much labor per hectare. The situation is related to the total population and total cultivated land in the two regions. In Java, about 70 million persons are concentrated on 5.6 million hectares of cultivated land. The Philippines has the same amount of cultivated land but only about 35 million people. A higher percentage of redundant labor is employed in Java than in the Philippines and there is a lower productivity per unit of labor employed. The high labor input in Java reflects the "share-and-share-alike" philosophy which entitles landless laborers to a share of the crop.

Rice income was measured as return above variable cost, since only variable costs are important in short-run decision-making once fixed costs have been committed to agricultural production. In the 1971 dry season in Sidomulyo, net return from local varieties was about the same as from modern varieties. In Cidahu, modern varieties gave a one-fourth higher net return per hectare than local varieties. The reason for the difference between the two villages is that in Sidomulyo in that season the yields of the local and modern varieties were about the same.

In Cidahu, small and medium farms had significantly lower net returns per hectare than large farms. These differences appear to be due to differences in yields. There is little sign that small farms are at a disadvantage when it comes to procuring cash inputs other than labor. In Sidomulyo the returns of the small and medium farms were not significantly different, and there was only one "large farm". Its hired labor costs were much higher than those of other farmers.

In Cidahu, two-thirds of the sample farmers earned income from off- and non-farm activities in the 1971 dry season. The smaller the farm, the more likely the farmer was to obtain income from off-farm activities such as farm labor, nonagricultural labor, trading, or transportation services. Farmers who received a smaller net return from rice found it more often necessary to do off-farm work to secure additional income. But those from larger farms who did work off the farm tended to have higher incomes from these outside activities . In Sidomulyo, differences in farm size did not produce differences in propensity to seek additional income. Moreover, farmers from the smaller farms obtained somewhat more income from such activities than large farmers.

Aside from off-farm and nonfarm income, farmers also obtained some additional income from backyard enterprises (pekarangan) and livestock. In the backyard, the farmer can raise a variety of crops such as papaya, banana, coconut, and vegetables. He can harvest these almost throughout the year and need not depend upon the season. A third of the sample farmers in Sidomulyo and half of the farmers in Cidahu were engaged in backyard production. Cidahu has more available farmland. Backyard income per farm, however, did not seem to be significantly different for the two villages. Livestock feeding was a source of income for 35 percent of the farmers in Sidomulyo and 21 percent in Cidahu. The difference in livestock income between the two villages was also not significant.

Change in levels of consumption during the period in which the modern varieties were being introduced is one criterion of increasing welfare among farmers. For most farm households the normal length of the rice shortage is two to three months each season, but for some it runs as much as four months. In the wet season it is usually most serious in February, March, and April, and in the dry season, in August, September, and October. Of seventy farm households in Sidomulyo, 35 percent reported no shortage in the 1968/69 wet season, compared with 33 percent in the 1971/72 wet season. The absence of change in Sidomulyo indicates that two-thirds of the farmers were not better off three years after general adoption of the modern varieties than before.

Although in normal times all families were rice eaters, during the shortage in the 1971/72 wet season, the number of rice eaters decreased by one-third in both areas. At the same time, however, the number of corn eaters increased by eight times in Sidomulyo (to 50 percent of the families in the village). The Cidahu farmers did not use corn as a substitute for rice. The consumption of most other food and household commodities also decreased during periods of shortage (other commodities include meat, eggs, salted fish, salt, cooking oil, kerosene, vegetables, sugar, soap, and cigarettes).

In interviews with several groups of the sample farmers, a number of major problems were identified with respect to rice growing and the Bimas program. In both villages, farmers believed that for optimum yields they had to apply heavy doses of the right chemical fertilizer at the proper time. They felt, however, that the Bimas program had not always met this requirement. They reported that fertilizer often arrived late, especially the type of fertilizer needed for basal application. Therefore, most farmers, particularly in Sidomulyo, did not apply this type of fertilizer (officials of Bimas reported that in 1971 the supply of basal fertilizer was far from adequate). Many farmers also said that they did not receive enough fertilizer from Bimas. As a result, they either applied less than was needed or, if they had the money they bought from private stores at 5 percent or more above the authorized selling price. The farmers in Cidahu complained about the rigid formalities followed in processing loan applications. Because of the resulting delays in obtaining credit, they felt that the credit period of seven months was too short. Sidomulyo farmers did not report difficulties in the processing of loan applications. One group stated, however, that the amount of cash credit that could be obtained from Bimas to apply to living expenses was too small.

The rice farmers who did not participate in the Bimas program were relatively worse off in terms of credit and farm input availability. Non-participants in Sidomulyo reported fewer troubles than those in Cidahu. Farmers in both villages stated that it was difficult to find enough seed conforming to specified standards of purity and germination. Water for irrigation was scarce, especially during the 1972 dry season (which was in fact a drought year), and was a main topic of discussion in these villages as it was with farmers throughout Indonesia. Farmers in Cidahu regarded plant protection as a serious problem. Modern rice varieties were considered less immune to the attack of pests and diseases. Farmers reported difficulties in securing effective chemicals during the attack of gall midge. Endrin, Dieldrin, Folidol, Demicron, and Aldrin were all expensive, and the results were often disappointing. In addition, Cidahu growers reported much loss from rats, especially in fields that were planted late. In both villages, farmers have said that the agricultural taxes and other contributions they must pay are too heavy.

In summary, the adoption of modern varieties began in both of the sample villages in the same year, the 1968 dry season. It was not initially an independent decision of the farmers, because participation in the Bimas program required farmers to plant modern varieties. Nevertheless, almost all the sample farmers in Sidomulyo moved quickly to the modern IR5 (PB5) variety, where the area planted to modern varieties increased year by year. By comparison, adoption of modern varieties in Cidahu was low. Serious attacks of gall midge resulted in low yield from modern varieties, and farmers began switching back to local varieties.

The differences in farm practices between the new and local varieties in Sidomulyo are in the amount of fertilizer used and the additional labor for weeding. In Cidahu, farmers who adopted modern varieties also tended to change their method of harvesting, using the sickle instead of the hand knife. This change required less labor in harvesting. Nearly all other practices were essentially the same.

Although more fertilizer was used on modern varieties in Sidomulyo, there was little effect on yield; modern varieties yielded only slightly more than local varieties there. Possibly the shorter maturity of the new varieties explains the preference there: Sidomulyo had an intensive double-cropping system (rice, other food crops, and sugar cane). In Cidahu, farmers said modern varieties gave lower yield than local varieties because PB5 was more susceptible to gall midge than local varieties. However, in both villages, yields of local varieties have risen sharply since the adoption of chemical fertilizer that came with the new varieties in the Bimas program.

In Sidomulyo, the modern varieties brought slightly lower net returns per hectare than did the local varieties. Gross returns for modern and local varieties were not significantly different. Production costs for modern varieties were somewhat higher than for local. As a result, the modern varieties gave lower returns than local varieties. In Cidahu, modern varieties brought a higher net return than did the local varieties. In Cidahu, the smaller the farm, the larger the percentage of farmers who obtained income from off-farm and nonfarm activities.

In brief, although sample farmers have responded well to the introduction of modern varieties wherever the factors that permit the adoption of modern varieties are all present, there is no sign as yet of any "green revolution" in the sample areas.

5
West Sumatra and South Sulawesi

Paul Deuster

Much controversy surrounds the "Green Revolution."
The term itself refers to dramatic increases in the production of certain food grains that is being achieved in
various parts of the world through the application of
science and technology to traditional agricultures. The
argued questions involve who is gaining and losing, how
much, and why. For two villages in Indonesia this chapter attempts to answer such questions by examining the
extent of adoption of high-yielding rice varieties,
chemical fertilizers, and pesticides; the degree of success in terms of production and income; and the direct
and indirect impact on village-wide income, absolute and
relative.[1] The basic data for this study was collected
through household sample surveys from one village in
West Sumatra and one village in South Sulawesi. Around
100 households in each village were randomly selected
and interviewed twice in the year. From the information
gathered, it is possible, among other things, both to
sum up the present income distribution and to reconstruct
the income situation as it was before the introduction of
the new technology.

In the two case studies, a number of measures are
utilized in examining changes in economic conditions attendant upon the introduction of new agricultural technologies. The economic impact of an innovation was divided into two components: the direct, immediate impact
that comes with the adoption and successful implementation of new inputs and/or methods and is experienced by
the participating farmers, and the indirect impact that
works its way from the adopting farmers to others in the
village through a number of linkage relationships.[2] For
purposes of analysis the linkages through which the impact of a change is transmitted are classified into the
following categories: (1) through inputs the farmers
use, (2) through the disposing and processing of the increased output, (3) through the use the farmers make of
their increased incomes, (4) through government actions,

(5) through income transfers that are based on non-economic reasons, (6) through common markets, and (7) through technical externalities of the new inputs and practices.

In addition to the linkages that connect participating farmers with others in the villages, the same types of linkages connect the others with still others as well as to each other and back to the original participating farmers. This means that any initial change will reverberate through the village until it dissipates itself or a new balance is achieved. In particular, any expenditure in the village could lead to further expenditures in the village as the initial expenditure is someone's income and that someone in turn could spend the income received. The cumulative result of such spending and respending is referred to in economic jargon as the "multiplier effect."

Inputs that farmers use include land, water, seeds, fertilizer, insecticides, credit, tools, animals, and labor. If the new practices require new inputs or increased amounts of old ones, local persons can benefit either by producing or supplying these inputs or as acting as intermediaries in the obtaining of them. On the other hand, if less is needed of something, local persons could suffer a loss of income. If increased yields call for more labor during harvest time, local villagers may gain by meeting this need, or on the other hand, if a change in harvesting practice reduces such opportunities, villagers may lose. Likewise, increased output may require changes or enlargement in processing, transporting, storing, and marketing facilities. For example, the demand for haulers may increase or horse-cart drivers may find their business of hauling paddy to market has improved. A larger volume of rice sold may open opportunities for local petty traders or induce outside middlemen to enter the scene.

If increased production leads to increased net incomes for farmers, the additional income may be consumed or saved in the form produced or exchanged directly or converted to cash and used for other items, savings, or investment. If local villagers make the goods wanted, provide the services desired, or serve as intermediaries in their marketing, they can benefit. For example, local craftsmen may find greater demand for their skills in building houses. A local producer of mats may experience less sales if the increased income leads the consumers to purchase more expensive items from outside the village.

The analysis includes consideration of the fact that regional, local and even national governments, through policies of taxation and expenditures, can redistribute the gains of increased production. For example, governmental units may capture part of the increase by taxes on the successful farmers and use the revenue to construct roads that benefit others. In addition to these economic transactions, others may gain by being the recipients of gifts or income transfers. Parents, mothers-in-law, nephews and nieces may share in the gains of more fortunate relatives. Contributions to the mosque may increase. The frequency and elaborateness of wedding celebrations or religious ceremonies may increase, providing more to guests and neighbors.

If the actions of farmers affect prices, then everyone who buys or sells in the same market is affected. For example, if increased demand for wage labor by some farmers drives up the wage rate, then all wage laborers and employers of such labor are affected. Or if increased rice production lowers the price of rice, all farmers who sell rice, whether or not they adopt new practices, and all consumers of rice are involved. In addition, it is possible that the new inputs or practices may have technical side effects or externalities that affect others. Fertilizer applied to one field may be carried by water to another or insecticides used to kill stem borers may kill the neighbor's ducks.

Finally, the same kinds of linkages that exist between the participating farmers and others in the village exist between others and still others. As a result, a single action can have a series of effects--a multiplier effect. Additional money or income in kind in the village will be spent/exchanged and respent/reexchanged again and again until it is removed from circulation either by being saved or being spent/sent outside the village. A basic question is how large is this multiplier effect and the answer depends mainly on the patterns of consumption/saving (what, how much, from where) and productive activities in a particular village, since these determine where the additional money is spent.

A wide range of variables are involved in conditioning the overall impact that arises from a particular technical innovation and the direct and indirect results experienced within a village economy. Thus, in the analysis of the two villages in West Sumatra and South Sulawesi, some consideration is given to such factors as: (1) the technical and economic characteristics of the innovation, (2) the arrangements and practices of the supporting institutions, (3) methods of introduction, (4) the economic relationships, patterns of resource ownership and response patterns existing in the recipient village, and (5) the social, cultural, political, and historical setting in which the changes take place. Even without specifications of the exact conditions and characteristics that invoke particular responses, the importance and relevance of these factors cannot be overestimated.

II

The first case involves a study of a village located in the upper end of a valley in the eastern part of the province of West Sumatra, approximately 140 kilometers from the provincial capital of Padang. A river cuts through the village land and several streams provide water adequate for rice growing during most of the year. The village contains around 2,000 people in roughly 300 households. The 99 households included in the sample average 6.1 members per household with 4.6 of their number over ten years of age. Of the heads of households, 80 percent are male and 83 percent are married. Their average level of education is 6.0 years of schooling, and the average age is 51.

The village people are Minangkabau, an ethnic group of over four million people who inhabit West Sumatra and are well-known by virtue of their having a matri-lineal society. The existence of this matri-lineal social structure has several important implications for how the introduction of agricultural innovation affects income distribution in the village. Basically, the women own the houses and rice lands, and the households are grouped into "clans" based on female descent. Each female child inherits from her mother an equal share of the mother's rice land, or more accurately each woman inherits life-long user rights to an equal plot(s) of rice lands. The land cannot be sold except under narrow, special conditions, and then only with the permission of the head of the clan, although to a certain extent this can be circumvented by mortgaging the land and never reclaiming. The result of these rules is that practically every family has some land. Since different branches of families grow at different rates, landholdings are not equal, but almost everyone has some land, with average farm size being .31 hectares. In addition, those who have more land are under social pressure to share-crop land out to those who have less, thus making access to land even more equally shared.

The major products of the village are rice and rubber, with each accounting for roughly 40 and 16 percent of the total net income of the village respectively. About half of all income is in non-cash form and only nine percent originates from outside (mainly gifts, pensions, and government salaries), although all the rubber and a significant portion of the rice are sold outside or to outsiders. Rice cultivation is still done mainly by hand, although water buffalo or oxen are extensively used to prepare the fields. The planting pattern is characterized by single transplanting and harvesting is done with a hand sickle. The only machines used are a simple, hand-turned separator of the rice from the

remaining bits of chaff, and gasoline engine-driven hullers to remove the hull and polish the rice. Generally,
two crops of rice are planted yearly, August/September to
December/January and January/February to May/June.

About a third of the land is used for sharecropping
and about a third of the farmers are sharecroppers. The
general sharecropping terms are a third of the gross production for the landowner with the farmer bearing alone
the costs of inputs. The rest of the farmers operate
their own lands, although this can vary from a situation
in which the household itself provides all the labor used
to the other extreme where the household assumes only a
supervisory role and hires others to do all the various
tasks. Indeed, wage labor is extensively used, especially in planting and harvesting. While there is a range of
combinations for payment (meals and/or wages), usually
labor is provided two meals and paid in cash.

A survey of the village in 1972-73 indicates that
the adoption of the new rice technology has been quite
extensive with all but one of the sample households using
a new rice variety, and all of the households using
chemical fertilizers to a reasonable level of dosage. In
respect to total area cultivated, over 98 percent of the
rice land among the sample farms was being cultivated
with the new varieties. Moreover, production figures indicate that these farmers were achieving yields of almost
three tons of milled rice per hectare, with net income
(return to the household's labor, land and capital) running about $300 per hectare. By Indonesian standards
these figures constitute a substantial level of production and income.

A comparison of rice yields prior to the adoption of
the new varieties indicates that sizeable production increases have been attained with the new technologies.
Thus, in the pre-adoption period, estimates indicate an
approximate figure of 45,450 kilograms of milled rice
equivalence as the total production of the households in
the sample, whereas with the use of the new varieties
production has increased to 178,570 kilograms, or roughly a 293 percent increase in total output. Much of this
increase can be attributed to the introduction of double
cropping, as the new varieties have a much shorter growing season, thereby making it possible for farmers to
harvest a rice crop twice a year. Nevertheless, these
production increases also reflect a substantial rise in
yields per hectare per cropping, with the new varieties
adding a full 85 percent increase.

A comparison of farm income for the pre- and post-
adoption phase for the new varieties indicates that with
the use of the new technology, total gross rice income has
increased by almost 200 percent. However, since costs of
production have risen even faster, net rice income has
gone up by a lesser figure of 140 percent. All of these

figures underestimate the amount of increase, as the 1972-73 year was not particularly good for rice production for reasons of drought and rat infestation. Finally, since the income tabulations are done on the individual household basis, it is also possible to compare the relative income distribution in the pre- and post-adoption phases for the new varieties. Using a Gini coefficient calculation, a commonly used measure of inequality, there is little indication of a significant change in relative income distribution, although individual households may have experienced a sharp drop or rise in relative standing.

In examining the larger impact or linkage effects of these increases in production and income upon the village economy, it becomes apparent that the changeover to the new varieties and the use of fertilizer has had a wide range of beneficial effects upon village welfare. Thus, in an assessment of the indirect economic impact on the input side of production, there has been a large increase in the demand for hired labor (mainly due to the movement to double cropping which has more than offset any decrease in demand due to the introduction of simple, hand-turned chaff-separating machines) and this has led to increased wages. Since most of the workers are coming from outside the village, increased earnings from this source do not amount to much for the village as a whole, although individual households may have gained substantially. A rough estimate is that income from casual labor has increased around 30 to 40 percent overall, adding around 2 percent to total village income. The value of land has also increased (or at least its mortgage value as the land is not sold outright). Although the percent share of the crop received by the landlords, who are local persons, has not changed, the amount received has increased in proportion to total rice production, that is, around 200 percent. However, since income to landlords of rice lands is small in terms of village total (3.3 percent of net income), addition to village income was around 2 percent.

With respect to other production inputs, a local agent handles fertilizer and credit distribution. He makes a small amount on each transaction, which accumulates into a sizeable total for the single individual, although it is not noticeable in the calculations of total village income. Finally, because of the availability and low price (one percent a month) of government credit for fertilizer and insecticides, local, informal money sources were seldom being used for agricultural credit. While there was increased demand for money to help finance traders of rice and other commodities, this increase probably was more than offset by the increase in the availability of local funds from increased incomes. There are few outlets for savings in the village other

than making loans to individuals, although this is a
risky proposition. Therefore, the overall result of the
technical changes on local lending is probably a lowering
of the real interest rate (although it is still very
high) and an increase, although small, in total income
earned through money-lending.

Visible economic benefits have been generated
through the handling of the increased output of rice production, although these changes are still less significant than those associated with the increased demand for
production inputs. Thus, in the last few years two small
gasoline hullers have been brought in by groups of local
individuals, replacing all but one of seven small, water-
driven mills. The result has been a shift in income between the two groups plus an overall increase in income
from this source because of the increase in rice production. Income from this processing activity has nearly
tripled, adding roughly one-eighth of a percent to village income. Finally, there has been a large increase in
the amount of rice sold. A significant proportion of the
trading in rice is handled by local traders, although
most is purchased by outsiders. Local horse-cart operators and motor vehicles from neighboring villages have
experienced increased demand for their services both in
hauling out the rice (and rubber) and in bringing consumer and building goods back into the village.

In examining how farmers dispose of their increased
incomes, the data indicates that a significant portion of
the increased rice production is simply consumed by the
households themselves. Another substantial portion is
saved for eventual use for such major expenditures as
building or remodeling homes and sending children away
to high school and even college. Finally, another part
is sold to obtain more of ordinary food and non-food
items, almost all of which are not produced locally. The
lack of non-farm productive activities limits the gains
to others from these expenditures. There are some who
have gained, particularly the operators of coffee, lunch
or petty goods stands, carpenters, and petty traders who
bring in goods and sell them at the weekly market, but
in terms of total income, these gains do not exceed two
or three percent.

A demand upon farm income through government actions
occurs in the form of various taxation measures. Local
officials collect, on behalf of the district, the land
tax (Ipeda) which, despite the changes in its rates over
the last years, has not been adjusted to the increase in
yields. The village keeps a small part of these collected taxes, passing the rest to the district level, which
carries out few activities which affect the village. The
village itself imposes a number of taxes, for example, on
the marketplace; the selling of cattle, rubber, and
rocks; and on households. Almost all the revenues col-

lected through these taxes go to pay the salaries of the
local government officials and in providing for the
operation and maintenance costs of the marketplace and
the government office. The total burden from these formal taxes was less than one-half of a percent of village
income. Finally, clan ties, family obligations, and Islamic exhortations result in a degree of non-economic
income transfers. At harvest time the clan leaders
generally arrange that some of the produce is given to
the more needy members of the group. However, only about
one and one-half percent of village net income was allocated as gifts to others in the village.

In assessing the impact of these changes in increased production and income on prices in the local market, it must be noted that the prices, especially of
rice, in this particular village are in large part determined by prices at the provincial level. In brief, the
village is part of larger regional markets, and hence,
local production did not by itself affect local price.
The fluctuations caused by external factors were too
great during the field work period (1972-73) to allow
any conclusions to be drawn. It can likely be anticipated however, that with increased production, lower rice
prices will be eventually experienced. In the labor market, the price of labor increased, making it more expensive for anyone who wanted to hire and enabling laborers
to receive more. Finally, as already mentioned, given
the increased availability of formal credit from government sources and local funds from increased income, the
real interest rate declined within the informal credit
market.

In summary, with the near universal adoption of the
new seed varieties and fertilizers, there has been an
enormous increase in rice production and net rice income
by over 190 and 140 percent respectively. The direct
impact of these increases has been substantial with an
attendant rise of 20 percent in total village income. In
assessing the indirect impact, the linkage effects have
also contributed to the income of many individuals and
to an increase in the overall total income. Moreover,
the size of the increases, including the multiplier effect, do reach substantial levels, although cumulatively
they do not approach the total of the direct effect. In
this context, the limited number of items produced in the
village keeps the linkage effects down. Finally, while
the new rice technology is associated with a rapid rise
in absolute levels of village income, the data indicates
that these changes have not been accompanied by any
significant modifications in levels of relative income
distribution.

III

The second village selected for investigation, located in the province of South Sulawesi, is on a different island and well over 1,000 miles from the first village. Not only are the two villages widely separated geographically, but they are quite different physically, economically, and culturally. The chosen South Sulawesi village is located about 35 kilometers from the provincial capital of Ujung Pandang on one of the region's major roads. According to the records of the Agricultural Office at the district level, the total area of the village is 30 square kilometers with 1190.31 hectares of rice land, of which 250 is irrigated. Except for steep, rock hills at the western extreme, the land is flat and low. One river cuts through the southern part and a major primary canal with branches provides irrigation. In the rainy season most of the village is subjected to flooding. The village inhabitants are Bugis, an ethnic group with strong Islamic beliefs. South Sulawesi is the traditional homeland of the Bugis people, who number over four million and thereby constitute one of the largest ethnic groups in this part of the island.

In the particular village under study there are approximately 5000 people living in nearly 1000 households. Administratively, the village is divided into nine lingkungan or hamlets. Some of these hamlets are located along the main road or along a side dirt road, while others can be reached only by walking a kilometer or two across paddy fields and fording streams. Formerly, these hamlets were independent, but about seven years ago they were united into one village. The 104 households included in the study sample averaged 5.3 members per household, with 3.4 of this number ten years or older, and with women serving as head of family in 12.5 percent of these households. For the heads of the households in the sample, the average age was 45.0 with the average level of education including 1.4 years of schooling.

In this village rice is overwhelmingly the crop of importance, with over 40 percent of the net income of the sample coming from rice cultivation. No other crop compares in importance to rice as tobacco is only beginning to be a dry-season crop and only a little corn, cassava, fruits, and vegetables are grown in the village. The major rice-growing season is the rainy period with planting in December and January and harvesting in April and May. On irrigated lands two crops are usually grown (the second harvest occurring in September/October), and the rain-fed rice land is usually left idle during the dry season. Rice cultivation is either done by sharecropping or by the owner himself with maybe some unpaid (except for provision of meals) help from relatives for the

difficult tasks. Average farm size for the sample is .69
hectares per household. Half of the farmers are owner-
operators while another third both farm their own plots
and sharecrop some additional land. The remainder are
pure sharecroppers. In the case of sharecropping, the
harvest, costs of fertilizers, and insecticides, and the
land tax are divided in two between owner and sharecrop-
per. The standing crop is usually divided before it is
cut and each arranges the harvest of his half. Finally,
land preparation is usually done by hand, although some
use livestock. It is possible to rent buffaloes or
cattle, but the price is high and is rarely done. No
hired labor is used except for harvesters who receive
one-fifth of what they cut with an ani-ani knife. Laborers from outside the village, sometimes relatives, but
often not, come for the harvest. In addition, no machines are used in the agricultural process, except for
small gasoline driven hullers.

A survey of the village in 1972-73, indicates that
among the sample farms, 80 percent of the total area
planted is under cultivation with improved or the new
high-yielding rice varieties. Out of the 92 households
in the sample actually cultivating rice, only 50 percent
are using chemical fertilizers, and of the area cultivated, about 60 percent is fertilized. However, the intensity of use is still low. The key determining factor
for both the adoption of improved seeds and the chemical
fertilizers is irrigation. All of the operators of irrigated land plant at least some of the improved varieties,
and over 40 percent plant at least some high-yielding
varieties. Also, over 85 percent of this group uses
chemical fertilizers. Of the farmers on the rain-fed
areas, almost 40 percent plant only local varieties and
less than ten percent plant any high-yielding varieties
at all. Finally, only 25 percent of this group uses
chemical fertilizers.

Production figures indicate that users of chemical
fertilizer have increased output from a base figure of
800 to 1,120 kilograms of milled rice per hectare per
cropping, whereas for non-users of chemical fertilizer,
production has risen from 860 to 985 kilograms of milled
rice. By Indonesian standards these production figures
are low, and at 415 rupiah per U.S. dollar, the net income
for the user of chemical fertilizer is only about $100
per hectare. A comparison with rice yields prior to the
adoption of the new varieties indicates that for users
of chemical fertilizers, total production has increased
slightly over 50 percent. This rise in output can be
attributed to an increase in area planted (10 percent)
and to increased yields (40 percent). For non-users of
chemical fertilizer, many of whom have changed from local
to national improved rice varieties, total production has
increased by 22.5 percent (7.5 percent for increases in

area planted and 15 percent for increases in yields). In
terms of total village output, there has been an 8.9 percent increase in area planted, a 29 percent increase in
yield per hectare per cropping, and a 40 percent increase
in total production.

A comparison of farm income for the pre- and post-
adoption phases for the new practices indicates that with
the use of the new technologies, total gross income has
gone up 48.7 percent. Since production costs have increased at a faster rate, net rice income has gone up by
a lesser amount of 44.0 percent. Whereas absolute income
has increased, the data indicates practically no change
in relative income distributions. Nevertheless, there
are growing disparities between geographical parts of the
village, with irrigated areas prospering at a more rapid
rate than is the case for the non-irrigated areas.

The indirect impact associated with these increases
in rice income can be traced through the different linkages or channels connecting participating farmers to
others in the village. In examining these it becomes
apparent that there was little indirect gain in this village. Through the use of inputs there has been little
spread effect in the village for a number of reasons.
Except for the harvest, households do not hire labor, and
at harvest many come from outside the village to take
advantage of this opportunity. The traditional payment
of one-fifth of what is cut and carried to the house is
substantially above going wage rates in other casual
employment. Landlords did experience proportional gains
in their share of the crop, but roughly 60 percent was
paid to landlords outside the village.

While in processing and marketing of the rice most
of the gains were contained within the village, these
gains were minimized by the fact that much of the increased production and income was consumed by the household itself in the form of rice. In processing, the
owners of hullers gained with little loss to others, as
almost all pounding had been done previously by hand
within the individual households. A few petty traders
and house-cart drivers have had some increased business
in helping to market the rice. The pattern of consumer
expenditures generally did not affect others in the village. Major expenditures involved home improvements,
marriages, tools, radios, and household furniture. Other
than being a wedding guest or helping to build or repair
a house, local villagers were not affected by these expenditures since they were for items not made locally.

Other economic changes due to other linkages can be
discerned with respect to the transmission of the income
gains associated with the new rice technology. While the
demands upon farm income from government taxation have
increased, the burden has been spread mostly on a per
household or head basis, rather than on an income or pro-

duction criteria, and most of the tax collected goes out
of the village for sub-district or district-level projects. Income transfers based upon non-economic transactions were rather insignificant as the weakness of
existing kinship ties and religious requirements led to
little giving of the increased gains to other members of
the village. While there is a religious tax, most were
either excused because of poverty or neglected to pay it.

The village lacks control over the potential effects
generated through common markets, as the price of rice in
South Sulawesi is largely determined by selling prices at
provincial market centers rather than by production increases at the local level. Finally, the multiplier effect, which can be used as an indicator of the indirect
economic changes generated by the increases in production
and income, was in this case, quite low. Production is almost exclusively rice and, therefore, a high percentage of
consumer items (roughly 90 percent) are purchased outside
the village. Thus, the village is unable to capture many
of the potential secondary gains associated with the rise
in income from the new rice technology because of the
lack of other local productive activities.

In summary, while far short of universal adoption,
major advances have been made in the acceptance of the
new rice technology in this village, with a full 50 percent of the farmers using chemical fertilizer. Nearly
two-thirds of the sample farmers were using improved
rice varieties and another 20 percent were cultivating
high-yielding varieties. The use of more modern inputs
has yielded certain economic rewards with total gross
rice income increasing by 40 percent. An examination of
the more indirect effects of these changes upon village
welfare indicates that increases in production and income
have been accompanied by only marginal transmissions of
secondary benefits within the local economy. Thus, much
of the income generated through the increased yields has
been transferred outside the village either to outside
landlords, to larger government units through taxation, or
to outside sellers and manufacturers of consumer items.
Nevertheless, the rice technology has contributed to a
rise in income levels, and the evidence further indicates
that, despite a geographic bias, these gains have been
fairly evenly distributed throughout the income levels
of the village economy.

An overview of the case studies reveals major differences between the two villages, both in the extent of
adoption of the high-yielding technologies, in the attendant gains achieved with respect to production and income, and in the indirect impact on village-wide welfare
which accompanied these changes in production practices.
In the one village in West Sumatra, adoption of both new
rice varieties and chemical fertilizers was much greater
than in the village in South Sulawesi. This difference

is most evident in the fact that 99 percent of all plantings in the West Sumatra case are of high-yielding types,
whereas in the South Sulawesi village, only 20 percent of
the plantings are of this type. This variation in extent
of adoption is easily attributed to the technological
suitability of the inputs to the two terrains. In the
West Sumatra case, the lands are irrigated and the new
varieties and fertilizer can be used without difficulty.
This is not true in the South Sulawesi village where only
21 percent of the rice lands are irrigated and where the
remaining rain-fed areas are generally subjected to
flooding. The available new varieties are not suitable
to this type of terrain.

The differences in the extent of adoption of the
high-yielding technology are visibly reflected in the
economic growth patterns for each village. Thus, the
farmers in the West Sumatra village have been more successful in increasing rice production and net rice income. These gains were achieved by both moving to
double-cropping, which the shorter-growing season of the
new rice varieties made possible, and in obtaining higher
yields per hectare per cropping with the use of newer
varieties and more chemical fertilizer. In the South
Sulawesi case, on the irrigated lands it is possible to
move from the traditional two croppings per year to almost three. However, this had not yet been done because
apparently it is too much work for the individual household. The persistence of traditional patterns of work
organization in this village, whereby the household alone
provides all the labor for rice farming outside of harvesting, acts as a barrier to triple cropping. An underlying issue concerns why some farm households are more
responsive to outside innovation, whereas other farmers
seem to be more resistant to technological change. In
this context, the question of why the farmers in one
village use modern inputs more frequently than those in
another is difficult to answer when only two cases are
involved and differences between the two are so many.
However, it is possible to speculate that key differences
in these two cases can be attributed to a number of
variables, and most importantly, to three factors. These
are the exposure and openness of the village population
to sources of external change, the level of education of
the farm population, and to problems of accessibility to
inputs and the marketing of farm outputs.

Concerning the first variable, exposure and openness are not easily quantifiable variables. The concept
refers to such facts in the West Sumatra case as: most
of the men in the village have spent, at least several
years outside of the village, strangers often visit, the
population adheres to a reformist, modernistic movement
in Islam, and the villagers are eager and open to inter-
change with the rest of the world. The South Sulawesi

situation is the opposite and the village tends to be
resistant to and apprehensive of the outside world.
Many of the villagers have never been more than a few
kilometers from the village despite a major road running
through part of the village, and few outsiders visit the
local area. Finally, a more conservative and orthodox
brand of Islam constitutes the dominant cultural pattern.
    A second factor which may partially account for
variations in responses to technological innovation is
the difference in education levels between the two villages. The average number of years of schooling for
heads of households in the West Sumatra village is 6.0
versus a much lower 1.4 for the South Sulawesi sample.
Finally, the last factor centers on the ease and sure-
ness of obtaining inputs and disposing of output. With
the help of a German technical team, fertilizer distribution in West Sumatra has been set up on a reasonably
efficient basis. In addition, West Sumatra serves as the
bread basket for two-neighboring provinces, and as a consequence, farmers are assured of having inputs when needed
and of being able to sell their output at a good price.
The situation in South Sulawesi is less favorable as
fertilizer distribution is plagued by a number of administrative problems and the province is more isolated so
that prices are easily depressed by abundant harvests.
    While the increases in rice production and income
were much larger in the West Sumatra village than in the
case of the South Sulawesi village, the percentage impact
on total village income was, in both cases, of about the
same magnitude: 19.8 percent versus 15.7 percent. This
lack of difference can be explained by the fact that income from rice is more important in the South Sulawesi
village than it is in the West Sumatra village (44.4 percent versus 29.9 percent). In both cases however, relative income distribution has remained practically unchanged, although there is a growing geographic disparity
in the South Sulawesi case. The lack of change in income
distribution in the West Sumatra case can be ascribed to
local Minangkabau customs which result in almost everyone having some land and hence most farmers are able to
participate in the Green Revolution. In this society, all
female descendants inherit equal users' shares of their
mother's land and the land cannot be sold except under
narrow, special circumstances. Finally, the direct and
indirect linkage effects associated with the increases in
rice production and income were much more effective in
spreading the gains of the increase in rice production in
the West Sumatra case than in the South Sulawesi one.
This was due mainly to the much greater use of hired
labor and to the greater variety of activities and enterprises in the one village over the other.
    From these case studies of the impact of the new
high-yielding technology on rice production and village

income, there are several policy observations that can be drawn concerning the limitations and potential of the Green Revolution. As noted in the South Sulawesi case, whether for reasons of certain social or cultural constraints or for a lack of access to irrigated rice land, not everyone can or will follow the Green Revolution, at least for the innovations presently available. Secondly, in both cases, the total impact in terms of village income was much less dramatic than the production changes. In brief, both of these observations should increase awareness that the Green Revolution is not a single panacea for rural poverty.

On the potential side, the high-yielding rice varieties and chemical fertilizers were being adopted and were being used successfully. A 190 percent increase in production in the West Sumatra village cannot be ignored. In addition, the indirect linkages offer potential opportunities, which if properly mobilized would offer a wider range of benefits to a larger number of people. For example, if employment is an objective to be fostered, then policies should be designed to encourage the use of labor as an input (over machines), the local production of inputs and consumer goods, the development of saving mechanisms that can channel resources to job-creating investment, and the use of local customs on job-sharing.

In conclusion, while certain policy observations can be derived from the case studies, caution must be exercised in trying to generalize from a two village study for Indonesia as whole or even to the outer islands. The country is too large and with too much diversity to arrive at any particular generalization. Nevertheless, the West Sumatra experience is most likely an unusually favorable case, while the South Sulawesi one probably falls more toward the middle range of adoption and degree of success for villages. For effective policy decisions, these studies support the absolute need for on-the-spot field work to discover the effects of an innovation. The impact of technological changes varies so greatly at the local level that conclusions on effects cannot be rendered by simply studying the general technical and economic characteristics of the innovation and its supporting institutions. Finally, this study has concentrated solely on narrow economic questions, grossly simplifying the interlocking economic nature of the village to do so. But for any final judgement on the success or failure of the Green Revolution, the broader political, social, and cultural consequences must also be examined.

NOTES

1. I would like to thank the Ford Foundation for a post-doctoral fellowship which made possible the field work in Indonesia

for a year and a half period (1972-73), during which the data presented here was collected. I am also indebted to the many organizations and countless individuals in Indonesia who assisted my research efforts and/or made my stay so enjoyable. Unfortunately,
they are too numerous to name more than a few here: LIPI, Economics
and Agricultural Faculties of Andalas University, Ir. Basyir Radya,
Economics Faculty and Research Bureau of Hasanuddin University, and
the Agro-Economic Survey.

    2. In pursuing this theoretical overview in greater detail,
one should examine the following sources: occasional papers from the
Employment and Income Distribution Project and others of Cornell
University, especially, John Mellor and Uma J. Lele, "Growth Linkages
of the New Foodgrain Technologies," no. 71; W. Graome Donovan,
"Employment Generation in Agriculture: A Study in Mandya District,
South India," no. 75; John Mellor and Mohinder S. Mudahar, "Moderniz-
ing Agriculture, Employment and Economic Growth: A Stimulation
Model," no. 81. Also see Montague Yudelman, Gavan Butler, and Rana-
dev Banerji, Technical Change in Agriculture and Employment in De-
veloping Countries (Paris: OECD Development Centre, 1971); A. T.
Mosher, Getting Agriculture Moving (New York: Praeger Publishers,
1966); and John Mellor, The Economics of Agriculture Development
(Ithaca: Cornell University PRess, 1966).

Part III

Employment and Income Distribution

Introduction

In recent years, issues of employment and income distribution have assumed much greater prominence in the
consideration of policy and planning objectives within
government circles. With the completion of the first
Five Year Plan (Repelita I - 1969/1974) it was recognized
that major gains had been achieved in stabilizing and
strengthening the national economy, but the pattern
of economic growth had not served to generate much improvement in the welfare of lower income households. In
the second Five Year Plan (Repelita II - 1974/1979) a
number of measures were adopted which seek to channel
more resources to the rural and urban poor. Most notable
in this regard has been the increase in allocations for
rural health and educational facilities and the funding
of various public works programs in generating more employment opportunities for lower income laborers. The
impact of these programs are still relatively limited,
given the enormous magnitude of the employment and welfare problem in rural Java. Further progress in addressing these issues will, in great measure, depend upon the
recasting of current policy priorities in a direction
which enables the employment goal to assume a more paramount role in the government's overall strategy toward
national development.

The following two essays are directly concerned with
issues involving employment and income distribution in
Java. In the first selection, Montgomery seeks to assess
the employment absorbing capacities of the major sub-sec-
tors of Java's rural economy. In calculating both labor/
output coefficients and total output ratios for each sub-
sector, it is found that paddy production ranks as the
most promising area for increasing employment. As the
author notes, this conclusion would seem to suggest that
much greater emphasis needs to be placed upon the expansion of irrigation facilities and improved water management in order to increase cropping intensity and total
area under wet rice cultivation. This emphasis would

likewise entail the building of water storage areas and
the tapping of ground water sources in order to provide
increased irrigation during the dry season. All of these
efforts are greatly dependent upon the effectiveness of
government programs to rehabilitate upland catchments
where deforestation and erosion have exacted a heavy toll
of watershed areas.

In the second essay the emphasis shifts to a direct
focus upon income distribution. The analysis examines
currently available data on income distribution in Java
during the 1960s and 1970s, in order to discern trends and
changes in relative and absolute levels of welfare in rural and urban areas. The authors draw a number of conclusions from the data. Thus, it appears that urban
elites have increased their share of the national income,
whereas the income shares of rural elites have remained
relatively constant. In this context, it would appear
that the benefits of economic growth have frequently
gravitated towards urban areas, and most particularly, to
the capital city of Jakarta. Finally, in terms of more
absolute standards, it appears that the level of living
in the rural sector may have declined for the bottom 20-
40 percent of the population. This latter conclusion
would seem to be consistent with the views of many observers familiar with the evolution of economic conditions in Java over the past decade, and it only serves to
add further weight in support of a development strategy
for enhancing income growth among low income rural households. This emphasis derives not only from a concern for
increasing basic welfare levels among the rural poor, but
is further premised on the need for enhancing consumer
purchasing power in spurring both agricultural and non-
agricultural production.

6
Employment Generation Within the Agricultural Sector

Roger Montgomery

In a recent article in the Far-Eastern Economic
Review, James Keddie reported on a 1970 ILO study which
estimated that 300 million new jobs would be needed outside agriculture in the less developed world before 1980.
According to Keddie, the ILO went on to say:

> In Java, it is estimated that of the one mil-
> lion people joining the labor force each year,
> only 140,000 find jobs, The major development-
> al challenge for the next several decades will
> therefore be one of devising strategies which
> serve to generate employment for a burgeoning
> labor force in Asia and more importantly in
> Java where population growth continues to
> rapidly increase the ranks of the unemployed
> and marginally-employed labor.[1]

Previously it has been shown that official Indonesian government estimates of unemployment do not disclose
the magnitude of the employment problem.[2] Four different
official estimates of the unemployment rate in Java have
been: 5.6 percent in 1961, 2.0 percent in 1964, 0.8 percent in 1967, and only 2.3 percent in 1971. Any casual
observer of the teeming masses in the capital city of
Jakarta can quickly deduce that these figures must be in
error. What in fact is to be seen here is a display of
the "discouraged worker" syndrome. People who cannot
find jobs for long periods of time define themselves as
not looking for work. Direct questioning of the labor
force through population censuses and labor force surveys
has not proven productive in estimating the severity of
the employment problem. Direct questioning has proven
even less fruitful in discovering ways in which labor may
be absorbed into the productive process, simply because
the productive process has yet to be examined simultaneously with an examination of the labor force in Indonesia. Unemployed persons and "discouraged workers" do not

know why they are not able to find work. If they did, they might be able to do something about it. Lack of trying is not the reason for their unemployment. Attention must therefore be focussed on employment rather than the unmeasurable unemployment.

The following essay is an examination of the demand for labor as it is generated by producing activities in six major agricultural sectors: paddy rice, other food crops, non-food crops, estate sugar, other agricultural production, and food processing. The area of actual field study involves a small section on the south coast of Java called the Special Region of Yogyakarta, a tiny place, but possibly the most densely populated rural area in the world.[3] In order to provide some background on the evolution and characteristics of the agricultural foundation in this area, the analysis is introduced with a brief ecological overview of the agricultural sub-system in Central Java, and is thereafter followed by an examination of labor-absorption patterns within the six agricultural sectors. A summary perspective includes a calculation of sub-sector variations in income elasticities and an identification of possible lines of action for increasing labor utilization within the larger agricultural economy.

I

In 1816, Raffles ordered a census which produced the figure of 4,615,270 inhabitants in Java.[4] Of these, there were estimated to be 685,207 inhabitants in the "native province of Yogyakarta." Raffles, although not in possession of an adequate cadastral survey, still attempted to give a population density for Yogyakarta, and neighboring Surakarta, which was 147.5 persons per square mile; a number which is equivalent to 57 persons per square kilometer. By 1971, the census figures show that Java's population had increased to 76.1 million, with population density at 576 persons per square kilometer, and the annual growth rate at 1.9 percent since 1961.[5] In this same period, the Yogyakarta region grew to 2.49 million and to a density per square kilometer of 785 persons. The importance of this population density can best be seen in comparison with other densely populated countries in Asia. According to population statistics published by the United Nations, in 1961, population density in China totalled 59 persons per square kilometer, whereas for Japan the figure was 252, and for Korea and Taiwan, 181.[6] In brief, the region of Yogyakarta and even the island of Java are truly unique in the burden of the world's population they must carry.

To understand how Java has been able to support such a large population and almost adequately employ the labor

force, one must examine its geography and soils. Java's
backbone is volcanoes, many of which are still active.
On the northern most border of the Yogyakarta region is
the volcano Gunung Merapi rising to 3000 meters and still
quite active. The andesitic materials that resulted from
volcanic eruptions have created vast areas of young ash
soils. In the four <u>kabupatens</u> (districts) within the
Special Region of Yogyakarta, Sleman lying directly north
of the city and Bantul directly south of the city have
almost entirely volcanic ash soils. The district of
Kulon Progo, directly to the west, has a mixture of soil
types, with grumusols and alluvial soils predominating
at lower altitudes and lateritic soils predominating at
higher slopes of the Sentolo hills. In the fourth and
poorest district of Gunung Kidul, directly to the east
and situated on a rolling mass of hills with limestone
base materials that predate the volcanoes, the soils are
so mixed that soil mappers have not yet successfully
mapped the region, but grumusols and shallow limestone
soils predominate. Many of the limestone soils have been
badly eroded by denudation of the forest cover. The
grumusols have the distinctly undesirable feature of containing a high level of montmorillonitic clay which results in heavy soil shrinkage and swelling causing considerable root damage to plants.

Although the limestone and grumusol soils (distant
from the volcano) have low fertility and many undesirable
characteristics, the soils in the vicinity of the volcanoes have such outstandingly desirable characteristics
from an agricultural point of view that they deserve special mention. The rivers draining the slopes of the volcano Merapi dissolve nutrients and carry new materials
by alluviation to many of the fields through the irrigation system. The remarkable feature of these waters is
their natural refertilization of the soil during the process of irrigation. It is perhaps this condition which
has enabled the Javanese to switch to annual cropping
without continued decline of soil fertility. Central
Java, and Yogyakarta in particular, has been regularly
refertilized, due to the regular volcanic activity of
Mount Merapi approximately every four years.

In terms of actual cropping patterns, the Javanese
have been quite skillful in exploiting the agricultural
potential of their rich soil and natural resource endowment. Historically, Java was known as the island of
Djuwawut, the place where millet was to be found. Millet
is today an exceedingly unimportant crop. By 1603, rice
was extensively grown and sawah cultivation was spreading. Two-thirds of the sawah in Java have been created
out of unleveled field since 1833.[7] Clifford Geertz has
made a polarity of the difference between upland (<u>ladang</u>)
or swidden cultivation as practiced in the outer islands
and sawah cultivation as practiced in Java.[8] Geertz is

correct in most aspects except for his characterization
of sawah as a monocrop regime. He has correctly observed
that rice, when grown, is grown alone. However, sawah
cultivators do grow numerous crops on their fields, and
while a particular field may be seen as a monocrop, a
Javanese farm is not a monocrop enterprise. Thus, between 1940 and 1962, the percentage of cropped land in
Java devoted to maize varied slightly from 22 to 23.2
percent. The area planted to cassava, sweet potatoes,
soybeans, peanuts, tobacco, pulses, tubers, and vegetables rose from 33.3 to 36.4 percent, and the percentage
devoted to rice suffered a drop, from 45 to 40 percent.[9]
Not all farmers are to be found planting the above
crops. Where the crops are grown and whether they are
grown in rotation with rice depends jointly upon the soil
type and water availability. On the volcanic ash soils,
rice predominates, and where continuous supplies of water
are available, it is not infrequent to find a continuous
(three crop) rice planting. With lesser availability of
water, rice is grown during the rainy season, followed by
a field crop such as peanuts, or soybeans. Numerous
other cropping arrangements exist where water supplies
are not assured. In the poor limestone soils, rice is
seldom planted; rather, a rotation (or even mixed field),
of manioc, peanuts, maize, beans and other crops is
grown. Given the proportion of harvested land that is
planted to rice, it is a mistake to say that the Javanese
farmer is a rice farmer. He is a rice farmer if he farms
irrigated volcanic soils; otherwise, he is a general farmer. Thus, in the Yogyakarta region, out of 317,173 hectares, sawah represented 19.7 percent, dry field area
represented 38.8 percent, and the area devoted to housing
and village compounds also planted to tree and fruit
crops was 27.2 percent. In addition, forests cover includes 6.4 percent, and other land, mostly not agriculturally usable, accounts for 7.9 percent.[10] Again, of
the eight major field crops that occupied most of the irrigated sawah and dry fields in the Yogyakarta region,
the following breakdown of harvested area was observed:
31.5 percent of the harvested area was cultivated in wet
rice, 14.2 percent in upland rice, 10.9 percent in maize,
20.9 percent in manioc, 1.2 percent in sweet potato,
10.5 percent in peanuts, 9.2 percent in soybeans, and
1.5 percent in sorghum and millet.[11]
The above totals still fall short of giving an adequate picture of the diversity which agriculture exhibits
in the Yogyakarta region. In addition to the above field
crops, numerous vegetable, fruit, tobacco, tree, and
fiber crops are grown by small-holders. Moreover, there
must be added the estate crops of sugar and Vorstenland
tobacco. In brief, tremendous diversification is already
practiced by Javanese farmers in the Yogyakarta area and
in many other areas of Java. The question must be

addressed, however, as to whether these cropping patterns are ideal from the perspective of absorbing labor.

II

With the above overview of the agricultural sub-system in Central Java and some perspective on the exceedingly wide range of cropping patterns followed by the peasant farmer, the focus of analysis must now move to an assessment of the relative labor-absorbing capacities of each of the six major agricultural producing sectors. In order to measure variations in labor demand a farm sample survey was conducted in eight villages, two per kabupaten, with a sample size of 138 farms.[12] The analysis will first involve an estimation of labor/output coefficients for the six agricultural sectors, followed by calculations of the total labor output ratios.

In considering the labor requirements for the first sector on paddy rice production, attention is initially given to findings across all farms which planted rice, followed by a breakdown by major rice varieties. Separate information is presented for male- and female-labor use, for it is in this sexual division of labor that many important differences occur which affect the structure of labor-use. Up to 16 different paddy-labor operations can occur, however, and some alternative processes exist for these activities. For instance, poorer farmers with no access to draft animal-labor broke land entirely by hand hoeing with no plowing. Also, in post-harvest operations, some farmers thresh, winnow, and then store rice, milling thereafter whenever they choose. Other farmers do not thresh, winnow, and mill their rice, but rather dry the stalk paddy and then hand-pound first the grain from the stalk paddy and then further pound the rice from the husk. Those who hand-pound have a high percentage of broken grain which is neither marketed nor marketable. Labor operations are distinctly (but not completely), segregated by sex; clearing stubble, plowing, hoeing, and harrowing are men's operations. Transplanting is almost completely a job for women, but weeding is done by both sexes. Water control and pesticide application are men's work, whereas harvesting, threshing, and winnowing, or alternatively, hand-pounding, are basically, but not entirely, women's work.

Valued at sampled-farmers' own estimations of sale value of their stalk paddy, 6,994 labor days were required in producing one million rupiah in gross output. The total labor used per hectare for one crop of paddy is 474 days, of which 315 are pre-harvest labor, and 159 are post-harvest labor. Of the pre-harvest labor operations, the vast majority are male labor; of post-harvest labor, the vast majority is female. On a per farm basis, only about 202 days of labor are used in paddy production annually. On the average there were 3.62 potential adult workers with 1,321 available days during the year. Thus, even if only family labor were used, paddy rice production would only occupy 15 percent of their time. Moreover, the labor-use figures above comprise all labor, family, hired, and exchanged with neighbors, and therefore less than 15 percent of available time was exerted in producing rice on one's own farm.

Of particular interest in Indonesia today is whether a significant change in labor use is happening with the introduction of new high-yielding varieties. Interest in differences among varieties takes two forms. The first concern involves possible differences in requirements per hectare, and labor requirements per million rupiahs of gross output. Evidence from various areas in Java (in particular, the Agro-Economic Survey), has suggested that the new IR varieties use more labor per hectare, at least in pre-harvest operations. Thus, many observers have concluded that employment creation has been one side effect of the introduction of the Green Revolution varieties. In order to address this issue in the Yogyakarta sample, the 111 paddy-producing farms were divided according to four major variety groups: (1) the IR varieties, (2) the variety C-4, also classified as high yielding, (3) traditional Javanese varieties, and (4) locally improved varieties. A review of this data indicates that labor used in IR variety paddy rice production is less, not more, on a per hectare basis than with Javanese varieties. The dramatic change that takes place is a substantial reduction in care taken of the IR5 rice plant before harvest in regard to such operations as hoeing, weeding, and even in water control--all of which are men's work. There is a dramatic change in sex composition of labor required. Slightly more female labor is required per hectare for IR varieties, but much less male labor is required. The new varieties do have somewhat (but not dramatically) higher yields in terms of physical weight, and thereby require correspondingly more labor to thresh, winnow, and/or hand-pound the higher yield.

Of greater interest in the context of this study are not differences in labor used per hectare, but differences in the labor used per unit of value of production. It has been stated above that the direct labor/output ratio across the sample was 6,994 labor days per million rupiahs, but this figure constitutes a weighted average of the higher labor requirements of traditional Javanese varieties and C-4, and the lower labor requirements of locally improved and IR varieties. Actually, the comparative differences in the labor requirements per million rupiah of paddy is quite large for each of the rice varieties. At the higher end of the scale, the direct labor requirement for C-4 is 8,748 days, and for traditional Javanese varieties 7,339 days, whereas for locally improved varieties it is 6,685 days, and for IR varieties, 6,604 days. In brief, if the composition of paddy production undergoes substantial change in the near future the overall labor coefficient must be expected to drop.

The calculation of the labor/output coefficient for the second agricultural sector (other farm food products) is derived from a weighted sum of individual crop labor requirements. Included in the sample are non-paddy upland rice, maize, soybeans, peanuts and a wide range of other vegetable and fruit crops. In the sampling process, labor is again tabulated directly by operation: clearing, planting, weeding, harvesting, etc. The overall labor coefficient for this sector is 2,997 labor days per million rupiahs, a total labor requirement which is much lower than the labor requirement for rice, (6,990). Likewise, when other farm food crop labor coefficients are compared with paddy rice labor requirements on a per hectare basis, it becomes evident that very few crops require as much labor as rice. The weighted average of these labor coefficients for other food crops gives a low figure of 181 days required per hectare, and this is only 40 percent of the labor required for paddy rice. Vegetable production exceeds this weighted average; manioc, soybeans, and peanuts were only slightly greater and crops such as maize, coconuts, peppers, and yard-long beans fall below the average. Low labor requirements for maize and manioc can be attributed to the fact that they are generally grown on limestone soils where water availability and yield reliability is minimal. In brief, in comparison with paddy rice production, other food crops, fruits, and vegetables do not require as much labor per unit of land, nor as much labor per unit of revenue output.

The estimation of the labor/output coefficient for the third agricultural sector of farm non-food production is again derived from a weighted sum of individual crop labor requirements. Of the eighteen non-food crops under cultivation, information was available for this study on only 8 crops, but these eight crops make up 93.9 percent of the total sector revenue. In terms of total agricultural production in the Jogyakarta area, non-food crops are relatively rare, occupying less than 10,000 of the 371,000 cultivated hectares in the region. Included in the sample are such crops as kapok, thatch palm, bamboo, and tobacco. The weighted average labor coefficient for this sector is 5,078 labor days per million rupiah, a figure which remains well below the total labor requirements for lowland wet-rice cultivation.

Calculations of labor requirements for estate sugar, the fourth agricultural sector, are based upon data gathered from the Madu Kismo Sugar Estate located in the Yogyakarta region. Cultivation practices on the estate

reveal a distinct difference between labor requirements
during the slack season and during the peak harvest and
milling season. The planting season begins in May and
during this month seedlings are transplanted from mountainous Kaliurang to fields in lowland Bantul. The growing cycle now takes about 14 months, although formerly
this period lasted for 16 months. Three weeks are needed
for breaking ground, hilling, and trenching of fields
which will be planted to sugar, whereas transplanting requires about a one-week period. After these peak labor
demand operations, all subsequent activities up to the
harvest period are spaced out over the growing period.
Possibly because of the day-length photosensitivity of
sugar, the sugar estate is very rigid in its desire to
have all ground breaking and planting done simultaneously
with a very large labor force,rather than spreading this
work over a longer period of time with a small labor
force.

The growing cycle for the sugar industry requires
that a distinction be made between labor requirements
based upon full- and part-time employees. For full-time
employees, the work year consists of seven months at six
days per week, but increasing to a seven-day work week
during the five months of harvest when the mill is in
continuous operation. Full-time employees therefore work
332 days per year. For part-time or seasonal employees,
the season is a continuous seven-day work week, and thus,
the total work period consists of about 150 days of employment per year. Based on this data the labor coefficient for the sugar estate sector can be estimated at
919 days per million rupiahs, a figure which is considerably lower than the direct labor/output coefficients
for the previous three sectors.

In order to further refine the calculation of the
labor coefficient, the employment requirements for sugar
production can be divided into two component operations,
(1) cane production and (2) the milling of cane for
sugar. The first process uses much labor, but adds little value,and the second function uses very little labor
but adds most of the final value. In many countries,
sugar production is accomplished by such a two-stage
operation with sugar mills buying cane from small growers. Even with this division, however, the actual process of cane production is still much less labor-using
when compared to paddy rice. On the Madu Kismo Sugar
Estate, 408,170 days of labor are exerted in the production of cane on 1,530 hectares of cultivated land. Thus,
the labor use per hectare is only 267 days per year, a
rate which is exceeded not only by paddy rice (almost
double), but several other food crops as well, including
tobacco, (370 days per hectare). Moreover, the figure of
267 days per hectare for cane production is an annual
figure; the higher figures for paddy rice, other food

crops, and tobacco are for crops lasting less than six months, allowing for second or third crops, and therefore higher labor applications per hectare on an annual basis. In brief, sugar production, when examined in close conjunction with other agricultural activities, is not a labor-using process. Neither is it comparatively labor-absorptive per hectare, even when sub-divided into its distinct production and milling components.

The fifth agricultural sector comprehends other agricultural production, and in this instance, primary attention is focussed upon animal husbandry as information was not available on labor used in either the very limited forestry or fishing activities in Yogyakarta. In animal husbandry, feed gathering is the most time-consuming operation. Approximately one-third of a day is required per small animal equivalent for food gathering. Sheep and goats (over one year) represent one animal equivalent, with cattle or buffalo (less than a year) representing three animal equivalents. Calculations must also be made of marketing time, another time-consuming operation for animal husbandry in Java. Finally, human labor is also involved in producing animal draft labor (plowing) values, and survey results in Yogyakarta indicate that just over 1,540 man-days were required to work draft animals in the production of one million rupiahs of income from plowing. Given this information on labor time (human) involved in the production of values of animal husbandry for (1) slaughter, (2) animals traded, and (3) draft animal labor, it is estimated that the direct labor/output coefficient for this sector is 731 labor-days per million rupiahs. This rate is much lower than the labor coefficients for the other five agricultural sectors.

The sixth agricultural sector concerns an assessment of labor requirements for the food processing and beverage manufacturing industry in Yogyakarta.[13] This sector includes manufacturing activities in the processing of milk, ice, ice cream, canned food, peanut and coconut oil, soft drinks, and a wide range of other food and beverage items. Included in the sample are 9 large firms, 106 medium-scale firms, and another 3,390 small-scale firms, of which 379 were seasonal in their operations. For the small-food processors, the data indicates that full-time firms operated a mean of 23.4 days per month, or 281 days per year, whereas for medium- and large-food processors, the figure is 300 days per year. Based upon number of labor employed and days in operation, and combined with gross value of output data, the direct labor/output coefficient for this sector can be estimated at 2,618 labor-days per million rupiahs. This coefficient rate is well below the labor requirements for the first three sectors involving paddy rice, other food crops, and non-food crops.

III

   With the above sectoral calculations of labor absorption in perspective, the analysis must now move to an
assessment of growth potentials in each sector and the
comparative differences which follow in the generation
of additional employment throughout the larger economy.
The latter task requires calculating the total labor/out-
put ratio for each sector. Whereas the computation of
direct labor/output ratios involves observable economic
conditions, the computation of total labor/output ratios
cannot be observed, as they are estimates of the entire
labor requirement placed upon an integrated economy by
the production of one unit of any particular good or service. Their estimation requires use of the Leontief
inverse matrix, a tool of proven value for structural in-
vestigations. While direct labor coefficients measure,
for example, the employment within the auto industry in
the production of autos, total labor coefficients measure
not only employment within the auto industry but also in
the glass, steel, rubber tire, paint, and other industries that supply intermediate goods and services. Total
coefficients are always greater than or equal to direct
coefficients.
   For comparative purposes, Table 6.1 gives both the
direct (observable) and total (estimated with inverse
matrix multiplication) labor coefficients for the sixteen
sectors of the Yogyakarta economy. There are only a few
small changes in the order of labor intensity of the coefficients, with paddy production losing its first place
to the service sector in terms of direct labor absorption. Food manufacturing and beverages rise from seventh
place (direct) to fourth place (total), and the major
decline in rank is mining, which drops from ninth place to
fourteenth. The six agricultural sectors are scattered,
showing little uniformity according to either definition
of labor/output ratio, with variations in rank for direct
L/O coefficients ranging from first through twelfth, and
for total L/O coefficients ranging from second through
thirteenth place.
   Although the rankings do not change substantially,
each of the sixteen sectors do not experience the same
proportional rise in labor demand generation when the
total labor/output coefficient is divided by the direct
labor/output coefficient. The ratio of total labor/out-
put coefficient to direct labor/output coefficient has at
times, been called an employment multiplier via backward
linkage or intermediate input use. This ratio has
nothing to do with Keynesian multipliers, but simply
shows a percentage rise in total labor demand generated.
For paddy rice, the ratio of the coefficients is 1.16 (a
16 percent increase in labor use via backward linkage).

Table 6.1
Direct Labor/Output Coefficients (h_i) and Total Labor/Output
Coefficients (L_i) for the 16 Sectors of the Jogyakarta Economy

	Sector	h_i (Labor days per million Rp)	Rank h_i	L_i (Labor days per million Rp)	Rank L_i
1.	Paddy	6,994	1	8,145	2
2.	Other Farm Food	2,997	6	4,574	7
3.	Farm Non-Food	5,078	4	5,314	6
4.	Estate Crop	919	11	2,371	12
5.	Other Ag.	731	12	2,194	13
6.	Food/Beverages	2,618	7	7,817	4
7.	Mining	1,174	9	1,853	14
8.	Textiles	957	10	4,455	9
9.	Other Mfg.	682	13	3,566	10
10.	Construction	3,146	5	5,622	5
11.	Electricity	547	14	1,196	16
12.	Transportation	2,513	8	4,555	8
13.	Trade	6,750	2	8,130	3
14.	Banking	427	15	3,383	11
15.	Rental	0	16	1,255	15
16.	Services	5,638	3	8,888	1

For other Food Crops, it is 1.53 and for non-food crops
it is 1.05. For the Sugar Plantation the employment multiplier is 2.58, and for Other Agriculture, and Food Processing the ratios are 3.00 and 2.99. For the remaining
ten non-agricultural sectors, the ratios of coefficients
range from a low of 1.20 for the Trade Sector to a high
of 7.92 for Banking, 5.23 for Other Manufacturing, and
4.66 for Textiles. These sharp rises in labor demand
generation in the non-agricultural sectors are considerably higher than those for the agricultural sectors
and they show very strong backward linkages for high
levels of labor-absorptive intermediate inputs.

Were there no other factors of production other than
labor, the total labor/output coefficient would reflect
the opportunity cost in terms of man days of labor fore-
gone in the production of one million rupiahs of output.
The total labor coefficients are a superior measure of
employment generation and show that services, paddy and
trade, are the most absorptive of labor and that no other
agricultural activity surpasses paddy in labor utilization. In this context, however, it must be noted that
the expansion of agricultural employment, as measured by

census changes from 1961 to 1971, has slowed perceptibly, growing at a rate of only 0.5 percent per annum, while population grew at 1.9 percent per annum.

The slow growth of agricultural employment is a phenomenon occurring in every Asian country and two factors seem to be associated with the decline in labor absorption. First, there is the natural pull of the cities, drawing rural people into urban activities via wage differences. More importantly, however, is the fact that the growth of agricultural output is by nature slower than that of industrial output, a condition which can be attributed to low-demand (income) elasticities for agricultural goods and an inelastic supply of land. With respect to low income elasticities, Table 6.2 gives demand elasticities for agricultural products in Indonesia. These calculations are in general higher than might be expected, even among low-income countries. In Table 6.3, the demand elasticities are compared with total labor-absorptive capacity (the L coefficients) one sector at a time. This comparison indicates that if any of the six agricultural sectors rate high on both labor-absorptive capacity and income elasticity, they will likely maintain their product position in the total bundle of goods produced as incomes rise.

The information in Table 6.3 demonstrates that as a rule, activities which are labor absorptive have little growth potential (in regard to rising income, not rising population), and conversely, those agricultural activities which are high in growth potential have little absorptive capacity. The two exceptions to this general rule are paddy production and food and beverage production. Paddy production has a very high initial rate of direct labor absorption, (h_i from Table 6.1 equals 6,994 labor days per million Rupiahs) but because of relatively low use of labor-absorbing intermediate goods, the total labor/output coefficient is only 16 percent higher. The diffusion of generated demand for labor by paddy throughout the rest of Yogyakarta's economy is slight. Nevertheless, income elasticities of demand for the final product, rice, are in the range of 0.6 and 0.8, which indicate that as incomes rise, rice consumption will be expected to almost keep pace with income growth. In regard to food manufacturing and beverage production, although employment directly within this sector is low, with a direct labor/output coefficient of only 2,618 labor-days per million rupiahs, the total labor/output coefficient is 300 percent higher, or 7,817 labor-days per million rupiahs. This high coefficient can be attributed to heavy backward linkage demands for labor engaged in the use of agricultural intermediate goods. Although income elasticity estimates are not available for many of the goods included in Manufactured Foods (Sector 6) those that were available were almost uniformly equal

Table 6.2
Indonesia Income Elasticity of Demand Estimates from Four Sources [14]

Sector	Product	(FAO, 1970-1980 study)	(FAO, 1975-1985 study)	(FAO, Perspective study)	(Deuster's Estimates)
I	Paddy Rice	0.70	.60	.62	.759
II	Other Farm Food				
	a) Field Crops				
	Maize	0.40	0.20	0.64	NA
	Cassava and Sweet Potatoes	0.20	0.20	0.13	0.138
	Peanuts and Soybeans	0.30	0.30	0.32	NA
	b) Fruits and Nuts	0.80	0.80	0.82	NA
	c) Vegetables	0.60	0.40	0.65	0.977
III	Farm Non-Food Crops				
	Cotton	0.80	NA	NA	NA
	Coffee	0.20	0.20	NA	NA
	Tea	0.60	0.60	NA	NA
	Spices	0.50	NA	0.50	NA
	Tobacco	NA	NA	NA	0.991
IV	Estate Crop Production				
	Sugar	1.37	1.10	1.00	NA
V	Other Ag. Production				
	Meat	1.32	1.60	1.32	1.581
	Eggs	1.20	1.20	1.20	2.635
	Milk	2.00	2.00	1.77	1.624
	Fish	1.00	1.00	1.00	NA
VI	Prepared Foods				
	Wheat and Bread Products	1.00	0.40	1.00	1.095
	Soy and Coconut Oils	1.00	1.00	1.00	NA

Note: NA = not available

Table 6.3
Comparison of Labor Absorptive Capacity (L)
with Income Elasticities

Product	Sector	Labor Absorption	Income Elasticity
Paddy	I	High	Moderate
Other Farm Food	II	Moderate	Low (except fruits & vegetables which are moderate)
Farm Non-Food	III	Moderate	Low to Moderate
Sugar	IV	Low	High
Other Ag.: An. Hus.	V	Low	High
Manufactured Food, Beverages	VI	High	Moderate to High

Definitions   High: L over 7000   High: Elasticity equal to or greater than 1

Moderate: L between 4000 and 7000

Moderate: Elasticity between ½ and 1

Low: L below 4000

Low: Elasticity below ½

to one. Thus, the prospect for rapid labor absorption
is greater in food manufacturing than in any other agricultural sector because of the consonant high labor use
and sanguine prospects for expanded demand as incomes
rise.

Aside from low-income elasticities, agricultural
growth in Java is also constrained by an inelastic supply of land. In the Yogyakarta area, all land with sufficient water is already in use and expansion in land
use can only be achieved through major improvements in
irrigation. Recent reports from the Kali Progo Irrigation project indicate that many areas in the Yogyakarta
area will receive additional dry-season water supplies.
Capital costs for subprojects within the overall plan
range from a high of Rp 147,000 per hectare for the Kulon
Progo subsystem, to a low of Rp 53,000 per hectare for
the Sapon Subsystem. Project benefits are expected to be
approximately six-tenths of an extra rice crop and about
seven-tenths of an extra non-rice field or vegetable

crop. Thus, capital/first year gross-output ratios range from a high of 1.20 to a low of 0.43 and capital/first year value-added ratios go from a high of 1.77 to a low of 0.64. These capital requirements are quite low when compared with industrial capital/output ratios.

Irrigation expansion is important because more labor cannot be absorbed in agricultural production without relaxation of the water constraint. Low-capital requirements and high-labor requirements for increased agricultural production indicate that irrigation should then be the priority area of concern. Moreover, the activity of constructing new irrigation systems is itself a labor-absorbing process. The construction sector has a high initial direct labor/output ratio (3,146 labor-days per million rupiahs) which ranks fifth among the previous-listed sixteen-sector activities. Similarly, it has a high total-labor requirement for the entire Yogyakarta economy (5,622 labor-days per million rupiahs gross output) which also ranks fifth among the sixteen sectors.

In summary, the key to increased labor utilization in the Yogyakarta economy is through expansion of agricultural production of those products which are labor absorbing. This does not include all agricultural products. For instance, estate sugar production and animal husbandry are not labor-absorbing activities when compared to field-crop production, nor when compared to the processing and manufacturing of foodstuffs and beverages. Traditional Javanese agriculture has already devised the most labor-absorptive technology in the world, the cultivation of rice on irrigated sawah. Under these conditions, if the supply of land was not constrained, employment expansion could continue apace with rising income due to the high income demand effects exhibited by rice, which for many is still a luxury good. Nevertheless, the evident constraint is the unavailability of new land, an obstacle which can only be overcome through increased irrigation and an attendant increase in multiple cropping. What is called for is not diversion or regulation of existing water supplies during the rainy season, but instead, storage and impoundment of water for dry season use. The Kali Progo irrigation improvement studies show that the capital costs are not high per hectare, and the benefit streams are quick to begin and quick to surpass the present value of the irrigation capital costs. Irrigation is therefore clearly the first priority for further research if labor absorption within rural areas of Java is to be a meaningful goal.

NOTES

1. James Keddie, "The Mass Unemployment Explosion," The Far Eastern Economic Review, 82, no. 52 (December 31, 1973): 41.

2. Roger Montgomery, "Migration, Employment and Unemployment in Java: Changes from 1961 to 1971 with Particular Reference to the Green Revolution," Asian Survey, 15, no. 3 (March 1975).

3. Research for this study was undertaken in the special region of Jogyakarta from 1971 to 1973. Special thanks are due to D. G. Sisler who directed this study to completion, and to J. Mellor and J. Vanek, whose guidance and advice were exceptionally useful.

4. Widjojo Nitisastro, Population Trends in Indonesia (Ithaca: Cornell University Press, 1970), p. 19.

5. Biro Pusat Statistik, Sensus Penduduk 1971: Serie B, No. 2 (Jarkarta: 1972).

6. United Nations, World Population Prospects as Assessed in 1963: Population Study No. 4 (New York: United Nations, 1966), p. 27.

7. Clifford Geertz, Agricultural Involution (Berkeley: University of California Press, 1968), p. 34.

8. Ibid., p. 35.

9. Sie Kwat Soen, Prospects for Agricultural Development in Indonesia: With Special Reference to Java (Wageningen: Centre for Agricultural Publishing and Documentation of Wageningen, 1968), p. 51.

10. Sir M. McDonald and Partners, Kali Proyo Basin Study (London: Sir M. McDonald and Partners, 1971), p. 9.

11. Biro Statistik, Yogyakarta, Statistik Pemerintah Daerah, Istimewa Jogjakarta, 1969 (Yogyakarta: Biro Statistik, 1969), 2:69.

12. Details on basic-farming characteristics of the 138-sample farms are as follows: average-landholding-per-farm (sawah, tegal, and pekarangan) is .455 hectares; average sawah planted to rice in the wet season is .228 hectares; average number of draft-animals per-hectare of sawah is 2.13; percent of families owning at least one cow or bull is 26.8 percent; average-family-size is 5.56 persons; and average number of children over 10 years of age is 1.86 per family.

13. Labor information for this sector is derived from the following two published industrial censuses conducted by the Central Statistical Bureau: Sensus Industri 1964: Hasil Pentjatjahan Untuk Sektor Industri Ketjil Dan Rumah Tangga (Census of Small and Cottage Industry) (Djakarta: Biro Pusat Statistik, 1964), 2a; and Survey Perusahaan Industri Tahun 1971, Ind/3: Banjaknja Perusahaan Industri, Mesin Tenaga, Banjaknja Tenaga Kerdja Diperintji Menurut Djenis Industri di Tiap 2 Daerah I dan II (Census of Large- and Medium-Manufacturing Industries: Machinery, Labor-force employed, Detailed According to Industry and Province and District) (Djakarta: Biro Pusat Statistik, 1971).

7
Income Distribution and Levels of Living in Java, 1963 and Beyond

Dwight King and Peter Weldon

The problem of equity and the social aspects of Indonesian development has so far produced little time-series analysis of sufficient scope for policy relevance. The reasons for this deficiency can perhaps be found in the logistical difficulties and great expense of large-scale surveys, the predilection among scholars--themselves impressed by ecological and cultural diversity--against macro analysis and standardized field procedures, the lack of recognition that consumer expenditures may be a preferable, albeit surrogate indicator of income, and the official preoccupation with changes in per capita income measured by total national product divided by population which begs questions of distribution. In an effort to partially offset this deficiency, this paper represents an attempt to synthesize Java-wide data pertaining to income distribution beginning in the mid-1960s and stretching into the 1970s, as recent as there are data available. The importance of examining the distributional pattern accompanying a national economic growth rate pegged at 6 to 8 percent per year in Java/non-Javan terms is fully recognized. Unfortunately, there are not sufficient sources of data to allow extension of the analysis beyond Java. Java, of course, is an extremely important area in which to measure both growth and distribution, given its population size and central role in determining national development policies. Although the following analysis is intertemporal within Java, less error prone than inter-country comparisons, this study finds its context among the literature on other Southeast Asian countries where, regardless of policy mix and growth rates, the general picture is one of worsening distribution.[1]

The only source of Java-wide comparable time-series data on income distribution is found in the four rounds of the National Social and Economic Survey (SUSENAS) on consumption expenditures, carried out in the 1960s by the Central Bureau of Statistics with United Nations guidance

and support, except for the brief period when Indonesia
withdrew its membership. The unit for data collection
has been the household and only common (excluding board-
ing houses, hospitals, jails, etc.) households were enumerated; household members were defined as those who live
together in the same dwelling unit and share their principal meals. Consumption of home-made and home-grown
items were evaluated and entered the calculations, as
were consumption of gifts and wages paid in kind. Expenditures on non-consumption (e.g., debt payment, land and
buildings) and household enterprise were excluded. Compared to the first three rounds, the sample size in the
latest round is rather small and apparently has greater
reliability in rural than in urban areas.

The analysis of urban areas for the period can be
supplemented from two additional and independent data
sets. The first set is provided by the Cost-of-Living
Survey, also carried out by the Central Bureau of Statistics in four of the largest Javan cities in 1968-1969.
While details of the survey have been reported elsewhere,
it is worth noting that in the field operations, some
families (including foreigners) with abnormally high expenditures were exempted from the survey and that the
technique of data collection involved a combination of
closed question schedules and daily recording of expenditures in an account book for the duration of one week,
the latter presupposing literacy.[2] Thus, a slight bias
away from the extremes on the distribution of income can
be assumed. Finally, in each of the four cities considered here, income was understated; reported expenditures usually exceed reported income/receipts. Therein
lies the rationale for using expenditures as a proxy for
income in this analysis.

A second and independent source of data on the same
four large cities comes from a large market and media
survey carried out in late 1970. The sample has been described previously, but it is useful to point out the
number of households in the sample (Jakarta, 1,978; Surabaya, 607; Bandung, 630; Yogyakarta, 342) and the fact
that the·survey did include foreign households which
might give it a slightly upward bias. The survey collected data on both household and individual income; the
former will be utilized for consistency with other surveys and also because they are considered more reliable,
given some of the weaknesses in the individual sample.

II

In rural areas from 1963 to 1970, there apparently
was very little change in the distribution of income and
there were no clear trends in the proportion of total income accruing to equal population quintiles. This lack

of change should not obscure a very clear pattern of inequality with the upper 20 percent receiving double its
equal share of income and the lower 20 percent receiving
less than half of its equal share. Apparently, the gap
has not widened, relatively speaking, and may have narrowed very slightly: a condition made evident by the
change in the lowest quintile's share from 7.6 percent in
1963-1964 to 8.7 percent in 1969-1970. Such relative improvement probably occurred during an overall absolute
decline in rural areas, as will be shown subsequently.

In urban areas several consistent changes toward increasing inequality are visible. The 20 percent of the
population with the highest income increased their share
about 13 percent, from 36.7 to 41.5 percent. The next
highest income group remained relatively stable, but the
shares of all the other population quintiles slightly
declined. The unweighted average for Bandung, Yogyakarta, and Surabaya, shows the distibution was more skewed
in the largest cities, but since there is no data available specifically for these three cities at an earlier
time period, trends specific to them in contrast to all
urban areas (as defined in the 1961 Census), are not
known. Fortunately, however, SUSENAS has in three out of
its rounds distinguished Jakarta within the urban category. Data specific to Jakarta indicates that the top
quintile gained 22 percent, or increased their share from
42.6 to 52.0 percent; an upward move which is much more
than the increase in urban areas in general. It can be
hypothesized that the other three large cities mentioned
above also experienced similar trends so that, in general,
large centers of economic activity experienced increasing
inequality of income distribution during the period 1963
to 1970.

The consistency of the general urban trend shows an
increasing concentration of income at the top. In contrast to the lowest population quintile in the rural
areas of Java, whose relative position was not eroded,
the poorest quintile's share of income in all urban areas
declined from 9.5 percent in 1963-1964 to 7.8 percent in
1969-1970. This urban figure excludes Jakarta where the
lowest economic group seems to have held its own. The
gains of the top quintile in Jakarta have been at the expense of the second and third quintiles. The 20 percent
plus gain in share by the top quintile in Jakarta, undoubtedly, accounts for a severe movement of the Gini
index from .311 in 1967 to .438 in 1970; a trend which
contrasts with the less severe change in urban areas excluding Jakarta.

Large cities probably accounted for most of the increased inequality in urban areas of Java. As in Jakarta, the top quintile in both Bandung and Surabaya showed
gains and again at the expense of the second and third
quintiles that fell behind, relatively speaking. In all

three cities, in addition to Yogyakarta, the gap between
the lowest and the middle population quintiles has narrowed. Yogyakarta presents a different picture from the
other three cities with the top quintile almost static
and the bottom quintile increasing its share by more than
60 percent. Whether in fact these represent trends or
are more likely artifacts of the 1970 sampling procedures
cannot be clearly determined. Nevertheless, they useful-
ly draw attention to differences which have emerged or
may be emerging in the major growth centers of Java.

The changes described above are all within certain
areas or sectors, e.g., within rural areas, within urban
areas, and within Jakarta. Equally important are comparisons between those areas. For example, the increasingly unequal distribution of income in urban areas has
been noted, but how have urban areas fared in comparison
with rural areas or with Jakarta? Is the differential
between rural and urban and between Jakarta and other
areas growing or declining?

These questions can be illuminated through comparison
of per capita means and medians calculated from the same
SUSENAS data used throughout this paper. Comparing rural
and urban areas (excluding Jakarta), it appears the rural
population improved their position slightly during the
economic chaos of the mid-1960s, but that it declined
slightly between 1967 and 1970. The percentage of rural
to urban median income dropped from 73.5 to 71.7 percent,
and the ratio between mean income declined from 65.9 to
64.1 percent. Much clearer is the decline of both rural
and urban areas with reference to Jakarta. The magnitude
of the decline was greatest for urban areas and is seen
in both the ratio of means and of medians which respectively fell from 80.9 to 69.7 percent and from 87.7 to
70.9 percent between 1963 and 1970. This suggests that
overall income growth in Jakarta far outdistanced other
urban areas and rural areas. It is interesting to note
that the ratio between Jakarta and rural median incomes
(but not mean incomes) stayed almost constant at about
50 percent, which suggests the above decline of urban
areas relative to Jakarta occurred in real terms, and thus
cannot be explained away by price-level differences.
Only if both the mean and median ratios had declined
would an explanation be plausible based primarily on
higher inflation rates for Jakarta. This finding also
substantiates the earlier finding of declining equality
in Jakarta by showing that, during a period of rapid
growth and increased income in Jakarta, there was constancy (though differences in magnitude) between the income position of the majority of Jakartans and the rural
masses over time. In terms of median income levels, it
can be seen that relative to Jakarta, other urban areas
fell from a median income of about 20 percent lower than
Jakarta's median to 30 percent lower in just eight year's

time. In rural areas, median income, although constant
in trend, was about 50 percent less than in Jakarta and
30 percent less than in other urban areas.

The above data also enables one to estimate the proportions of the populations which are very poor, elite,
etc., although given the absence of sufficiently comprehensive measures in income it would be preferable to have
data on education, occupation, literacy, and food consumption in order to construct a more sensitive and meaningful index of stratification. Looking first at the
elite end of the distribution, it is apparent that the
richest 10 percent of the population in urban areas (excluding Jakarta) is increasing its share. These figures,
based only on the last three SUSENAS surveys, which provide an adequate number of income groupings for decile
analysis, are as follows: for 1964-1965, 23 percent; for
1967, 25.2 percent; and 26.7 percent for 1969-1970. In
rural areas their share has been almost constant at about
25 percent for these three time periods. The proportion
is higher in the largest cities, with Jakarta being the
highest at 32 percent, and Surabaya the lowest at 28.7
percent, (based on the Cost-of-Living Survey 1968-1969).
Of this 30 percent share held by the wealthiest decile in
the largest cities, two-thirds of it was in the hands of
the very wealthiest 5 percent of the households. In Jakarta this meant the richest 5 percent had a share of
total income similar in size to the share of the poorest
45 percent of the households (and it may be recalled
these data exclude high-income foreign households).

III

The relative distribution of income is important in
that it shows how the economic pie is divided within the
society. Yet much of the current interest in income distribution is not simply due to a concern with relative
inequality. It is also a concern with absolute stan-
dards-of-living in terms of calorie intake and nutrition
levels, clothing, sanitation, health, education, etc. It
is hypothetically possible that a given quintile of the
population could be relatively worse off than before, but
due to an overall improvement in economic conditions, be
better off in absolute terms. Conversely, relative improvement could mask an overall decline in levels-of-
living.

The search for indicators that adequately measure
absolute material well-being is particularly complicated
in the case of Indonesia. Besides the usual sparseness
of data comparable over time, the hyper-inflation of the
mid-1960s makes any effort based on prices or other monetary units a rather doubtful enterprise. One method recently used was to convert consumer expenditure or income

into "rice equivalent" at the price of rice prevailing at the date consumer expenditure was surveyed.[3] A "poverty line" was designated at 240 kilograms and 360 kilograms of rice equivalent per capita per year for rural and urban areas respectively; using this base measure, about 50 percent of the Indonesian population was believed to be below the poverty lines in 1969-1970. In time series analysis, however, this method is nearly unusable because of the imprecision that arises in determining the prevailing market price of rice when prices fluctuate not only within markets but also between regions. The government rice subsidy program in Indonesia is a complicating factor in the use of this measure because of the effect on market prices and government employee consumption levels.

This criticism does not deny the importance or the usefulness of developing measures of dietary habits that can be applied on national samples at different periods of time. The SUSENAS surveys gathered information on quantities of various foods consumed in addition to expenditure in monetary units. It is clear from these surveys that the amount of rice consumed is a function of income and that consumption levels are higher in urban than in rural areas. A trend might also be discerned of increased consumption by the top three quintiles in both rural and urban areas. But perhaps the most striking finding is the lower quintile constancy in amounts of rice consumed. This finding further substantiates a number of studies that have noted the inelasticity in rice consumption relative to other food groups and also the greater inelasticity of food consumption in developing countries compared to developed countries.

Before conclusions about level-of-living are drawn from constancy in rice consumption, several factors should be noted. One is that during the eight-year period under consideration the real price of rice fell; a fact which likely represents both an increase in production and a large government subsidy program. A second relevant item is that the proportion of total consumption expenditure spent on food has remained fairly constant within income quintiles, although it varies between quintiles and between rural and urban areas. For instance, in rural areas, the proportion for the highest income quintile is about 75 percent, for the lowest about 80 percent, and in urban areas, the proportions are 65 and 75 percent respectively. Thus, it seems likely that at best, the lower income quintiles of the population remained relatively stable in their level-of-living, given the configuration of a declining real price for rice, increasing real prices of non-rice food items, and constant proportions of total expenditure going for food. At worst, the level-of-living for the lower quintiles of the population deteriorated, as real prices of non-rice food items increased more than the concommitant decrease in the real price of rice. In any case, the level-of-living, as measured by consumption of food, does not appear to have improved for the lower quintiles.

This finding of improvement for the upper income quintiles, but no change or decline for the lower income quintiles in absolute levels-of-living, can be further checked in an analysis of trends in a shortened time period by looking at two of the SUSENAS surveys carried out during relatively stable economic conditions. For this time frame, 1967 to 1969-1970, calculation of price indexes, and their application as a deflator to expenditure on all food in current rupiahs, has at least fair reliability. Total food expenditures can be compared in constant rupiahs for equal quintiles of the population, ranked as usual according to total expenditure (income). A recently proposed price index especially for food in rural areas of Java has been used as a deflator.[4] The rural food index was used because it better reflects the urban areas as defined in SUSENAS than the urban food index which is based on the largest cities. From these calculations it appears total food expenditure in constant rupiahs increased for the top three income quintiles and decreased for the bottom two, except for the second and third quintiles in the rural areas where the pattern is reversed. If the population is divided according to a 40 percent (top) and 60 percent (bottom) proportion, the top 40 percent gained 8 percent in rural areas and 13 percent in urban areas, while the bottom 60 percent fell 28 percent in rural areas and 14 percent in urban areas, the latter in spite of some suspected underdeflation resulting from applying a rural food index in urban areas. These percentage changes may not be too reliable in terms of magnitudes since the time period has been shortened and leeway is necessary for various errors. They are largely consistent, however, with the trends in income distribution reported previously, and with the average annual decline of 1 percent in total per capita calorie consumption of six basic foodstuffs during the period 1968-1971, reported earlier by Timmer.

Mears, a long-time observer of the Indonesian economy, reports findings consistent with those shown above; namely, that "the per capita calorie availability from all five foodgrains appears to be no higher in 1975 than it was in 1960."[5] He offers two possible explanations: "Does this suggest that the calorie content in the diet satisfied the average Indonesian so that as income rises he trades off calories of less desirable foodgrains for those more desirable? Or does it mean that incomes have not risen for the lower income individuals who might have been expected to consume more calories as their incomes rose?" The authors of this paper are not in a position to answer the first question, but findings in this paper would seem to constitute a positive answer to Mears's second question.

In attempting to ascertain directions in the post-1970 period, data from three sources was assembled; a media and marketing survey conducted by a private research organization, a trial labor force survey carried out by the Central Bureau of Statistics, and the preliminary rounds of the 1976 SUSENAS. The most important data source is the last, but the full 1976 SUSENAS was not yet available at the time this paper was written. The first survey collected data in 1976 on household income and household expenditure for Jakarta (1959 HH) and Surabaya (1041).[6] Nine income categories were used, precluding the use of decile analysis. Basically, the results are consistent with those reported earlier in this paper. The share of the top quintile population in Jakarta in 1976 was about 49 percent, in contrast to the 52 and 47.7 percent for 1970 and 1968-1969 respectively; these three figures for the lowest quintile were 4.9 percent, 7.1 percent, 7.5 percent, indicating a sharp decline between 1970 and 1976. The Gini coefficient dropped very slightly in 1976 to .430 from .438 in 1970.

The 1976 situation in Surabaya is in more dramatic contrast to the situations reported earlier. The Gini coefficient rose to .484 from the 1970 and 1965-1969 figures of .328 and .332. The top quintile's share moved to 52.3 percent from 47.9 percent (1970) and 42.8 percent (1968-1969), while the lowest quintile's share dropped to 3.73 percent from 10.6 percent (1970) and 8.0 percent (1968-1969). The sharp drop in the share of the bottom quintile needs to be more carefully examined, but unfortunately there are not the data on hand for such an effort. In any case in the post-1970 period, for both Jakarta and Surabaya the inequality of income distribution seems to have increased.

The second data source, the 1976 trial labor force survey, offers some data for rural areas in East, Central, and West Java, though, the sample areas and sizes preclude much direct time-series comparisons with data used previously in this paper.[7] Samples on expenditure questions included urban surveys of Bandung (313), Surakarta (252), and Pasuruan (301), whereas, the rural areas were surveyed fairly near these urban areas in the regencies of Bandung (325), Karanganyar (334), and Pasuruan (324). The only direct comparison that can be made is for the city of Bandung, where previously the Gini index from the trial labor force data was .475, indicating increasing inequality consistent with that of Jakarta and Surabaya. The Gini indexes for Pasuruan (East Java) and Surakarta (Central Java) were .472 and .521, and these figures are very much in the range of the 1976 figure computed for Surabaya and would seem to indicate that income distribution in at least some Javan cities outside

Jakarta is becoming less equal at a more rapid rate than
is the case for Jakarta. This tentative finding would
not necessarily preclude a continuing increase in the
other urban-Jakarta differences found previously, but
this relationship cannot be tested at this time because
of a lack of data. It is likely, however, that Jakarta's
post-1970 efforts at providing basic kampung facilities,
stabilizing rice prices and other policies may have
slowed the increasing inequality found in the 1963-1970
period relative to this same phenomenon in other Javan
cities, where such government programs have not been as
extensive.

    For the three rural samples of the trial labor force
survey, the Gini indexes were .443 (East Java), .408
(Central Java), and .482 (West Java). It is difficult to
generalize from these calculations because of the small
sample sizes and the possible atypicality and urbanness
of the sampling areas, although it is clear that these
Gini indices are much higher than those for rural Java in
the sixties. These figures also contrast with the Gini
coefficients calculated from results of the first four
months (January-April) of the 1976 SUSENAS.[8] While these
four months are not necessarily representative nor typical of the entire year, comparisons can be made with data
for the same time period of the 1970 SUSENAS, again for
Java and Madura. Basically, the findings show a situation of increasing inequality in urban areas and little
change in income distribution in the rural areas. The
Gini index for the rural areas are .298 and .295. The
income shares for the lowest quintile in rural areas are
8.7 percent in both 1970 and 1976, and in the urban areas
these shares were 7.7 and 5.5 percent respectively. In
the rural areas the shares of the top quintile were 39.3
percent (1970) and 39.7 percent (1976); the contrast in
the urban areas is again much greater, 41.0 percent
(1970) and 47.4 percent (1976). Mean per capita income
(unadjusted) increased in urban areas by 429 percent and
in rural areas by 347 percent in the 1970-1976 period,
clearly increasing the rural-urban income differences reported above. While the 1970 figures for the first four
months are not the same as those for the total 1969-1970
SUSENAS sample, they show considerable contrast with the
1976 figures. Using data for the first four months of
1970 and 1976, it is found that the percent of rural to
urban median income has fallen from 63.2 to 56 percent;
the figures for mean income are 60 and 48.5 percent.

    The analysis for the post-1970 period does not touch
on absolute income and consumption levels of Indonesia's
rural and urban poor. Concern with the distribution of
income often obscures concern with absolute levels, and
while the dramatic income increases reported in the 1970-
1976 period might have benefited both the urban and rural
poor, this should not be assumed. Careful analysis of

the consumption data in the 1976 SUSENAS should be done
in order to further illuminate these issues.

NOTES

    1. Acknowledgement and thanks is given to Roger Montgomery for
his assistance and also to Thee Kian Wie and Hendra Esmara for useful discussion in the preparation of this paper.
    2. R. M. Sundrum, "Household Income Patterns," Bulletin of
Indonesian Economic Studies 10, no. 1 (March 1974): 82-105.
    3. Sajogyo, et al., Usaha Perbaikan Gizi Keluarga (Bogor: Lem-
baga Penelitian Sosiologi Pedesaan, 1974).
    4. Gustav F. Papanek and Donna Dowest, "The Cost of Living,
1938-73," Ekonomi dan Keuangan 23, no. 2 (June 1975): 181-206.
    5. Leon Mears, "Indonesia's Food Problem, PELITA II/III,"
Ekonomi dan Keuangan 24, no. 2 (June 1976): 99-121.
    6. Computations were based on unpublished computer print-outs
from the Indonesian Central Bureau of Statistics.
    7. These calculations are preliminary.

Part IV

Village Dynamics

Introduction

Many observers of contemporary Java have marveled at
the seemingly infinite capacity of the smallholder agricultural sector to absorb an expanding labor force within
the limited confines of the island's rural economy. Numerous speculations have been advanced in seeking to account for the high elasticity of village Java in accommodating to increasing population pressure. One of the
most interesting perspectives on the processes of adaptation to population growth has been advanced by Clifford
Geertz, in his examination of the underlying ecological
dynamics of wet rice cultivation. According to this
view, the agronomic characteristics of wet rice cultivation provide opportunities for attaining higher levels of
productivity through increased labor inputs, and it is
proposed that it is precisely this condition which has
enabled Java to absorb an endless stream of new entrants
into its rural labor force. Geertz referred to this
adaptative response as a process of "agricultural involution," and for the past two decades this theory has held
sway, explicitly or implicitly, in much of the scholarly
interpretations of agricultural development and rural
change in contemporary rural Java. In a great many instances the theory acquired the attributes of a kind of
weltanschauung of Javanese reality, as many sought to expand its application in explaining a wide range of social
as well as political characteristics in the evolution of
contemporary Indonesian society.
    In recent years, the concept of involution has been
subjected to more systematic scrutiny as a number of
scholars have advanced research findings which suggest
that Geertz's interpretation is in need of major revi-
sion, if not abandonment, as a framework for analyzing
the structure of continuity and change in rural Java.
The following two essays represent an analytical exposition of some major new modes of conceptualization in understanding the impact of population growth upon the organization of agricultural production and technological

change in the Javanese village.

The author of the first essay advances the position that the process of involution is beginning to give way to increased population pressure and the emergence of a more commercially based agricultural practices. Work opportunities in wet rice culture are assuming a much less prominent role in the available employment spectrum as household labor allocations among small farmers and landless households are distinguished by the fact that family members are compelled to spend long hours working in a diverse range of off farm occupations at relatively low levels of productivity and returns to labor. In brief, many laborers are having to work longer hours to maintain a constant, if not deteriorating level of household welfare. These conditions are associated with the decline of traditional arrangements for work-sharing and the dissolution of those patron-client ties, which in the past, assured that wealthy villagers responded to the basic welfare needs of lower income households. The author implies that these changes reflect a deeper process of ongoing transformation in the social and economic arena at both the local and national level. Thus, the Green Revolution has provided an impetus for larger and middle-sized farmers to adopt a more entrepreneurial response in maximizing returns on their holdings at the expense of reduced returns to hired labor.

The second essay pursues many of the themes advanced in the first essay in greater detail, further dissecting the involution theory into its component parts and holding in juxtaposition the many changes both historically and currently underway in transforming the structure and organization of agricultural production within village Java. It is suggested that, from a larger perspective, the concept of involution may have been bound to a particular set of temporal and circumstantial conditions, and it therefore fails to capture the full complexity and sweep of historical change within Javanese society. From a contemporary perspective the author summons forth a wide range of evidence in proposing that current processes of change in the technology and social organization of Javanese agriculture are fundamentally labor displacing, a conclusion which stands in opposition to the presumed labor absorptive capacities of the rural economy as reflected in the involution thesis.

The above two essays represent a major contribution in opening the door to rethinking and redirecting the mainstream of analytical and empirical inquiries on the dynamics of change and continuity in Javanese agriculture. In the past much has been unquestioningly assumed about village and household responses to population growth and technological innovation. It would appear that much is to be gained in discounting such precon-

ceived notions in order to examine afresh the processes
of labor allocation and absorption in the Javanese rural
economy.

8
Population, Involution, and Employment in Rural Java

Benjamin White

Most post-war studies of the Javanese rural economy have pointed to Java's "population problem" as an important component of present poverty and as a serious obstacle to future development. The prospect that Java, already one of the poorest and most densely-populated agricultural regions in the world, will double in population from 80 to 160 million within the next 35 or 40 years is a natural if uncomfortable starting-point in considering the problems of improving (or some would say of even maintaining) levels of living in the Javanese countryside within the next few decades.

Java's population history is different from that of many other countries presently experiencing rapid population growth. The classic "population explosion" in Third World countries has normally involved a relatively sudden and recent surge in population growth rates at some time during the present century, although in some countries this has not occurred until after the Second World War. Java is unusual because of the early beginning and long duration of its population growth: during the past 160 years, since usable population estimates began to be made, average annual growth rates seem rarely to have dropped below 1 percent, and only rarely to have exceeded 2 percent, resulting in an extraordinarily long period of relatively steady and continuous growth from about 5 million in 1815 to 80 million today. The causes of this growth are a matter of debate which need not be discussed here; but it is important to remember that population growth in Java is nothing new, but rather has been a perennial feature of life since at least the beginning of the colonial period. The annual rate of growth between 1961 and 1971 censuses was 1.9 percent - less than that of Sumatra (2.8), or Kalimantan (2.3), or of many other Asian countries where growth rates may reach 3 percent, but still sufficient as noted above to double population in about 36 years.[1] As was said in the 1940s and has been said many times before and since, "Java is filling up...."[2]

There is nothing necessarily alarming about projections of future population totals in themselves. As Missen suggests, "they are only meaningful as with populations generally, when considered in terms of the capacity of the economy to absorb or use them, a principle which those brought up in the renewed neo-Malthusian fervour of the past few years should remember."[3] Numerous observers have considered Java overpopulated since the early 19th century, and one wonders what colonial officials may have thought after the census of 1930 (when the population was found to be 41.7 million) about the possibility of supporting almost double that number on Java by 1974. For those who now doubt the possibility of supporting a doubled population on this small and crowded island, there is perhaps some comfort in the fact that previous alarms have been consistently, if only partially mitigated by the extraordinary resilience of the Javanese village economy in the face of population growth and innumerable other external pressures. Some aspects of this resilience will be subjected to critical examination below, but its conventional formulation is well-known: a combination of increasing internal complexity in the distribution of land and labour opportunities in the labour-intensive techniques of irrigated rice cultivation, and in the distribution of the agricultural product an extremely absorptive if ultimately self-defeating process whereby output per hectare increased with the growth of population while output per capita remained the same. These processes were called by Boeke, "static expansion," by Geertz, "agricultural involution," and by both authors "shared poverty."[4] Despite this resilience, however, there is evidence of declining real per capita incomes and levels of nutrition during the present century, and in recent years, some authors have begun to suggest that the Javanese countryside is approaching the "limits of involution:" "various pieces of contemporary evidence... indicate that during the period of independence the traditional elastic qualities of the Javanese village and indeed of rural Java as a whole (have) reached a point of extreme strain."[5]

In considering the problems of population and poverty in rural Java, it must be assumed at the outset that such strictly demographic measures as birth control and assisted out-migration are palliatives rather than solutions. It must also be understood that given the already serious problems of overcrowding and unemployment in Java's rapidly growing urban populations, and the dismal labour absorption record of recent industrial development, the rural population cannot be viewed as a potential reserve of labour for urban industrial development. Solutions to rural poverty must therefore be sought primarily in the rural economy itself, in the opening-up of opportunities

for the productive absorption of a growing rural labour
force.

It thus becomes a matter of great importance to examine the existing structure of the Javanese rural economy,
to determine what are the present barriers to the more
productive use of labour and what kinds of changes might
result in the removal of these barriers. Given the great
variations that many researchers have noted, even between
adjacent villages in Java, this is clearly an enormous
task, demanding research in many villages and on many
levels before any answers or practical solutions can be
confidently proposed. The purpose of this paper is to
examine briefly two features commonly regarded as characteristic of "population pressure" in Java: "unemployment" or "underemployment," and the general notions of
"involution" and "shared poverty" mentioned above. Exam-
ples will be drawn from some recent studies and from
field research undertaken by the author in a Javanese
village in 1972-73.

II

"Overpopulation" or "population pressure" are, of
course, relative terms. Rural densities in the southern
part of Central Java alone may vary, for example, between
about 380 per square kilometer in Kabupaten Gunung Kidul
(where per capita incomes are probably the lowest in all
Java) and over 1400 in adjacent Klaten, but there is no
clear correlation between these crude densities and any
conventional indicator of economic welfare. Population
pressure, or a population problem, can only be measured
by relating crude population figures to a complex set of
variables, some of which relate to the natural and some
to the man-made environment. Of greatest importance are
the land types available within a given area, and particularly the ratio of irrigated rice land (sawah) to unirrigated gardens (pekarangan) or other dry land (tegalan); the quality of that land, and of its water supply
through rainfall or irrigation, and various other more
external determinants of land use - for example, the
presence or absence of government-imposed cultivation of
sugar or other plantation crops, and the existence of
specialized markets for the products of various agricultural or non-agricultural activities. Thus, the proximity
of large urban centres, or of roads leading to them, provides opportunities for many kinds of specialized crop
production, for particular trades and crafts, and for
various kinds of wage labour away from home.

Broadly speaking, it might be said (if the statement
can be simply accepted as a useful over-simplification)
that population densities have adjusted themselves to
such factors as these to give a more or less uniform

degree of relative population pressure all over Java.
The village of Kali Loro (Yogyakarta), which was the subject of the author's own research, has a crude population
density of 730 per square kilometer, and thus falls
slightly above the average density for Central Java as a
whole (about 650 per kilometer if including Yogyakarta);
not surprisingly its ratio of sawah to total cultivable
area is also close to the average for Central Java as a
whole (34 percent in Kali Loro, and about 40 percent for
Central Java).[6] The village was in fact chosen because
it appeared "typical" of the region, in terms of crude
density, land types and quality, and other factors such
as distance from a major urban market centre; but it is
more important to remember that just about any village in
Java, whatever its crude population density, makes as
good a subject as any other for the study of population
pressure.

What then does population pressure mean in terms of
its general effects on rural economy? Much of the literature goes little further than telling what one would
expect, that because of the pressure of people on resources, landholdings are small, per capita incomes low,
diets deficient in quantity and quality, employment opportunities scarce and so on. Such relationships (between people and food, people and land, and people and
employment) are used by Bennett in his attempt to measure
population pressure in East Java, from which he concluded
that, "while each of the three scales . . . has indicated
different degrees of population pressure, each emphasizes
in quantitative terms the existence of far too many people for the existing technology."[7] But these characterizations, however accurate, tell little about the specific
patterns of economic activity, the modes of gaining a
livelihood, that one would expect to find in these villages where there are "far too many people."

Many village studies point also to the existence of
large numbers of landless households and of uneven distribution of holdings among those who do own land. It
should be noted (because this is not always made clear)
that this feature of village life in Java is not an automatic consequence of high population/land ratios, in that
equal distribution of landholdings is quite compatible
with situations of acute land scarcity even if it does
not usually occur. Indeed, attempts to relate inequali-
ties in landholdings to overall land/man ratios may meet
with surprising results. Maurer, comparing four villages
in Bantul (Yogyakarta), found that the proportion of landless households was highest in the villages with the best
overall land/man ratios: "One could say that in the village where the overall economic situation is the worst,
the economic situation of a larger number of families is
better than in the village where the overall economic
situation is the best."[8]

Thus, although the economic structure of any Javanese village will reflect a combination of these two factors, it is important to distinguish the effects of absolute resource scarcity ("pressure of people on resources") from the effects of differential access to those resources ("pressure of people on people").

Myrdal, in Asian Drama, complains that Western concepts of unemployment and underemployment do not adequately "fit" the realities of Asian societies.[9] Given the inappropriateness of Western categories of labour force analysis, and the inadequacy of official statistics in Asian economies on "numbers of unemployed persons," etc., Myrdal proposes a framework for the analysis of labour utilization in which the level of labour utilization is expressed as the product of three ratios: (1) the participation rate (the portion of the total labour force normally performing some work); (2) the duration of work among participants (in terms of average weeks per year, days per week, hours per day etc); and (3) labour efficiency (level of output for a given number of work-hours). He deplores the general unavailability of this type of information and stresses that to obtain it, "the labour utilization approach requires behavioural studies founded on observations of the raw realities."[10]

It is highly instructive to compare conventional views of labour utilization patterns in rural Java with the few studies based on "observations of the raw realities" that are available. According to the "involution and shared poverty" approach, it is assumed that, while the opportunities for productive labour are scarce, these opportunities are generally shared. Thus it might be said that few individuals are unemployed, but the great majority are underemployed, or in Myrdal's terms, the "participation rate" is high but the "duration of work" is low. Myrdal himself shares this view of the situation in Java. Citing Boeke and Geertz, he asserts: "in Java an increase in the absolute number of participants in the agricultural labour force has apparently been associated with a reduction in work duration by those already engaged in agricultural production."[11]

Many authors observe, as evidence of the same phenomenon, that the working-day for agricultural labourers in Java is reckoned in terms of a unit of 3-4 hours. Labourers normally work in the rice fields only in the morning (from about 6:30 to 10:00 a.m.) and are only rarely invited to return in the afternoon for another 3-4 hours. Farmers also tend to follow this practice, although based on the research undertaken in Kali Loro it appears it is not mentioned by the above authors how the rest of the day is spent. Since, as will be seen, most have paid little attention to economic activities other than the cultivation of rice or another major staple, it is assumed by default that much of potential working-time is dissipated in enforced idleness. Thus Kattenburg notes in his study of a village near Salatiga (Central Java): "it is apparent . . . that the working-day is not over-full."[12] Shared poverty, it seems, implies not only shared work but also shared idleness.

When examining some attempts to fill this picture with more detail it appears that the more directly obser-vational the research methods, the more qualifications are needed in this conventional conception of labour uti-lization. Penny and Singarimbun, in a recent study of population and poverty in the village of Sriharjo in Ban-tul (Yogyakarta), devote a chapter to demonstrating that there are "too many people for the work" - which might be ably re-phrased more optimistically (since growing num-bers of people are an unavoidable reality, and one must hope rather for improvements in their labour opportuni-ties) as "not enough work for the people."[13] They sub-stantiate this statement with a table showing the number of days of work (either self-employed or as a wage la-bourer) done per adult male in a random sample of 75 households over one 180-day rice season (rainy season 1969/70).[14] The data were collected in a survey in which people were asked at the end of this season to recall how many days or hours of work they had done in a variety of occupations; a "full day" of work was considered to be 6 hours in rice cultivation and 8 hours in other activi-ties. The results are remarkable.

Out of the 180 days, on average only 18 days per per-son were spent in rice cultivation; 33 days per person in the production of coconut-sugar (a pekarangan product and a major source of income in this village); and 28 days in various other forms of non-agricultural work. Of these latter 28 days of non-agricultural work, 17 were in low-status jobs with poor returns (duck tending, common la-bouring, tile making, local market official, bicycle re-pairs, barber, carrying tradegoods and stone collecting); 11 were in higher-status jobs (clerk, factory labourer, telephone operator, school teacher, hospital orderly). Thus it appears that only a very small amount of working time was spent in rice cultivation (22 percent of all actual working time, but only 10 percent of all potential working time), and furthermore, that the adult males of this village spent only 78 of the 180 available working days doing work of any kind. If 8 hours are taken as the standard of potential daily working hours, then it must be concluded either that this sample were unemployed for approximately 200 days per year, or that they were able to work for an average of only 3.3 hours per day. Thus, their work-duration rate (whether in days per month or hours per day) was only about 41 percent.

The first of these conclusions is of great impor-tance. By showing the small amount of the male popula-tion's time devoted to rice cultivation (in a village

with a relatively normal amount of sawah - some 40 percent of the total cultivable land), it suggests that the
understandable preoccupation of rural economists and
policy-makers with Java's rice problem has led to a relative neglect of the study of possibilities for improved
productivity in other areas of rural production. This
point will be returned to later; for the moment, however,
some doubts can be raised about the validity of the second conclusion, that less than half of available working
time is actually spent in work of any kind.

In a study of "land, food, and work" in the three
East Javanese villages previously used in Bennett's study
of population pressure (see above), Edmundson and his
assistants followed the demanding procedure of accompanying 54 adult males during most of their waking hours,
noting down their activities during the day and the
amounts of time spent in each.[15] Research of this intensity, of course, involves some risk that the methods of observation will influence the behavior of the person observed; there is no way of knowing whether the subject is
working more or less than normally because of the observer's presence. Edmundson found the average time spent
daily in productive activities to be approximately 6.25
hours, and that once again a relatively small proportion
of this time was spent in the cultivation of rice or
other staple crops. He concluded: "the Javanese villagers worked harder and perhaps spent a greater proportion
of their time working than any comparable group of Western workers with whom I am familiar."[16]

Using different research methods in Kali Loro, it was
found that hours were even higher than those reported by
Edmundson. As part of a study of the economic importance
of children, the author and/or some local assistants made
regular visits to a sample of households every six days
and ascertained from the household members (both male and
female adults and children) how they had spent the 24-
hour period immediately prior to the interview, and how
much time was spent in each activity. Altogether, more
than 90 households were visited in this way but the data
presented below refer to a subsample of 20 households
(104 individuals), for whom an entire 12-month cycle of
time-allocation data (60 visits per household) has been
analyzed. The material thus covers 6,240 "person-days"
of activities, spread evenly over the year. The sample
of 20 households is approximately representative of the
total village population in terms of access to land, with
the exception that the 3.5 percent of households who own
more than one hectare of sawah (and who between them own
40 percent of all the sawah in Kali Loro) are not represented.

The household data from Kali Loro indicates that
adult men did a total of 8.17 hours of work per day
throughout the year while adult women did 11.1 hours

daily. If the work of household maintenance and child-
bearing are excluded and only "directly productive work"
are counted, the men spent 7.9 hours daily in these activities and the women 5.9 hours. Although, as in Sriharjo, two crops of rice were grown on most of the sawah in
Kali Loro, only 25 percent of the men's total working
time (or 28 percent of their total "directly productive"
work) was spent in rice cultivation.

Thus, one of Penny and Singarimbun's conclusions (the
small amount of time devoted to rice cultivation) is
fully confirmed; but the other (the low average duration
rates of annual or daily work), seems to be contradicted
by both Edmundson's material and the findings on Kali
Loro. If again, eight hours are taken as the standard of
a full day's work, then Edmundson's sample of adult males
and the work patterns recorded in Kali Loro come quite
close to achieving "full employment" in terms of work-
duration rates. Since the three studies mentioned cover
only a total of five villages it obviously cannot be concluded that one is correct and the others wrong; however,
on methodological grounds alone there is justification
for the view that the more direct methods of observation
will more closely approach Myrdal's "raw realities."

It may be noted in parenthesis that the material on
Kali Loro is more complete in one respect than other studies of labour utilization in Java, in that it includes
the female part of the adult labour force (who in fact
outnumber their male counterparts in rural Java). Despite the five hours daily that women spent in housework,
cooking, childcare, etc. in Kali Loro, they also spent
close to six hours daily in "directly productive" activities. Examination of the income data collected by Ann
Stoler for the same sample of households indicates the
importance of both the amount and type of cash and real
income contributed by women; the neglect of women's work
is another aspect of much research on rural employment
conditions which fails to do justice to reality.[17]

III

The crude picture of labour utilization in Kali Loro
could have been as easily deduced - without the laborious
process of recording daily patterns of labour allocation
- from simple consideration of the kinds of productive
work accessible to most of the population in this village. These considerations again imply that the employment situation in villages like Kali Loro is not characterized by low participation rates ("no work to do"), nor
by low work duration rates ("not enough work to do"), but
by low labour productivity or labour efficiency, which
for a landless or near-landless household means "a lot of
work to do, with very low returns."

Much has been written about the low and possibly declining returns to labour in Javanese rice cultivation.
Sajogyo, for example, citing a study of three villages in
Klaten (Central Java), estimates that the average level
of labour productivity ranged from 0.8 kilograms of
milled rice per man-hour (with local rice varieties) to
1.2 kgs/man-hour (with new "miracle rice" varieties).[18]
For labourers, the real returns to their labour are of
course lower than this, and they appear to have sharply
declined during the last few years despite the higher
yields made possible by the use of improved varieties,
fertilizers, and pesticides. Makali, in an interesting
study of 20 Javanese villages over the 5-year period
1968/9-1972/3, shows that the real wage for a half day's
work (expressed as the amount of rice that can be purchased with it) had declined by about one-third during
this period.[19] In Kali Loro, in 1971 and 1972, a man's
wage for a half-day in the sawah would purchase 2/3 kg of
rice and a woman's slightly less than ½ kg, but by late
1973, men's wages barely reached ½ kg and women's barely
1/3 kg. Women's lower wages (for transplanting) are compensated by their subsequent higher wages at harvest
time; they are paid a share in kind (bawon) of the amount
they harvest, varying from 1/6 or even less to 1/12, depending on their relationship to the farmer's household.
Ann Stoler's research on harvesting in Kali Loro found
the average wage for a harvester from a landless household (who has no harvesting opportunities to offer in return and is thus often paid a lower share) to be about
1.4 kg of milled rice per half-day, while for landowners
the average wage was as much as 2.2 kg.[20]
While it is generally stressed that returns to labour
(for both farmer and wage labourer) are low in rice cultivation, it is not so often noted that they are even
lower in most of the other productive activities in which
most people spend the majority of their time. In Kali
Loro, women handloom-operators in local factories, paid on
a piecework basis, were earning not more than Rp 80-100
for a long day of up to 12 hours. Small traders (mostly
women), with less than Rp 500 in capital, made profits of
Rp 50-100 per day of trading depending on the distance
(and consequent hours of walking) between markets, which
varied from 4 to 24 hours for the full travelling, buying, and selling time. In the preparation of various
food items for sale, coconut-sugar (gula jawa) makers
made about Rp 40-50 for a total of 8 hours of labour: 2
hours tapping the trees (men), 4 hours of boiling the sap
down (women), and about 2 hours of firewood collecting
(often done by children). The income is halved for those
who do not own coconut trees but sharecrop those belong-
ing to others. Makers of lontong (cassava which is
boiled, pounded into paste, rolled into rings, and fried
- a very labour-intensive process in which the whole

household is usually involved) were making about Rp 3½ per hour. In the most common handicraft activities, women made about Rp 1½ per hour weaving pandana-mats (tikar), and men about twice that much weaving split-bamboo mats (kepang). For households with sufficient capital to invest in tools or a bicycle, returns to labour can be increased Rp 15 per hour for a carpenter, with a set of tools worth Rp 15,000, or about Rp 20 per hour for a trader carrying Rp 3,000-worth of goods on a bicycle worth Rp 8,000-12,000. All of the above estimates on wages were made for early 1973, during which time the price of rice in the Kali Loro market ranged from rupiah 50-70 per kg (Rp 415 = U.S. $1.00).

The extent of any household's involvement in activities such as these in Kali Loro depends primarily on its access to sawah. Of the 478 households surveyed, 20 percent had no access to sawah (as owners, sharecroppers, or renters), and a further 43 percent cultivated less than one-fifth of a hectare. A household of average size in the village (4.5 persons), eating an average of 1/3 kg of rice per person per day, would require 540 kgs of hulled rice per year; one-fifth of a hectare of sawah, if double-cropped, produces in average years just over 500 kgs of unhulled rice once the costs of the necessary inputs (not counting unpaid family labour) have been subtracted. Thus, over 70 percent of the households in Kali Loro do not have enough sawah to attain even their annual rice requirement, let alone their other needs in food, clothing, school fees, etc. The great majority of households must therefore obtain a substantial part of their income (for 29 percent of the households, all of their income) either from wage labour or from other activities of the kind described above, in which the returns to labour are much lower than in rice cultivation. As returns to labour decline, then obviously the number of daily hours of labour required to attain a given level of living must increase.

If the various productive opportunities were ranked in order of their returns to labour (with harvesting at the top, mat-weaving at the bottom, and so on), one would expect to find that households would, whenever possible, choose the available combination of activities with the highest total returns to labour. Thus, for example, women will often stop or reduce their trading or mat-weaving activity during harvest time to take advantage of the better returns in harvesting. Men may remain at home, cooking and babysitting to free their wives for the harvest; young children may herd livestock or cut fodder when there are wage-labour opportunities for their fathers, or they may cook and babysit while their father cuts fodder and their mother is planting rice, and so on. Mat-weaving is normally done only at times when there is no more productive activity available, particularly at

night, or when one cannot leave the house (weaving, cooking, and babysitting are often combined). It is hardly
surprising that there are virtually no "full-time" mat-
weavers (exceptions are elderly women who can do no other
kind of work), for at some times of the year when rice
prices are high and mat prices low it would require 20
hours of weaving per day to provide one adult with rice.

Each household survives on a basis of extreme "occupational multiplicity" and a highly flexible division of
labour among household members.[21] Since the returns to
labour in most occupations can barely support an adult
let alone a whole household, the burden of subsistence is
shared by men, women, and children together. Each household's income is derived from a great variety of sources
which constantly change in response to available opportunities according to the season, the state of the market,
and even the time of day; and each individual household
member has normally not one or two occupations, but a
great number in which he/she engages in differing combinations and for differing lengths of time in response
both to his own opportunities and those of the other
household members. An individual in Kali Loro may, for
example, spend two hours collecting coconut sap, three
hours in the sawah, two hours cutting fodder, two more
hoeing in the garden, two more weaving a bamboo mat, and
a few hours fishing in the dark, all in a single day; it
would not be surprising therefore, if retrospective employment surveys failed to achieve a realistic picture of
work duration rates!

The slack periods in the rice cultivation cycle between each planting and harvest (approximately from January to March and from June to August during the years of
my observations) are the lean seasons (paceklik) when
prices are generally rising, labour opportunities in agriculture most limited, and returns to labour in other
occupations lowest. But the majority of households,
without stores of rice or other savings during these
periods, have no choice but to continue putting in long
hours of work for lower returns in order to survive.
Thus, we may expect that - contrary to conventional characterizations of "seasonal unemployment" - the agricultural cycle will be marked not by seasonal fluctuations
in the total "directly productive" work input per day,
but rather by involuntary changes in the allocation of
working time between agricultural and non-agricultural
occupations. This is confirmed by observations in Kali
Loro. Comparing the five markedly "busy" and seven
markedly "slack" agricultural months for men and women,
it is found that, while the percentage of total "directly
productive" working time devoted to agricultural work declines from 48 to 29 percent (men), and 36 to 11 percent
(women), there is no significant change in the total
daily input of "directly productive" work for either sex.

Like "general" idleness, seasonal idleness is a luxury which most of the population at Kali Loro cannot afford.

One should of course be cautious in drawing general conclusions from this crude picture (based on a small sample of households observed during one year in a single village) of rural employment and the variety of means by which households piece together a livelihood. However, if the conditions described above are a general characteristic of Java's rural economy, then conventional conceptions of rural employment, involution, and shared poverty will require some modification. The "pressure of people on resources" means not only that returns to labour in rice cultivation and agricultural wages are low, but also that the rural population as a whole is increasingly squeezed out of rice cultivation and into a large variety of other activities in which the returns to labour are even lower; the result in terms of average work duration is a longer, not a shorter, working day.

Some developments in the organization of rice production in recent years seem likely only to accelerate this process of channeling labour increasingly into less productive non-rice occupations. Mention can first be made of the decline in real agricultural wages noted above, which makes other sources of income increasingly necessary to supplement those wages if levels of living are to be maintained. Secondly, several recent publications have documented the ways in which large farmers and landlords have recently begun to limit the number of harvesters in their fields or to reduce the wages given them, particularly by the employment of a small number of male harvesters using sickles and paid a cash wage rather than larger numbers of women, harvesting with the small-bladed ani-ani and paid a share of what they harvest.[22] Similarly, the dramatic rise in the use of small machine rice-hullers, owned by wealthy villagers, to replace hand-pounding in the processing of the rice harvest has resulted in the loss of another relatively lucrative labour opportunity for women. In Kali Loro the wage paid to women for hand-pounding (before the introduction of hulling machines in the late 1960s) was one-tenth of the amount hulled. Although many households still hand-pound their own rice for their daily needs, hand-pounding for wages (in which the returns to labour approached those of harvesting) has completely disappeared. One result of this change in Kali Loro was a dramatic rise in the number of women traders operating with tiny amounts of capital, a condition leading to further saturation of the market system and presumably (although this is harder to document retrospectively), further diminution of their profits. In the 478-household sample, almost 40 percent of women over 15 years of age are now engaged in some form of seasonal or year-round part-time or full-time trading.

It has been suggested that these changes are evidence
that involution and shared poverty have now reached their
limit and are breaking down. This question is difficult
to approach in such a general form, because there is room
for doubt whether involution and shared poverty as Geertz
defined them were ever adequate as characterizations of
the political economy of Javanese village life. However,
it is instructive to consider the more specific question
why so many traditional labour arrangements in agriculture seem to be breaking down in recent years. All of
the changes mentioned above serve the function for the
wealthy farmer or landowner of cutting the costs of rice
production, at the expense of smallholders and landless
labourers. It is remarkable that these changes should
have occurred within the space of a few years, and at a
time when high-yielding varieties have opened the possibility of greatly increased returns to rice farming even
without these cost-cutting measures. It seems, on the
face of it unlikely that these changes can be ascribed
simply to population pressure; rather, one must recall
the distinction made earlier between the effects of absolute pressure of people on resources and the effects of
differential access to those resources, which is a matter
of political economy.

The beginnings of the Green Revolution in the late
1960s, more or less coincided with major political and
economic changes at the national level, whose consequences at the village level should not be underestimated.
On the one hand, the "opening up" of the Indonesian economy has produced, among other things, an influx into city
markets of expensive and mostly imported luxury consumption items (Hondas, radios, luxury textiles, and so on)
and a concomitant wave of "consumerism" which has not
failed to affect many wealthier villagers. On the other
hand, with the "closing down" of most forms of political
activity at the village level, powerful individuals in
the village depend much less than before on the kinds of
support which "patrons" generally need from their "clients;" furthermore, the altered political climate makes
much less likely the kinds of pressure from below which
labourers have previously brought to bear in Java when,
for example, traditional harvesting arrangements have
been threatened. For the wealthy villager, land and its
produce are becoming less a source of local power through
redistribution of wealth within the village (and consequent maintenance of a loyal following who will, within
limits, protect their patron's power and privileges), and
more a source of cash to be spent outside the village, on
luxury items, on obtaining higher education and salaried
jobs for their children, and so on. Borrowing the term
used by Scott in his analysis of the dynamics of Southeast Asian patron-client relations, it can be said that
there has been a recent shift in the relative "bargaining

power" of richer and poorer villagers.[24] These phenomena obviously require much more detailed analysis and have been described here too starkly and simplistically. In Kali Loro there are many wealthy landowners who still own no motorcycles or hulling-machines, who dress simply and give traditional harvest shares and other forms of security to those who depend on them; but there are larger numbers who spend more of their wealth than before outside the village and redistribute less than before to their fellow villagers.

The above analysis indicates that, while the overall availability of productive opportunities in rice production and other activities may be seen as a function of population pressure on resources, it cannot understand the distribution of those opportunities among the population without reference to other factors. Similarly, it seems that shifts in the political economy of the Javanese village - particularly in the uses to which wealth is put, and in the relative bargaining power of richer and poorer villagers - offer more plausible explanations than population pressure of the recent cost-cutting changes in the behavior of wealthy landowners.

Whatever the outcome of these and future changes may be, it is clear that rural development programmes must aim at improving the conditions of production both in and out of the sawah, and at providing not "much work" but more productive work to those who need it most. These programmes require a better understanding of the existing "raw realities" of labour utilization, and this understanding must be based on intensive research in which the basic units of observation are neither individuals nor "occupations" but whole households. Finally, it is hard to envisage long-term improvements in the labour productivity and incomes of the majority of the rural population without a shift in attention from the "pressure of people on resources" to the "pressure of people on people." While the former (largely irreversible) condition has reduced the average household availability of sawah in Kali Loro to 0.2 ha, it is the latter condition, as manifested in the distribution of access to land and other resources, which determines the continuing inability of the majority of households, either singly or in cooperation, to achieve sustained increases in the productivity of their long day's work.

IV

Thus far the analysis has been concerned with the general effects of population pressure and some other factors on the rural economy in Java. In conclusion it may be interesting briefly to reverse this focus and consider the possible effects of rural economy on population dynamics. It was noted earlier that because of the generally low returns to labour, the burden of household subsistence must be shared by men, women, and children alike. Thus, while the material conveyed above is more complete than some other studies in that it includes women's work, an understanding of labour utilization in household economies - the basic "atoms" of rural economy - is still incomplete if consideration is also not given to the contribution of children.

For the same sample of 20 households in Kali Loro, the average work inputs of all children six years of age and over, according to age, sex, and type of work, were compared with those of adults. The data reveals that the contribution of children is clearly substantial, both in the work of "household maintenance" (childcare, housework, firewood-collecting, etc.), which may free adults for more productive work, and in certain types of "directly productive" work (especially handicrafts, animal care, and agricultural wage labour for girls, and animal care for boys). It should be remembered also that the biologically-determined subsistence requirements of children are less than those of adults, as are their culturally-determined actual consumption levels (children in Kali Loro do not smoke or chew betelnut, or give slamentan feasts, and their average expenses on clothing up to the early teens are less than those of adults); so that the productive value of children, relative to their drain on household income through consumption, is higher than the data would indicate.

There is thus a possibility that under conditions of low labour productivity and extreme occupational multiplicity in the household economy, the economic advantages of large families lie not only in the provision of old-age security to parents (a factor recognized by many authors), but also in the economic contribution of children from an early age. The author has given further consideration to this question in earlier papers in which it was suggested that both in the colonial period and at present, population growth in Java has not been the result of villagers' apathy or irrationality or of the non-availability of birth-control methods, but rather a response to an economic system imposing conditions of production on the household economy such that the economic advantages to parents of relatively high fertility outweigh the economic costs.[25]

If high fertility is advantageous to successive generations of parents its results are the opposite for their successive generations of children, who must grow up in an increasingly crowded and under-productive economy in which working hours must become even longer if the meagre level of subsistence is not to decline. It is not surprising then that many of the children of Kali Loro, when they reach adulthood, decide to leave the village, and in many cases to leave Java. Measures of out-migration are difficult to obtain in the absence of adequate village records; however, some idea of the extent of out-migration from Kali Loro is obtained by examining the present place of residence of children of the older women (aged 50 and over), in the sample of 478 households. Of 465 children who have left the parental household, only 209 remained in Kali Loro, 31 had left the village but remained in the kabupaten (regency); 122 had left the regency but were still in Java, mostly in the cities of Jakarta and Yogyakarta or in smaller towns in Central and East Java; and 103 had left Java for Sumatra (with a few to Kalimantan and Sulawesi) in search of opportunities that might in some degree free them from this vicious circle of poverty, inequality, underproductivity, and population growth.

NOTES

1. All 1971 figures and 1961-1971 growth rates are taken from the following sources: Geoffrey McNicoll and S. Gde Made Mamas, The Demographic Situation in Indonesia (Honolulu: Papers of the East-West Population Institute, 1973), no. 20.

2. J. H. Boeke, The Structure of Netherlands Indian Economy (New York: Institute of Pacific Studies, 1942), p. 163.

3. G. J. Missen, Viewpoint on Indonesia: A Geographical Study (Melbourne: Nelson, 1972), p. 257.

4. See J. H. Boeke, Economics and Economic Policy in Dual Societies (Haarlem: Tjeenk Willink and Zoon N. V., 1953); Clifford Geertz, "Religious Belief and Economic Behavior in a Central Javanese Town: Some Preliminary Considerations," Economic Development and Cultural Change 4, no. 2 (January 1956): 134-158; and Clifford Geertz, Agricultural Involution (Berkeley: University of California Press, 1963).

5. Missen, Viewpoint on Indonesia, p. 259.

6. This name of the village is a pseudonym.

7. See Don Bennett, "Three Measurements of Population Pressure in East Java," Ekonomi dan Keuangan Indonesia (March-April 1961): 97-106; and Don Bennett, "Population Pressure in East Java" (Ph.D. thesis, Syracuse University, 1957).

8. Jean-Luc Maurer, "Some Consequences of Land Shortage in Four Kelurahan of the Kabupaten Bantul," (Yogyakarta, mimeograph).

9. Gunnar Myrdal, Asian Drama (New York: Pantheon, 1968), 2: Chs. 22-23, and 3: Appendix 6.

10. Ibid., 2:1027.

11. Ibid., 2:1090.

12. P. M. Kattenburg, A Central Javanese Village in 1950 (Ithaca: Cornell University, Southeast Asia Data papers), no. 2:15.

13. D. H. Penny and Masri Singarimbun, Population and Poverty in Rural Java: Some Economic Arithmetic From Srihardjo (Ithaca: Cornell International Agricultural Development, 1973) no. 41.

14. Ibid., p. 28, Table 16.

146

15. Wade Edmundson, "Land, Food, and Work in Three Javanese Villages" (Ph.D. thesis, University of Hawaii, 1972).

16. Ibid., p. 143.

17. See Ann Stoler, "Garden Use and Household Consumption Patterns in a Javanese Village," Masyarakat Indonesia 3, (1976); Ann Stoler, "Some Economic Determinants of Female Autonomy in Rural Java," (mimeographed paper presented at the Agricultural Development Council RTN Workshop on "Family Labour Force Use in Agricultural Production," ICRISAT, Hyderabad, February 2-3, 1976); and Benjamin White, "Production and Reproduction in a Javanese Village" (Ph.D. thesis, Columbia University, 1976).

18. Sajogyo, "Modernization Without Development in Rural Java," (mimeographed paper contributed to the Study on Changes in Agrarian Structures, organized by the Food and Agricultural Organization, Bogor, 1974).

19. Makali, "Upah Buruh Tani Pada Tanaman Padi Dikaitkan Dengan Kenaikan Produksi dan Harga Padi Selama Lima Tahun di Dua Puluh Desa Sampel Intensifikasi Padi Sawah di Jawa" (Relations between Wages in Rice Agriculture, Increased Yields and Rice Prices over Five Years in Twenty Javanese Villages in the Rice Intensification Study Sample) (Bogor: Survey Agro Ekonomi, 1974).

20. Ann Stoler, "Some Socio-Economic Aspects of Rice Harvesting in a Javanese Village," Masyarakat Indonesia, 2, no. 2 (November 1975): 24-35.

21. "Occupational Multiplicity" (the necessity for individuals or households to combine several economic activities in order to subsist) has been discussed by Lambros Comitas, "Occupational Multiplicity in Rural Jamaica," in L. Comitas and D. Lowenthal, eds., Work and Family Life: West Indian Perspectives (New York, Doubleday-Anchor, 1967), pp. 156-173.

22. See for example William Collier, Gunawan Wiradi and Soentoro, "Recent Changes in Rice Harvesting Methods," Bulletin of Indonesian Economic Studies 9, no. 2 (July 1943): 36-45; William Collier, Suentoro, Gunawan and Makali, "Agricultural Technology and Institutional Change in Java," Food Research Institute Studies 13, no. 2 (March 1974): 106-120.

23. William Collier, et al., "Agricultural Technology and Institutional Change in Java," pp. 106-120.

24. James Scott, "The Erosion of Patron-Client Bonds and Social Change in Rural Southeast Asia," Journal of Asian Studies 32, no. 1 (November 1972): 5-37.

25. Benjamin White, Production and Reproduction in a Javanese Village; Benjamin White, "Demand For Labour and Population Growth in Colonial Java," Human Ecology 1, no. 3 (1973): 217-236; and Benjamin White, "The Economic Importance of Children in a Javanese Village," in Moni Nag, ed., Population and Social Organization (The Hague: Mouton, 1975).

9
Agricultural Evolution in Java

William L. Collier

During the past two decades many scholars have sought recourse in the concept of "agricultural involution" in explaining Java's seemingly unending capacity for absorbing larger numbers of laborers within its already densely populated rural economy. The concept of involution had its beginnings in the 1952-1954 "Modjokuto Project," where Clifford Geertz and a team of several other social scientists undertook an interdisciplinary study of certain institutional, economic, and cultural features of rural society within a small village area in East Java. Applying the concept to modes of agricultural production and distribution in rural society, Geertz went on to refine his ideas about involution in a number of publications, and finally authored a book bearing the title of <u>Agricultural</u> <u>Involution</u>. Thereafter, the concept of involution gained widespread recognition in the discourse of scholarly work on Indonesia. Nevertheless, the elegance and consuming attractiveness of the involution theory has frequently given rise to its acceptance under conditions where there should have been more on-going questioning of its validity in not only explaining events as observed in the 1950s, but also in trying to determine the theory in understanding events in the 1970s. The following essay addresses this task and hopefully provides some new insights on the dynamics of agricultural change in Java. The first part of the essay examines the concept of involution and its adequacy in explaining certain continuities with respect to the structure of rural society, whereas the remainder of the analysis undertakes an examination of involution theory in terms of its relevance in explaining more recent evidence on the character of agricultural change within rural Java.

I

Trying to fully comprehend Geertz's conception of agricultural involution is very difficult because of the imprecision associated with this concept. His main definition of involution appears to be as follows:

147

> Wet-rice cultivation, with its extraordinary
> ability to maintain levels of marginal labor
> productivity by always managing to work one
> more man in without a serious fall in per-
> capita income, soaked up almost the whole of
> the additional population that Western intru-
> sion created, at least indirectly. It is
> this ultimately self-defeating process that
> I have proposed to call agricultural involu-
> tion.[1]

This definition implies that over a long period of time,
rice production could absorb additional labor without a
reduction in income per person to these laborers. In
Geertz's view, the process of involution was most visibly
apparent in rice growing, with the movement toward double
cropping, more careful regulation of irrigation water to
the fields, careful weeding around the rice plants, selection of each rice grain to be harvested, and the use
of hand-pounding in milling the rice.[2] Related to the
land itself, he described the growth of intricate share-
cropping arrangements as more evidence of involution.[3]

Geertz extended his ideas of involution from the
rice fields to just about all activities in rural Javanese villages, especially in the low-land, well-irrigated
sugar cane areas. In his view, the village responded to
the intrusion of the sugar cane, and the land lease system in the following manner:

> The mode of its (village) adaptation was
> again involutional. The basic pattern of
> village life was maintained, in some ways
> even strengthened, and the adjustment to
> the impingements of high capitalism ef-
> fected through the complication of estab-
> lished institutions and practices. In
> land tenure, in crop regime, in work orga-
> nization, and in the less directly economic
> aspects of social structure as well, the
> village . . . faced the problems posed by
> a rising population, increased monetization,
> greater dependence on the market, mass la-
> bor organization, more intimate contact
> with bureaucratic government and the like,
> not by dissolution of the traditional pat-
> tern into an individualistic rural prole-
> tarian anomie, nor yet by a metamorphosis
> of it into a modern commercial farming com-
> munity. Rather, by means of "a special kind
> of virtuosity," a sort of technical hair-
> splitting, it maintained the overall outlines
> of that pattern while driving the elements
> of which it was composed to ever-higher

degrees of ornate elaboration and Gothic
intricacy.[4]

Extending his ideas beyond the low-land rice areas,
Geertz stated that "involution too has proceeded relent-
lessly onward or perhaps one should say outward, for a
process which began to be felt first in full force mainly
in the sugar regions is now found over almost the whole
of Java."[5]

Various scholars have attempted to clarify the concept of agricultural involution. First among these individuals is Otto van den Muijzenberg, who tested the
idea of agricultural involution in the Philippines. He
notes that, "although there has been some criticism of
minor points of the concept and theory, no fundamental
critical discussion has yet taken place."[6] In this context, it may seem obvious, but van den Muijzenberg made
a contribution just by separating the two concepts of
agricultural involution and shared poverty. He classified agricultural involution as the productive side and
shared poverty as the consumption (or distributive) side
of the situation in rural Javanese villages.[7] It may be
easier to test these concepts if they are separated in
this manner; one being production oriented and the other
consumption/distribution oriented. However, there is a
difference with respect to distribution, if it is thought
of as distributing work opportunity, a definition which
places it closer to the production function.

A major oversight on the part of Geertz is the fact
that he apparently does not include off-farm labor by
farmers in his analytical framework. In most of the recent studies on Javanese agriculture it has been defi-
nitely shown that the rice farmer secures a significant
share of his income from other sources, and if this other
income is included, then the income per man may have increased rather than remained constant or decreased as
Geertz speculated. In summarizing his work, van den
Muijzenberg found the following:

> Thus, the third level at which we should con-
> sider the involution/evolution question re-
> quires consideration of all the resources both
> agricultural and non-agricultural, local and
> non-local, available to the villagers. As
> long as a significant proportion of their in-
> come comes from outside the village these con-
> siderations must involve other terms than just
> the productivity per hectare of sawah. Geertz
> fails to adopt this approach even when he is
> dealing only with the sawah as a resource.
> His conclusions on evolution in the Javanese
> sawah ecosystems are based solely on rice pro-
> duction and he does not include in his calcu-

lations even the yields from second crops
let alone the land rent from and wages earned
at the sugar mills using the sawah land.[8]

Another dimension of the involution thesis which is
generally ignored in discussing agricultural institutions
in Java, is the fact that the island is characterized by
great regional differences in its social and economic
structure. Of course, the first major difference is between the Javanese regions in Central and East Java, and
the Sundanese regions in West Java. Then, the East Javanese regions are much different than the Central Javanese
regions, which can, in turn, be separated from the Yogyakarta region. Further, an Agro Economic Survey project
has noticed major differences between the situation on
the north coast of Central Java and the south coast of
Central Java. Great caution must therefore be exercised
in doing research in one area and then trying to generalize for other areas. In this context, Geertz did his
work in East Java, and White's work on Kali Loro is in
the hilly region of Yogyakarta. The Agro Economic Survey
had a sample of 20 villages in the best irrigated areas
throughout the island, but concentrated on the north
coast of Central Java. One of the studies by members of
the Agro Economic Survey concluded that various institutional changes were preventing the further spread of involution, and perhaps reversing it.[9] Yet, this assertion
is based primarily on research in the north coast area.

Besides the problem of differences between regions,
there is also the fact that peasants vary in their responses to the economic situation within a particular region at any one time. In this context, it must be
stressed that Geertz did his field work in a relatively
unusual period of time, for the entire country was suffering from inflation and the after-effects of the Second
World War and the revolution. Unfortunately, Geertz was
not able to compare the area where he did his field work
with periods before or after, when conditions were more
stable. Only one study has been able to undertake such
comparisons in measuring peasant responses to different
economic conditions, and this is the very useful research
by G. H. van der Kolff. Van der Kolff examined rice production in one region in East Java in 1922 and again in
1936, which gave him a marvelous opportunity to compare
the two periods. In 1922, the country was enjoying prosperity and farmers were receiving a high price for their
produce, whereas in 1936 the country was suffering severely from the global depression.[10] Prices for rice were
depressed, and very little money was in circulation at
the village level. By stretching the point somewhat,
there are similarities in the situation in 1922 and the
1970s, which were relatively stable and prosperous, and
the conditions in 1936 and the 1950s, when the country

faced severe economic problems and instability. Thus, villagers in 1936 showed much more solidarity between rich and poor than in 1922; the wages to rice field laborers were lower and they had to perform more work in an operation than in 1922; the share-cropping arrangements favored the tenant in 1922 and the landowner in 1936; cash wages were paid for planting, weeding, and harvesting in 1922, and paid in kind in 1936; labor was relatively scarce in 1922, and over-abundant in 1936. If van der Kolff had only been in the area in 1936, he would have drawn much different conclusions about rice production than if he had only been there in 1922. Studying the two periods gave him an invaluable opportunity to examine the villagers' reactions in each period. It is possible therefore, that if Geertz had done his field work in 1922 rather than 1952, his concepts of involution and shared poverty would have been much different.

In addition to the work of van der Kolff, another Dutch scholar with many years of experience in Java gives a different view of the situation than does Geertz. Egbert de Vries wrote in 1931 that:

> The situation of the farmer before 1830, so before the cultuurstelsel, can be described as that of a small cultivator with ample land for a family-undertaking, strongly restricted but also strongly supported by forceful communal ties. His land tenure rights, . . . were fairly durable; only there was a redistribution of the land in case of population growth.

> Although the cultuurstelsel in Pasoeroean did not lead to the excesses which happened elsewhere, it nevertheless destroyed the class of well-to-do farmers, substantially reduced its agricultural income, and destroyed the important social relations in the village. The countryside was proletarized, the communal tenureship with regularly rotating shares soon became a general feature. Rice cultivation declined as a result of retardation of the planting-time and diminishing care.[11]

Geertz argued that rice cultivation became involuted, while de Vries observed that less labor and care were used in rice production. Geertz extended his concept to social relations which he believed became involuted, while de Vries felt that these relations were destroyed rather than reinforced and involuted. Based on de Vries' long experience in Java, his access to all the Dutch materials, and his field research in the early 1930s, it would seem that his observations should be given considerable

weight in assessing the direction of rural change. One
only wonders why de Vries never commented on the involution concept.

Closely related to the concept of involution, is the
idea of shared poverty. Logically, it follows that if
villagers share job opportunities on the production side,
they are just as altruistic on the consumption side. At
times, in the discussions of these two institutions, the
concepts are used interchangeably, and it is difficult to
decide if the writer is talking about one or the other.
Geertz described shared poverty in the following manner:

> . . . The involutional process also worked
> its peculiar pattern of changeless change on
> the distribution side. With the steady growth
> of population came also the elaboration and
> extension of mechanisms through which agricul-
> tural product was spread, if not altogether
> evenly, at least relatively so, throughout the
> huge human horde which was obliged to subsist
> on it. Under the pressure of increasing num-
> bers and limited resources Javanese village
> society did not bifurcate, as did that of so
> many other "underdeveloped" nations into a
> group of large landlords and a group of op-
> pressed near-serfs. Rather it maintained a
> comparatively high degree of social and eco-
> nomic homogeneity by dividing the economic pie
> into a steadily increasing number of minute
> pieces, a process to which I have referred
> elsewhere as "shared poverty."[12]

By and large, the set of mechanisms producing this
fractionization of output seems to have been centered
less on land ownership than on land-working. Consequently, according to Geertz, there is involution of production
and of distribution. Yet, what is distribution? At
times he seems to be saying it is distribution of work
opportunities, and at other times the sharing of the results from the production process--the economic pie. In
this case, it would seem to add to clarity, if agricultural involution is viewed as the process of production,
and shared poverty as the distribution and consumption of
the products of production.

Perhaps the most critical shortcoming in the shared
poverty thesis is the fact that Geertz does not take into
consideration the huge schism in village society between
those who have land and those who do not. In not discussing the landless and how they gain a share of jobs on
the production side and a share of the results on the
consumption side, he is ignoring almost one-half of all
villagers. Geertz further states that there were no
large landlord groups in the villages. It is likely,

however, that this is incorrect for two reasons. First, a large landlord in Java is in most cases considered as someone possessing more than three-fourths of a hectare of land. Koentjaraningrat, in his study of a village in south Central Java felt that, "in fact, by central Javanese standards, two hectares of land is considered a large holding, and this is usually subdivided into small parcels that are cultivated by others, following the various share-cropping systems, by renting, or by pawning."[13] In comparing this small land-holding size to the situation in other rice plains areas such as Thailand and the Philippines, Java would not appear to have large landlords. If it is viewed, however, from the perspective that only a very small number of farmers control most of the village rice fields, then there are landlords. While for reasons of social and governmental pressure, a farmer cannot appear to own a large amount of land, some do, in fact, control a considerable amount of land through long-term renting and share-cropping arrangements.

In a context where ownership and control of land is divided in an unequal fashion, it would seem unlikely that much sharing takes place between people across these economic strata. Indeed, much of the evidence suggests that people with land are sharing their wealth with those in the same class and usually with their relations or close friends, and that the poor are simply sharing their poverty amongst themselves. Thus, in his study of a Javanese village, Koentjaraningrat provides information on the social ties of villagers which seems to indicate that there are definite limits to the sharing of wealth and poverty. First in importance to a Javanese household is to have good relations with close neighbors, then others in the same hamlet, and lastly, with households in other hamlets.[14] Kinship ties outside of the nuclear family are quite limited, and most important are relations among farmers who have fields in the same area. Koentgaraningrat does not specify that relations with the landless, other than close neighbors or relatives, have much importance to the Javanese household, and it is difficult to believe that, in these circumstances, a farmer would willingly share his resources with others in the village, especially if they are from a different social class. In partial agreement with this finding, are the comments of Selosoemardjan, who notes that there are strong communal norms in Javanese society which require the surplus wealth of the individual to be shared with others in the community, but with relatives being given first priority.[15] He suggests that there is sharing in a rural Javanese community, but it is differential and relies on kinship ties and neighbor ties. If a landless laborer has no wealthy patron, then in his own group there may still also be sharing, but it is a sharing of very little.

In her penetrating study of rural Java, Margo Lyon portrayed the problem in the following way:

> But what do these trends--admittedly involu-
> tional in one sense, but nevertheless true
> social and economic changes--imply in terms
> of changes in village stratification? The
> cash economy and the processes described by
> Geertz may have allowed the village to absorb
> more people, but they also changed the rela-
> tionship between people within the desa (vil-
> lage). It may be that most people had a
> niche in the system and that a situation of
> "shared poverty" prevailed, but increased
> poverty and hardship also accentuated rela-
> tively small differences in economic and so-
> cial rank within the village. The "fine web
> of work rights and responsibilities" may not
> be to the point, for, given the rising level
> of conflict in village society in recent de-
> cades and the increase in relative deprivation,
> what are minute changes in and of themselves
> are no longer minute in their larger context.
> Thus, accompanying the occurrence of involu-
> tion is a process of social and economic dif-
> ferentiation, promoted by the increased divi-
> sions, and involving changes in land use,
> ownership, and control.[16]

If the village is viewed in this context, with involution being associated with differentiation, then it
seems to imply that shared poverty must be declining as
involution increases. In a situation where there are not
enough resources to ensure survival for everyone, then as
conflicts among different groups develop, it seems much
less likely that individuals will share with someone in a
competing group. Although the Javanese have as much or
more social conscience as anyone, Geertz implies too
much in his concept of shared poverty. Lyon very clearly
states the problem:

> . . . the increasing irrelevance of the con-
> cept of "shared poverty" since colonial times,
> at least to those segments of the rural sec-
> tor at either end of the economic spectrum,
> created the conditions for a radically dif-
> ferent view of the village social and econo-
> mic scene on the part of some of its members.[17]

II

In his theory of involution Geertz advanced the position that the most important feature of rice production in Java is its ability to absorb increased numbers of cultivators per unit of cultivated land. According to Geertz, increases in labor-use simply reflect the capacity of wet-rice agriculture to yield more output in response to intensified cultivation practices. Thus, meticulous improvements in land preparation, transplanting techniques, irrigation management, and other aspects of the growing process, allow for marginal gains in production output and for incremental enlargements in labor input. It would seem therefore, that improvements in seed variety would also be accompanied by advances in production and labor-use, for involution concerns a process whereby improvements in the quality and management of land, water, seeds, etc., allow for higher levels of production and labor absorption. Thus, the current widespread adoption in Java of the new high-yielding varieties should be accompanied by increases in labor-use. Indeed, there is now sufficient evidence available on the use of the HYVs in advancing a preliminary assessment of involution theory in explaining farmer responses to the Green Revolution technology.

At the time the "Modjokuto team" was in East Java, the total production of rough rice (gabah) in Indonesia was 10,483,000 tons in 1952; in 1967, just before the introduction of the HYVs from IRRI, it was 14,280,000 tons; and thereafter, it increased to 23,100,000 tons in 1975.[18] Due to intensification and extensification, production increased by 240,000 tons per year before the widespread use of the HYVs, and 1,102,500 tons per year after this period. The latter increase reflects the fact that, beginning in 1968, the Government very actively promoted the use of the HYVs throughout the country. In the 1968/69 wet season, only 2.5 percent of the total rice area was planted in the HYVs, but this increased to 40 percent in the 1974/75 wet season.[19] In this context, and following from the involution thesis, one would expect that the widespread adoption of the HYVs would have yielded sizeable gains in increased labor-use per unit of cultivated land. Nevertheless, recent research indicates that there appears to be little difference in labor inputs for the cultivation of HYVs, as opposed to local varieties. Indeed, based upon several studies in East Java, where major increases in output have been achieved through the use of the HYVs, less labor is being used in their cultivation than what is normally used in the growing of local varieties.

The above conclusions are supported by data gathered by the Agro Economic Survey from a sample of 600 rice

farmers in 20 villages, all in Java, and all located in
the better irrigated areas. Based on this data, the results are rather mixed when comparing total pre-harvest
workdays per hectare of rice cultivated.[20] In West Java,
the average workdays per hectare to grow local and national varieties was 240 workdays as compared to 270
workdays to produce high-yielding modern varieties.
In contrast, in East Java, the representative farmers
used an estimated 260 workdays to grow the local/national
varieties and 230 workdays to grow the HYVs. Comparing
labor-use for the larger farmers in the sample, the average workdays per hectare were 220 in West Java, 195 in
Central Java, and 190 in East Java for the local/national
varieties; and for the high-yielding varieties, the estimates were 330 in West Java, 200 in Central Java, and 210
in East Java. If this data is combined for the three
provinces, and size differences are eliminated, then the
results are as follows:

	Local/national Varieties	HYVs
Hired labor (workdays/Ha)	185	190
Family labor	55	50
Total labor	240	240
No. of observations	531	91

Based on these estimates, it appears that there was little
labor-use difference in growing local and high-yielding
varieties. Indeed, based on the East Java sample, which
has the most observations for each variety, the local
varieties grown by the representative farmers use more
labor than the HYVs. These conclusions seem to be corro-
borated by the studies of Soelistyo in East Java, and by
the research undertaken by Montgomery in the Yogyakarta
area. Thus, Montgomery estimated that the high-yielding
varieties use an estimated (47 observations) 317.9 man-
days of labor per hectare, with the local varieties (56
observations) using 317.6 man-days per hectare of pre-
harvest labor, whereas Soelistyo found that there was no
significant difference between high-yielding and local/
national varieties in terms of labor-use per hectare in
irrigated areas.[21]
     The above comments relate to pre-harvest cultivation
practices, but perhaps the most dramatic evidence of institutional change with respect to agricultural involution is the shift from the bawon harvesting system to the
tebasan system. In this context, it may be that Geertz
first perceived his ideas on involution as he was watching a Javanese (bawon) rice harvest. Thousands of people
crowd into a village for the open rice harvest. Indeed,
the traditional system of rice harvesting with the ani-
ani in Java permits large numbers of people to join the

harvest in order to acquire a share (bawon) in kind. In the past, it would seem that this method of harvesting reflected the farmers' social concern for the poor and rested upon his role as a patron distributing benefits among his many clients within the village. These patron obligations were further reinforced by traditional patterns of communal loyalty and mutual assistance among kin and between neighboring households within the village. As would be expected, serious problems begin to appear when population growth gives rise to unemployment and to greater competition over the limited resources available in any one village. Thus, in many areas the bawon tradition, which was once a safety mechanism to support everyone in the village, has gradually been transformed into a method by which increased numbers of harvesters extract a greater share of the harvest from sawah owners in meeting their own income needs. A typical traditional harvest scene now involves women and young girls arriving early in the morning in large numbers and gathering along the edges of a rice field which they believe will be harvested. When the owner appears there is a great rush to enter the field, and to secure a strategic position in using the ani-ani to cut and bundle as much paddy as possible. An entire one-hectare field can easily be finished in one hour because as many as 500 to 1000 people may join the harvest. Once the rice is cut, the tempo slows down because it is no longer a race with one's neighbor. Each woman carries her harvested rice to the owner's house where his wife separates the bundles according to the local bawon custom into two shares, one share for the harvester and one share for the owner. Every step of the way there are attempts by these harvesters, especially if they are from outside the village, to increase their share. A description of the problem is given by Utami and Ihalauw:

> Uncontrolled numbers of harvesters result
> in various kinds of losses to the farmer:
> large numbers of harvesters cause more
> stamp-down loss, dropping loss, and left-
> over loss; in carrying the rice from the
> field to the farmer's house, losses occur
> through stealing or through real transpor-
> tation loss; and finally there are losses
> due to the distribution of shares and han-
> dling losses.[22]

With increasing frequency, it now appears that many farmers are seeking to reduce their traditional harvest costs by selling their rice crop before the harvest to a middleman who is called a penebas. The penebas usually buys an almost mature crop, and then arranges to recruit a limited number of laborers to undertake the actual harvest. Usually, a larger farmer or a wealthy person, the penebas is likely to come from the village itself or a nearby town. This so-called tebasan system has appeared in a number of locations, especially along the north coast of Java, and has been present for many years in other areas, but its original function was to shift the risks associated with harvesting and marketing from the farmer to the entrepreneur. Only recently has it been used to limit the number of harvesters and lower the total-harvesting wage. If the farmer did not sell to a penebas it would be difficult for him to break away from traditional social obligations in opening his field to all available harvesters. However, the penebas is considered to be a middleman and not constrained by these traditional obligations to the rural community. Although, as tebasan and its role in limiting harvesters becomes firmly accepted in the village, there are indications that farmers can then limit harvesters without using tebasan.

The profitability for the farmer in adopting tebasan as an alternative harvesting method and its advantages over the bawon system are made fully apparent in an Agro Economic Survey study of the two villages of Rowosari and Banyutowo in Central Java.[23] In these villages the traditional harvest shares were 1:8 or 1:9, which means the harvester theoretically received 11.1 percent or 10 percent, and the crop owners 88.9 percent or 90 percent, but the harvesters were actually able to secure a bawon of 1:6 or 14.2 percent of the rice they harvested, which in turn increased the farmers' harvest costs. Rukasah, in his very interesting study of income and expenditure patterns in Karawang regency in West Java, discovered that the share for harvesters varied from 19.3 to a high of 27.1 percent instead of the standard 20 percent.[24] For the operators, these share-wages were quite expensive, but since there was a surplus of harvesters each harvester did not earn much. However, with the adoption of tebasan, harvest costs were greatly reduced. Thus, in the above mentioned two villages in Central Java, it was found that the penebas had been able to force the harvesters to take a reduced harvest share of 1:11 and 1:12, or 8.3 percent and 7.6 percent of the amount they harvested. Utami and Ihalauw noted an even greater difference in their studies, with harvesters receiving a bawon of about one-tenth from a farmer and one-sixteenth from a penebas.[25]

Using yield estimates secured from some of the sample farmers, and data on shares and wages under various conditions from the villages of Rowosari and Banyutowo, the costs of harvesting can be calculated. If it is assumed that harvesters can manage to secure a 1:6 actual share (bawon) using the ani-ani rice knife on local rice varieties, then the farmers' estimated harvesting costs

were $31.93 per hectare in Rowosari village and $28.00 in
Banyutowo village. Comparing these farmers' actual harvesting costs with the $16.04 and $13.60 per hectare that
it costs the penebas to harvest local rice variety crops
with the ani-ani, it is evident that harvest costs are
reduced by 50 percent in using the tebasan harvesting
method.

To estimate the impact of tebasan on labor-use in
the rice harvest is very difficult, because the farmer has
no idea how many people join his bawon harvest. Even an
attempt to count the number of people in a harvest proves
difficult because people continuously enter the field,
either as harvesters or gleaners, until the harvest is
finished. In Banyutowo the author witnessed two harvests
and counted the harvesters. The first was carried out by
a farmer and the second by a penebas. In both of these
harvests, sickles were used to cut the high-yielding variety paddy crop. In the farmers' harvest, the area was
.24 hectares and about 100 people joined the harvest,
which averages out to 425 people per hectare. In the
sawah that was harvested by the penebas, the area was .54
hectares, and 105 people were involved, or 194 harvesters
per hectare. An even greater difference has been reported in Jepara Kabupaten. Utami and Ihalauw noted that
96 harvesters were working in a field of .20 hectares, or
480 persons per hectare. At the same time, 50 meters
away, only 3 persons were harvesting a field of .14 hectares, or 21 persons per hectare.[26] In the first field,
the farmer-owner carried out the harvest, and in the nearby field a penebas supervised the harvest of this purchased crop. Comparing these numbers with a reported 675
persons per hectare on relatively large fields, and an
amazing 973 persons using the ani-ani per hectare on less
than one-hectare fields--both for farmer harvests--in
Karawang Kabupaten near Jakarta, one can easily visualize
the reduced employment impact of tebesan.[27]

In some measure, the sharp decline in labor-use with
the use of the tebasan system can be associated with the
adoption of sickles in replacing the ani-ani knife. Returning to the above two-village study, and based upon
interviews with tebasan buyers, there were 56 percent
fewer harvesters when using sickles rather than the ani-
ani in Rowosari, and 43 percent fewer in Banyutowo. In
both types of harvest the penebas restricted the number
of persons. More important than just limiting the numbers of harvesters, the penebas used the same persons in
each harvest, which severely restricts the number of people who benefit from harvesting.

One final comment is in order concerning the harvesting function and its decline as a labor absorptive
mechanism, and this relates to the process of gleaning
the field after the initial crop cutting. Traditionally,
the rice harvest takes place in two stages. First, the

harvesters (penderep) cut the stalks with their hand-held
knives (ani-ani) and receive a certain share of the
amount they harvest. Next, one or two days after the
harvest, poor villagers would enter these fields and
gather for themselves the stalks of rice that were missed
by the harvesters. In recent years, however, with increasing population pressure, this institution has come
under stress, with more people vying for the limited resources available in any one village. Thus, with more
people harvesting, the race to cut as much rice as possible is intensified. Harvesters miss the harder to find
stalks of rice, and tramp down other stalks before harvesting it. Likewise, since more people join the harvest, the amount any individual can harvest has declined.
Since a larger amount of rice is missed and women receive
smaller shares from the harvest, more people have begun
to participate in the gleaning process. No longer is
gleaning (ngasak) delayed for a day or two, rather it
takes place in many areas just after the harvest, and in
some villages it occurs simultaneously with the harvest.
An example of this problem is the following:

> In Rowosari the penderep harvesters and the
> pengasak harvesters begin at the same time
> which makes it difficult to distinguish be-
> tween the penderep and the pengasak. The
> ngasak harvesters also may take paddy that
> is not a remnant. Sometimes the paddy is
> intentionally missed by the penderep, thus
> leaving it for the pengasak to harvest be-
> cause these people are part of the penderep's
> family. As everyone files out of the field
> some will say they are pengasak and the crop
> owner has no way of disproving it. The ngasak
> problem and the large number of harvesters cre-
> ate considerable tension in the harvest between
> the owners and the harvesters. This is a major
> reason why the farmers sell their rice to a
> penebas buyer. If a sickle is used to harvest
> the rice, then no paddy is left in the field--
> which eliminates the ngasak harvest.[28]

Again, Stoler notes the various changes in the organization of harvesting and gleaning in her observations of a
village in Central Java:

> Those excluded (from the bawon harvest) may
> ask permission to glean (ngasak) what is left
> after the harvesters have combed the field.
> Gleaners have always been present at harvest
> time; formerly, however, they were small chil-
> dren and old women from the poorest families
> who were neither agile nor skilled enough to

keep up with the quick pace of the harvesting
group. With more crowding of the land and
more landless families, gleaners now comprise
a more diverse group of women . . . . Several
factors have affected the gleaning system.
Formerly, when water was unavailable for the
dry season, harvested rice stalks were left
to decompose in the fields. Thus, gleaners
could come at their leisure without asking
permission and seek out the few panicles missed
by the harvesters the day or two before. Now
that a second rice crop is planted, harvesters
are followed directly by men who slash, burn,
or plough the remaining stalks back into the
earth for quicker decomposition. Others carry
the stalks home for fodder and garden mulch.
Thus the gleaners must be there on the day of
the harvest between the harvesters and cleaners.[29]

In summary, the above-mentioned changes in cultivation practices and the contraction in labor-use associated with these transformations provides ample evidence
that something other than the process of involution is
acting as a prime-mover in the allocation and distribution of production functions at the farm level. The concept of involution implies the presence of certain social
mechanisms and communal norms, whereby the needs of the
many maintain ascendancy over the wants of the few.
Nevertheless, the above evidence suggests that these
mechanisms are under some degree of stress and that the
presumed equilibrium between labor supply and labor absorption is giving way to a condition where the values of
efficiency and profit assume a much more pronounced role
in the economy of agricultural production.

III

In his early work, Geertz states that the emergence
of agricultural involution, as an underlying dynamic in
the organization of agricultural production, in great
part rests upon the fact that "the peasant has made certain that no effective labor saving innovation would get
a foothold in his crowded economy."[30] This resistance
against technological innovation is stressed by Wertheim
in his study on social change in Java between 1900 and
1930. He mentions that a rice field owner who replaced
the ani-ani with a sickle to reduce the number of harvesters would ostracize himself from the village community.[31] He further indicates that the village's social
system was one of disguised unemployment, and that the
villagers' system of values prevented innovations or
technical improvements because it would cause misery and

distress for a large portion of the people in the village. While in the past traditional norms and sanctions
within the village may have served to sustain a relatively static or steady-state condition with respect to technological change, the already mentioned adoption of
sickles as part of the tebasan harvesting system would
seem to suggest that age-old checks upon innovation are
beginning to give way as the village becomes more en-
meshed in the process of technical and economic change.
Indeed, there is now ample evidence of labor-saving technologies being adopted in practically every component of
the production process.

Using a sickle rather than the hand-held ani-ani
knife to harvest rice is one of the more obvious signs of
this evolutionary change in the Javanese countryside.
Although it has been mentioned in the previous section
that the adoption of sickles is associated with the use
of the tebasan system, in fact, however, there is now
evidence that their use is beginning to occur outside of
the tebasan harvests. Resistance to the acceptance of
the sickle has been reduced by its use in tebasan, and
many farmers apparently feel much less enfettered by tradition in opting for a more profitable but labor-displacing technology. The reasons for this higher profitability are as follows: (1) harvesting with an ani-ani takes
longer and the farmer must spend more time in the field
supervising the operation; (2) harvesters tend to select
only the panicles with the most rice if they use an ani-
ani, as this increases the amount they harvest in competition with others; (3) if harvesters use the ani-ani, then
the farmer must hire someone to clear the stubble from
the field. While the use of the sickle brings certain
benefits in terms of higher profits, the cost in labor
displacement is quite substantial. With sickles, only
about 75 man-days are needed to harvest one hectare (25
people for 3 days), while with the ani-ani, 200 or more
man-days may be used.[32] Moreover, using a sickle is
harder work than cutting rice stocks with an ani-ani, and
when the sickle is used, many women and older people are
simply unable to participate in the harvest. Although
only recently occurring on a wide scale, Smits, in his
careful counting of labor-use in rice production in 1926,
found that the amount of hours spent to harvest with a
sickle per bau (.6 ha) can be assumed to be half of the
amount of hours needed if the harvest is done with the
ani-ani.[33]

Along with the sickle, another technological change
in evidence is the use of weighing scales to determine
harvest shares. The usual procedure has been for harvesters to bundle the stalks together in the field, carry
them to the rice owner's house, and then the owner's wife
would divide these shares by hand. Normally, before
reaching the house, harvesters will have already selected

the largest bundles so that when the wife divides the
bundles between herself and the harvester, there is not a
free choice, for often the harvester has already declared
which bundles she considers to be her own. Of course,
these bundles are usually larger, so that instead of a
one-sixth share, the harvester may actually secure a one-
fourth share. Social pressure by the harvesters prevents
the owners' wife from redistributing the bundles. Nevertheless, with the widespread adoption of scales or volume
measures, it has become increasingly more difficult for
harvesters to acquire more than their specified share of
the harvest; with the scale the owner can determine ex-
actly what the laborer should receive.

Another labor displacing technology which has begun
to appear in Java, although not in large numbers, is the
mechanical rice thresher. Traditional threshing methods
in Java are quite labor intensive, with the threshing
being done in the owner's house, using either home-made
threshers that resemble a bicycle, or threshing by hand.
If it is a high-yielding variety that has been cut with a
sickle the rice is threshed by hand on mats in the field,
and then sacked and carried to the owner's house. Thus,
a large number of landless laborers will lose one more
income source if more modern mechanical threshers are
widely adopted by larger farmers and rice huller operators in Java. In addition to changes in threshing technology, mechanized weeders are also finding their way
into the production process. With the adoption of improved cultivation practices involving the use of
straight-line transplanting of seedlings, rotary weeders
are now being used as a substitute for labor intensive
hand weeding. In one observation Sinaga notes that:
"The tendency is for hand weeding (women) to be replaced
by landak/caplak (toothed/rotary weeders) used by men and
only possible when straight-row planting is used; this
type of planting is almost universal in Sukagalih. Eight
man-days weeding with the landak replaces approximately
20 women-days of handweeding."[34]

Other forms of mechanization are also gaining a
foothold in Java, and the potential for their widespread
use would seriously reduce levels of labor-use in the
rice producing sector. Thus, larger rice farmers in certain areas, particularly in West Java, have been using
hand tractors (power-tillers) for at least ten years and
perhaps even longer. Observations in one village indicate the following:

> In one of the villages there are nine padi
> tractors owned by the larger farmers. These
> farmers want padi tractors and feel it is
> better to use these tractors than hired la-
> borers. One padi tractor can plow one hec-
> tare of sawah in one day and half of the night.

> During the soil preparation period one padi
> tractor could handle approximately 24 to 30
> hectares, a process which would otherwise
> entail ten laborers and seven carabao and
> one person with each carabao to prepare one
> hectare of sawah. If the nine padi tractors
> were each used on 20 hectares of sawah, in
> the preparation period, this would displace
> from 2060 to 5400 man-days of labor . . .[35]

A detailed study of hand tractors found that, "without a
concomitant increase in production, employment losses for
each 5-hp tiller adopted and used at three-fourths utilization are an estimated 128 and 688 days per year for the
displacement of carabao and manual methods, respectively."[36] In some areas there may be a need for tractors in
order to prepare the soil quickly enough for the next
rice crop. A common complaint in some locations is that
there is a shortage of laborers for soil preparation.
Nevertheless, if tractors are widely adopted in the
heavily populated areas of Central and East Java, there
could be a large displacement of landless laborers. It
was the judgement of those interviewed who owned tractors
that a farmer should own seven acres of rice field and
have effective control over 20 acres before it is profitable to operate a padi tractor.[37] With these large-size
dimensions it may be difficult for most farmers to purchase tractors. Nevertheless, problems may arise, if organizations or contractors purchase tractors to be rented
out to farmers. Since in the heavily populated areas
there is a scarcity of pastures and therefore a scarcity
of carabao, it is entirely feasible that the soil-prepa-
ration-contractors who now use carabao would, in the future, shift to tractors.
     One of the most dramatic examples of technological
change concerns the decline of hand-pounding as the most
commonly used method in the processing of rice. In the
past, a small farmer typically would have women hand-
pound the rice for his family's consumption, while the
rice he sold would be in the form of padi or gabah (un-
husked rice). Hand-pounding would be done by family members, if only for a small daily amount; and by laborers
if a large amount was needed for a special occasion. A
large farmer would use hand-pounding laborers for the
rice his family consumed, and would sell either padi or
gabah. The small rice traders employed a large number of
female laborers to hand-pound rice. Beginning in the
early 1970s, hand-pounding was gradually supplanted by the
use of small-scale hullers, as the dominant technology for
rice processing, and although it is difficult to estimate
with any precision, it now appears that on Java alone,
much more than 50 percent of the total harvest is milled
by hullers.

The widespread adoption of small-scale rice mills simply reflects the fact that this more modern technology brings a higher rate of return than is the case with hand-pounding. This advantage is demonstrated by the following cost calculations. Based on survey data, it is estimated that the average labor can pound 31.2 kg of gabah in an eight-hour day. If she receives 10 percent of the product, and this is valued at Rp 42/kg, and if, in addition, she receives two meals per day, valued at Rp 25 each, then she receives a daily wage of Rp 180. This converts into a figure for average cost of hand-pounding of $1.45 per 100 kg. By comparison, the average cost to the farmer of using a huller is $0.54 per 100 kg, including the value of the by-product kept by the miller. This difference represents a substantial increase in efficiency at prevailing prices, and the beneficiaries are those farmers who would otherwise have hired laborers to pound their rice, and the huller operators and buyers of rice, to whom prices of milled rice may be around Rp 5 per kg lower than what would have prevailed if hand-pounding had remained in practice. The losers, on the other hand, are those wives of small farmers and landless laborers who would have normally gained additional income from hand-pounding. These are the people who can least afford such a drop in income, as the number of alternative work opportunities for them is quite limited. Although some of the displaced women will have found work in other endeavors, these are usually activities with lower returns. The hand-pounding of rice was a relatively high-paying job for these village women, some of whom could support themselves through the year from this income. In effect, the shift from a traditional technology to a more modern technology has eliminated one of the important income sources for landless villagers. Singarimbun, in his revisit to the village of Sriharjo, has the following comments on this change:

> However, the largest change in the village is that involving the women who formerly worked hulling rice. Before the advent of the mechanical rice hullers, a hard day's work could yield a woman two kilograms of rice, according to a formula giving her one-fifteenth of the product of her work. Now, there are three rice mills in Sriharjo, and most of the women who formerly worked in this industry have lost a major source of income. When I asked five of these women what alternative employment they would seek, they answered that there was no alternative work for them. "Then what will you do?", I asked. "We will eat more carefully (Le nedha ngatos-atos)," they replied. This expression, however desperate, is at least

accurate, because they now are forced to borrow money for food, and the interest rate is
substantial. If they borrow Rp 100 they generally have to pay back Rp 120 five days later.[38]

Assessing the overall magnitude of the shifts in income and jobs in hand-pounding is still not possible with
any great degree of accuracy. A report by Suparmoko, et
al, confirms estimates of the number of hand-pounding
laborers displaced in one rice season by the introduction
of the hullers.[39] They estimate that 3,701 laborers per
huller were displaced in a sample kecamatan in West Java,
3,229 laborers per huller in Central Java, and 482 per
huller in East Java. This wide difference in the East
Java sample is caused by laborers working longer hours
and more days. In addition, the hullers in West and Central Java processed much more rice per season because of
less competition from other rice mills. In the West and
Central Java samples, laborers worked 5 to 6 hours per
day for 20 and 11 days respectively, but in East Java it
was 11 hours per day for 48 days. If these numbers are
multiplied by the number of hullers in Java in 1971, then
an estimated 7,721,360 people in one season were displaced, though these people were clearly not full-time
laborers. The total loss in laborer earnings attribu-
table to the introduction of hullers seems to be on the
order of U.S. $50 million annually in Java.[40] This re-
presents a substantial diminution of income for large
numbers of landless households and small farmers.
The above-mentioned evidence indicates that technology change and the substitution of capital for labor is
beginning to permeate many aspects of Java's rice economy. The concept of involution suggests that technology
functions in the service of labor absorption, and that
embedded within the fabric of rural society are stric-
tures which inhibit the adoption of labor-saving production processes. Nevertheless, the notion that the economy of Javanese society can remain immune to the penetration of new technology must be put aside in order to
fully understand the current level of receptivity to new
labor-displacing technologies. Obviously, some of these
transformations can be attributed to interventions emanating from the larger policy and administrative arena
which stands above the village, but the evidence would
seem to suggest that the locus of these permutations are
also rooted within the village itself, and that the evolution of change within the village is a much more dynamic process than what would be otherwise envisaged in
the imagery of agricultural involution.

IV

Embedded within the concept of involution is the assumption that labor markets are highly responsive in accommodating additional labor, and that contained within
the organization of wet-rice agriculture are elasticities
which allow for high rates of labor absorption. Thus,
Geertz notes that, "by continuing and re-emphasizing traditional values stressing labor and the right to work,
historically defined fair shares for labor and a deep-
seated reluctance to sell the land to outsiders," the peasant has placed a premium upon maintaining a highly labor-intensive rice economy.[41] Thus, in situations . . .
"of increasing labor supply and constant output, workers
will characteristically be willing to restrict their own
effort to let a new man into the line . . ."[42] Geertz
further indicates that,

> examples of the operation of such values in-
> clude the obligation of a man with a relatively
> large amount of land not to work all of it him-
> self, even if able to do so not to work it en-
> tirely with wage labor: but to allow kin, po-
> litical dependents or poorer neighbors a chance
> to share in its cultivation. Contrariwise,
> such a man is expected to permit others to use
> his labor on their fields, even though he has
> no personal economic reason to offer it. The
> "fair shares" idea means that even the most
> moderate form of "Taylorism" in the direction
> of agricultural labor is very difficult of
> accomplishment; even in the most highly mone-
> tized areas, for example, meals are still pro-
> vided workers. The reluctance to alienate
> land to outsiders (it is forbidden by law to
> alienate it to foreigners) tends, of course,
> to prevent the development of large land-
> holdings.[43]

The concept of "fair shares" and the adaptability of
Java's rice culture in dividing up a fixed or only gradually increasing work load among a rapidly expanding labor
force may have been the dominant feature of agricultural
production in the 1950s, at least in the Modjokuto area,
but recent evidence suggests that is far from the case in
providing an appropriate characterization of Javanese
agriculture in the 1970s. In particular, many studies
now indicate that admission into the ranks of the employed is becoming much more limited, as landowners, in
response to an increasingly labor-abundant economy seek
to maintain and/or expand profits (and reduce costs as
well), whereas wage-labor, now competing for fewer jobs,

strives to sustain the level and permanency of its income producing sources. In this context, it appears that a variety of institutional arrangements are beginning to emerge which allow for more limited access to the labor market, a condition which is, in turn, accompanied by an attendant decline in work opportunities for many of the rural poor.

The attenuation of rural labor markets is perhaps most dramatically exemplified in the emergence of contract labor, a method of labor recruitment which some farmers are apparently employing in both their pre-harvest and harvesting operations. Thus, appearing now in some of the Agro Economic Survey's sample villages is evidence that contract (borongan) labor groups are being increasingly used by farmers to prepare their fields. Contractor groups usually consist of several farm laborers who own or have access to a carabao and agree to plow and spade (hoe) for a fixed amount of money. Only rather wealthy laborers can contract to do plowing because of the need to possess or acquire a carabao. An example of how this new mode of labor organization works in practice was examined in some detail in Gemarang, a village in East Java, during the dry season of 1973.[44] It was discovered here that if the farmer uses contract labor for the soil preparation, he employs two people with a carabao who plow the field, with four or five people then using a large hoe in spading the soil. Usually, for the contractor team, it takes from two weeks to one month to finish this soil-preparation operation. They will receive a total of 10 dachine (1 dachine = 62 kg of dry padi) per hectare for this labor at the harvest time, which means they are paid four or five months later. Thus, the farmer does not have to pay them in the planting period when he is short of cash. When the contract system is used in the wet-season, some of these farmers will give the contractors the right to sharecrop their sawah in the dry-season as an incentive to carry out the soil preparation without pay. Because of the poor irrigation facilities in the village, the danger of a crop failure is much greater in the dry-season, and in effect, the contract system serves to shift some of this risk over to the contract labor. Another reason for the farmer preferring this system is that he has more control over contract work: the laborers do a better job because of their desire to sharecrop his land in the dry-season and to do contract work for the farmer in the next wet-season. One other benefit is that the contract system allows the owner to limit his recruitment of labor from among his own relatives, neighbors, and clients. From the contract laborers' point of view, it is a preferable system because their wage is higher than for non-contract labor, and they are assured of work for up to one month. However, they must have a carabao and enough capital to supply their families with food until the harvest. Thus, for most landless labor they have neither the carabao or sufficient rice to carry them over to the harvest in order to engage in this kind of contract labor. Moreover, not only is the system biased against lower income groups, it also serves to reduce total labor-use in land preparation.

There is another variation in the use of contract labor, and it appears that it is being employed with greater frequency in controlling access to the harvest. Although there are many variations and names, this practice is generally known as ngepak-ngedok, and it allows laborers to transplant and weed a specific block in the farmer's field, for which they receive the right to harvest the block for a one-fourth or one-fifth share. Observations of this practice are reported by van der Kolff, in his study of labor relationships in Javanese villages from 1922 to 1932.[45] Even before van der Kolff, there were reports of the ngepak institution. Thus, in the Adatrechlbundel II for the 1905 to 1910 period, mention is made of two methods of paying harvesters: bawon talunan and bawon laragan. Those women who transplanted the seedlings also got the right to harvest the field which was bawon talunan. If the harvester did not help transplant but was invited it was bawon laragan. If they transplanted the rice seedlings, they received one-fifth of the amount they harvested, but if only invited at harvest time, they received a one-fifteenth share.[46] More recently, Roekasah Adiratma observed in his research in West Java that,

> under a special type of harvesting system attempts are made to hold the number of harvesters to a minimum for every plot of rice field so that the harvesters can earn more each day. This system, called ngawesi, limits by contract the number of harvesters who have the right to harvest a plot of rice field. However, they are obliged also to cut the straw, and engage in part of the land preparation for the dry-season crop.[47]

The actual operation of the ngepak-ngedok institution was observed in 1973, when the author lived in a number of villages in East Java. In one of these villages the laborers transplanted and weeded the rice fields and received one meal, but at harvest time they secured a one-fifth share. Usually, the family would do this as a group for several farmers, and if they did not have enough members to handle the harvest, they would invite others to join and give them the traditional harvesting share from their share. The family group also guards the farmers' irrigation water, applies fertilizers, and does

all the operations except plowing, harrowing, and level-
ing the fields. To organize the operation for ngepak-
ngedok, the field is divided into blocks (petak) for each
family group. Usually, there are 13 to 15 blocks per
hectare. One farmer, who had a one-hectare field, said he
divides it into 14 blocks. If it is a large block, he
assigns two people, and it if is a small block one person
is involved. He is able to assign 25 people, all family
relatives, to these blocks, and at harvest time they
bring other members of their family to help harvest the
assigned blocks. In this particular case, a high-yielding rice variety was planted and sickles were used in the
harvest. Since the laborers each receive the same share
whether they use an ani-ani or a sickle, there is no resistance to using the sickle. One laborer may enter into
ngepak-ngedok agreements with 10 to 15 farmers, and a
small rice farmer's family would be ngepak laborers for
other farmers. Yet, on his own land, he would assign
ngepak laborers to cultivate and harvest his field. Custom requires that they assign blocks to others, though he
can do one block himself.

At the time of the field survey in 1973, the majority of the sample farmers in the four villages were using
ngepak-ngedok as the primary method for organizing the
harvest. They assigned ngepak rights to averages of 13,
42, 23, and 4 people per hectare in the four villages,
and each of these labor households would have ngepak
rights in 10 to 15 plots. Relationships between the farmer and the ngepak laborer were very close; many of them
were either relatives or neighbors. In effect, what
these farmers and their relatives were doing was to make
it appear to others that the fields had been assigned for
harvesting, in order that the harvest could be shared
within their exclusive group. If they do not use this
institution then they are under pressure to open the harvest to everyone, using many more laborers. In brief,
the ngepak-ngedok institution has evolved to prevent
large numbers of wandering laborers access to the harvest. It even prevents people from the same village
joining the harvest, and it thereby operates to improve
the farmer's income and reduce the number of laborers in
the harvesting process.

The above analysis of emerging institutions which
serve to constrain access to rural labor markets would
seem to suggest that the so-called "right-to-work" pre-
scription is losing some of its moral force as a cultural
norm, and that indeed, the evidence would also seem to
indicate that the other elements of the involution process, i.e., the concept of fair shares, and the prohibi-
tion against the selling of land to outsiders may be
losing their presumed hold over Javanese peasant society.
The concept of fair shares can certainly be questioned in
light of a recent study undertaken by the Agro Economic

Survey on changing wage levels in Java. This study indicates that from the 1968/1969 wet-season to the 1972/1973 wet-season, wage levels increased between 40 and 50 percent in the three provinces for plowing, 40 and 45 percent for spading, and 20 and 50 percent for transplanting.[48] Nevertheless, during this same period the price of rice for these laborers increased between 50 and 63 percent in the three provinces. Thus, real wages declined in all three provinces by a factor of 17, 17, and 27 percent for the three-work activities (plowing, spading, and transplanting) in West Java, by a factor of 33, 55, and 30 percent in Central Java, and by 52, 54, and 85 percent in East Java. Declining real wages must also be viewed in the context of increasing reports of land being sold to those who live outside the village. Land transactions are most difficult to document by field survey, but there have been frequent occurrences where the Agro Economic Survey has turned up cases of outsiders owning village land. This evidence suggests the possibility that village land is falling more within the orbit of commercial interests as barriers to outside control weaken in the face of increasing economic pressures from within the village itself.

In summary, a review of emerging trends in the organization of wet-rice cultivation on Java suggests that the imperatives of efficiency and profitability are beginning to exact their toll in the erosion of traditions where elasticities in the production function allowed for high rates of labor absorption within the rice-producing sector. It is likely that these changes were well underway in some areas long before Geertz advanced his theory of involution, and subject to different historical conditions within a particular region, it is likely that the presence or absence of attributes associated with involution, or its polar opposite, i.e., a more commercial agriculture, have varied in their influence upon the character of village and rural society. Thus, it may be that the concept of involution has never really adequately represented the rich and variegated processes of historical change in many areas of Java, and it is for certain that future research must now move beyond involution in understanding a rice economy which seems to be exhibiting a marked tendency towards exclusion, rather than absorption, in responding to a burgeoning labor force.

NOTES

1. Clifford Geertz, _Agricultural Involution_ (Berkeley: University of California Press, 1963), p. 80.

2. Ibid., p. 101.

3. Ibid., p. 100.

4. Ibid., p. 90.

5. Ibid., p. 126.

6. Otto D. van den Muizenberg, "Involution or Evolution in Central Luzon," in Peter Kloos and Henri J. M. Claessen, Cultural Anthropology in the Netherlands (Amsterdam: 1978), p. 141.

7. Ibid., p. 143.

8. Ibid., p. 151.

9. William L. Collier et al., "Agricultural Technology and Institutional Change," Food Research Institute Studies 13, no. 2 (1974): 181.

10. G. H. van der Kolff, The Historical Development of the Labour Relationships in a Remote Corner of Java as They Apply to the Cultivation of Rice (New York: Institute of Pacific Relations, 1936), pp. 22 and 42.

11. E. de Vries, "Landbouw en Welvaart in het Regentschap Posoeroean," (Ph.D. thesis, Wageningen, 1931), p. 36.

12. Geertz, Agricultural Involution, p. 97.

13. Koetjaraningrat, "Tjelapar: A Village in South Central Java," in Koetjaraningrat, ed., Villages in Indonesia (Ithaca: Cornell University Press, 1967), p. 251.

14. Ibid., pp. 261-263.

15. Selosoemardjan, Social Changes in Jogjakarta, (Ithaca: Cornell University Press, 1962), p. 83.

16. Margo Lyon, The Basis of Conflict in Rural Java (Berkeley: Center for South and Southeast Asia Studies, University of California, 1970), p. 27.

17. Ibid., p. 28.

18. Adelita C. Palacpac, World Rice Statistics (Los Banos: The International Rice Research Institute, 1976), pp. 15-16.

19. Ibid., p. 36.

20. William L. Collier and Achmad T. Birowo, "Comparison of Input Use and Yields of Various Rice Varieties by Large Farmers and Representative Farmers," (Bogor: Agro-Economic Survey, mimeographed, 1973), p. 7.

21. Soelistyo, "Creating Employment Opportunities in the Rural Areas of East Java," (Yogyakarta: 1975), p. 256, and R. D. Montgomery and D. G. Sisler, Labor Absorption in Jogjakarta, Indonesia: An Input-Output Study (Ithaca: Cornell University, 1974).

22. Widya Utami and John Ihalauw, "Some Consequences of Small Farm Size," Bulletin of Indonesian Economic Studies, (July 1973): 53.

23. This survey is based on data from interviews with farmers and harvesters in the kabupatens of Kendal and Pemalang in the wet season of 1972/1973.

24. Rukasah Adiratma, "Income of Rice Farmers and Their Marketable Surplus of Rice in Krawang District," West Java (Ph.D. thesis, Bogor Agricultural University, 1970), p. 123.

25. Utami and Ihalauw, "Some Consequences of Small Farm Size," p. 55.

26. Widya Utami and John Ihalauw, "Farm Size: Its Consequences on Production, Land Tenure, Marketing, and Social Relationships in

Klaten Regency," (Salatiga: Satya Wacana University, mimeographed, 1972), p. 17.

27. Adiratma, "Income of Rice Farmers," p. 119.

28. Collier et al., "Agricultural Technology and Institutional Change," p. 177.

29. Ann L. Stoler, "Rice Harvesting in Kali Loro: A Study of Class and Labor Relations in Rural Java" (Paper presented at the 75th Annual Meeting of the American Anthropological Association, November 1976), p. 10.

30. Clifford Geertz, The Development of the Javanese Economy: A Socio-Cultural Approach (Cambridge: Center for International Studies, Massachusetts Institute of Technology, 1956), p. 35.

31. W. F. Wertheim and Siauw Giap, "Social Change in Java, 1900-1930," Pacific Affairs 35, (Fall 1962): 228.

32. William L. Collier, Gunawan Wiradi, and Soentoro, "Recent Changes in Rice Harvesting Methods," Bulletin of Indonesian Economic Studies 9, no. 2 (July 1973): 41.

33. M. B. Smits, "Arberdsaanwending in den Natten Rystbouw op Java," Landbouw, (1925-1926): 269.

34. Rudolf Sinaga, "Rural Institutions Serving Small Farmers in the Village of Sukagalih, Garut Regency, West Java" (Paper prepared for the ESCAP Expert Group meeting on Rural Institutions Servicing Small Farmers, Bangkok, December 1976), p. 6.

35. William L. Collier, Jusuf Colter, and Chaerul Saleh, "Observations on Recent Rice Problems at the Farm Level in Subang Kabupaten" (Bogor: Research Note no. 12, 1972), p. 3.

36. Richard Morris, The Potential Impact of Mechanical Land Preparation in the Indonesian Small-holder Production Sector (Los Banos: International Rice Research Institute, 1975), p. 101.

37. Collier et al., "Observations on Recent Rice Problems," p. 4.

38. Masri Singarimbun, "Note-Sriharjo Revisited," (Yogyakarta: mimeographed, 1976), p. 8.

39. Suparmoko et al., Penyerapan Tenaga Kerja pada Intensifikasi Penannaman Padi dan Pengolahan Padi di Jawa dan Bali (Yogyakarta: 1973).

40. Collier et al., "Choice of Technique," p. 36-45.

41. Geertz, The Development of the Javanese Economy, p. 35.

42. Ibid., p. 22.

43. Ibid., p. 114.

44. This study was undertaken by the author and is based on interviews with farmers, laborers and village leaders.

45. van der Kolff, The Historical Development, pp. 18-20.

46. Adatrechlbundel II, Vol. II, 1905-1910, p. 154.

47. E. Roekasahiratma, Income and Expenditure Patterns of Rice Producers in Relation to Production and Rice Marketed: A Case Study in Karawang, West Java (Bogor: 1969), p. 128.

48. Makali, "Upah Buruh Tani Tanaman Padi Dikaitkan Dengan Kenaikan Produksi Dan Harga Padi Selama Lima Tahun Di Dua Puluh Desa Sampel Intensifikasi Padi Sawah di Jawa" (Bogor: Agro-Economic Survey, 1974).

Part V

Rural Institutions

Introduction

An important feature in the analysis of rural change concerns the role of rural institutions and their contribution to enhancing levels of village participation in the development process. Most governments in third world countries have undertaken a wide range of local level efforts in institution building in seeking to expand access to public and private sector services. Thus, agricultural cooperatives, rural banks, and an array of other organizational modes have been introduced at the sub-district and district level, and most have been designed to facilitate interaction between center and periphery in raising agricultural productivity and rural welfare. The record of success in these organizational efforts has not been particularly impressive. Many of these newly created institutions have failed to establish close ties with the economies of their client villages, and where they have attained some degree of organizational efficacy, local elites are frequently able to acquire dominant control over their resources. Thus, many small farmers and lower income households are unable to gain access to the various benefits and services which these institutions are designed to provide in the form of agriculture credit, fertilizer, extension information, and marketing services. This condition of selectivity and unevenness in the distribution of organizational services seems to be particularly acute in those situations where disparities in social and political stratification are quite high at the local level. In this context, a critical question looms concerning the extent to which the achievement of productivity and equity goals in rural development can proceed without basic structural reform at the village level in allowing for greater access to land and other production resources.

In the following essay the author seeks to address some of the major issues involved in rural development in understanding how control over local level political and economic resources serves to influence the range and type

177

of responses to services proffered by outside government agencies. Attention is first focused upon the initial and later stages of colonial penetration in the special region of Yogyakarta in Central Java where, as an appendage of Dutch authority, the office of the village headman gradually assumed a pivotal role in exercising control over land and other local resources. The structure of village authority became more centralized and was simply submerged into a larger hierarchy of interests and organizations superimposed by the colonial administration, with the village headman now owing his primary allegiance to an outside chain of command rather than to his own local constituency.

With the achievement of independence in 1949, a number of changes were introduced which provided for greater village autonomy and the creation of village representative assemblies. This period of participatory village government was ended, however, in 1966 when the New Order regime sought to reestablish greater central government presence within the rural sector. It is the author's view that the demise of village self-government in the 1966 era, along with attendant government efforts to expand its role in local development, has served to enhance the position of the more privileged classes within rural society. In the economic arena, because of their access to larger landholdings and other related resources, local elites are first to benefit from government efforts to increase agricultural productivity. In the political arena, because of their close association with sources of power in village government, these same elites are also in a position to exercise substantial control over the various resources and benefits channelled through the rural bureaucracy. With these linkages to outside sources of political and economic power, traditional ties of reciprocity and exchange between local elites and their followings are being replaced by a more entrepreneurial and market oriented approach in the valuations applied to land, labor, and capital. Thus, the traditional prerogatives and bargaining power of marginal farmers and landless labor, in exercising their claims for security of tenure and employment as farm laborers, have diminished in step with the growing commercialization of the agricultural sector.

It is in this context of manifest disparities in access and control over public and private goods that the central government has sought to build new rural organizational structures in furthering its objective of enhancing agricultural productivity. The most notable example of this effort is the government sponsored BUUD village cooperative movement, an institution-building campaign designed to facilitate farmer access to production inputs and marketing services. While official pronouncements have enunciated the importance of having the

BUUDs stimulate the participation of smaller farmers and the general village populace in the development process, this has been a difficult task to accomplish, and in Mahoney's view the relatively limited impact of the BUUD can, in large measure, be attributed to the highly stratified character of village society. New organizational innovations emanating from outside sources either fall within the aegis of local elite influence, or they remain as mere appendages of the rural bureaucracy, and in neither instance do they develop broad based roots in the structure of village society.

The various themes addressed by Mahoney gives cause for some concern in assessing the prospects for building organizational channels to serve lower income households. It is likely that where control over village resources is less inequitable, more conventional institutional approaches can be adopted in enhancing access to government services. Where such conditions do not prevail, and intra-village disparities are much greater, the challenge remains of identifying modes of organizational intervention which can more effectively respond to the needs of those at the lower end of the economic scale.

10
Local Political and Economic Structures

Timothy Mahoney

Questions concerning the differential impact of agricultural development on opposing classes of rural society are a central theme in many recent analyses of the "Green Revolution." In general, the majority of these studies conclude that the spread of the Green Revolution has primarily benefited the wealthier and more powerful members of the rural populace. Studies of Indonesian agricultural development provide evidence that similar developments are occurring in the archipelago, particularly on the island of Java, the country's major rice producing area. Thus, research conducted by the Agro-Economic Survey, the main data source for farm-level rice yields for Java, concludes that it is the large farmers who are the primary adopters of the new high-yielding varieties of rice.[1] In a separate study of agricultural practices in rural Java, it is reported that larger farmers apply four times as much fertilizer per hectare as small farmers.[2] Further evidence that it is the large farmers who are disproportionately benefiting from the introduction of the new technologies is available from bank records which list the average landholdings of Bimas participants. In a study conducted by the FAO in the Daerah Istimewa Yogyakarta, it is noted that while the median size of wet-rice holdings in the province is between 0.25 and 0.50 hectares, the average acreage involved in the Bimas loan operations ranges between 0.75 and 0.84 hectares.[3] Comparable findings regarding the Bimas credit program are recorded by Staub, Alexander, and Saleh and by Bryant.[4]

Few studies on Indonesia have examined the structure of village stratification and the implied uneven distribution of political and economic resources as a possible determining factor in explaining differences in large and small farmer responses to the Green Revolution technology.[5] The primary purpose of this paper is to explore the potential of this perspective as an analytical tool for examining rural development in the Javanese countryside.

The paper will be generally confined to an analysis of
recent events in the Daerah Istimewa Yogyakarta and will
focus on the interaction between village level political
and economic structures. In addition, the analysis will
address issues related to the impact of these structures
upon existing agricultural development programs. The
focus in the final section will be on the activities of
the BUUD/KUD, or farmers cooperative organization.

I

The Daerah Istimewa Yogyakarta (DIY) is one of the
twenty-six provinces of the Republic of Indonesia. Located on the southern coast of Central Java, the DIY has
played a unique role in Indonesian history. Its boundaries lie within the historic heartland of Kejawen or
"Java Proper," which has served as the center for many
of the classical Javanese Kingdoms. The last of these
great empires, Mataram, was located in Kartasura, 50
kilometers northeast of the present day city of Yogyakarta. In 1755, a rebellion led by Prince Mangkubumi divided
Mataram in half. The reigning Susuhunan maintained control of the state of Surakarta, and Prince Mangkubumi became the ruler of the newly established Sultanate of
Yogyakarta. The creation of the "Independent" Sultanate
coincided with the Dutch takeover of the area, and after
several rearrangements between the rulers of Surakarta
and Yogyakarta, under the supervision of the Dutch, the
area of Yogyakarta became what is presently known as the
DIY.
The current system of village administration in the
DIY, particularly the close relationship between land and
political organization, is to a great extent the by-
product of an administrative structure which came into
existence during the Mataram period (late 16th to early
17th century). The Javanese state of this period has
been described as one of concentric circles revolving
around the Sultan, who was the sole source of power and
authority.[6] The innermost circle of the state, referred
to as the Keraton, included the Sultan and his family as
well as other high-ranking members of the nobility. Surrounding the Keraton was the nagara, or capitol city,
which was primarily inhabited by low-ranking nobles. The
third circle, called the nagara agung, literally "greater
capitol," was the primary source of princely revenues.
This area was divided into appanages--"sectors of land
and their population, over which a prince, or occasionally a high-ranking priyayi, was granted the right to levy
taxes in the name of the Sultan."[7] The fourth and final
circle of the realm was referred to as the manca nagara,
or "foreign land." In the manca nagara, which made up
the largest portion of the realm, the power of the Sultan

was of far less consequence. As was the case in the
nagara agung, the Sultan did appoint bupati-polisi to help
maintain law and order in these areas.

Following the establishment of the Sultanate of
Yogyakarta (1755), almost the entire rural area of what
today is included in the DIY became part of the nagara
agung. As mentioned above, the nagara agung was divided
into appanages in which high-ranking nobles, called
patuh, were given the right to levy taxes. Lands included in the appanage were customarily divided into five
parts. Four of these five parts were tilled by the villagers, with half of the produce being given over to the
patuh in lieu of taxes. The final one-fifth belonged to
the bekel, a local agent appointed by the patuh to carry
out his rights to levy taxes. The bekel was, in addition,
entitled to the free labor of the villagers to work his
land.[8]

As a consequence of the emergence of the appanage
system, the political structure of village society was
gradually altered. Autocratic patterns of local government developed as the office of the village headman, now
the bekel, greatly increased in importance. Political
power in the village became closely associated with control over land, as the rights to this singularly important
resource were transferred from the community to its appointed head.

By the mid-nineteenth century, the appanage system
had evolved into a complex network of power and privi-
lege, at the base of which was the economic exploitation
of the peasantry. Bekelships were, with increasing frequency, put up for sale to the highest bidder. To recover his expenditures for this position, a bekel often
made new demands of the peasantry, taxing gardens and
fruit trees, as well as the field produce.[9] In more general terms, these developments brought about an increasingly tighter supervision of the wong cilik (peasants),
who had little recourse but to accept these measures.

The appearance of Dutch enterprises in the last decades of the nineteenth century added an even harsher
element to an already overburdened system. Beginning at
this time, foreign capitalists were allowed to rent out
entire appanages for their sugar, tobacco, and indigo
plantations. As part of the rental agreement, all the
rights of the original appanage holder were transferred
to the plantation manager. In the process, demands for
the free labor services of the peasantry were sharply increased and the villager's access to arable fields was
significantly curtailed.[10]

The proliferation of the appanage system and the expansion of commercial enterprises in the rural areas of
the DIY significantly influenced existing patterns of
local government. The autonomy of the village unit, previously restricted by the institution of the appanage

system, was now seriously threatened by the intervention
of plantation operators in local affairs. The bekel, now
an agent of the plantation, became accountable to the
mandor, the company employee in charge of recruiting laborers and supervising work in the fields. The autocratic position of the bekel in local affairs remained un-
challenged, even strengthened, if he cooperated with the
mandor. However, if the bekel had the misfortune of dis-
pleasing his new superior, he could quickly end up behind
the "black doors" of the local jail.[11]

At the turn of the century, the abuses of local
authority encouraged by the intrusion of Dutch commercial
interests were opened to investigation. Government inquiries were held "with a view to liberating the villagers from the oppression of the village government."[12] In
1918, laws were put into effect which abolished the appanage system in the Principality of Yogyakarta. The
offices of both the patuh and the bekel were terminated
at this time. In place of the appanage system, a new
framework of rural administration, heavily influenced by
Dutch interests, was erected. At the top echelons of the
new system two separate lines of administrative control
were formed. One line manned by Javanese civil servant
appointees, remained primarily accountable to the Sultan.
The second, staffed by Dutch colonists, was placed under
the authority of the Dutch governor residing in Yogyakarta. At the local level, a new administrative unit called
the kelurahan was created. The head position in this new
unit, the office of the Lurah, was occupied by a locally
elected official. Finally, councils made up of all the
landholders in the kelurahan, were created and granted
authority in the name of the Sultan over the distribution
of village lands.

The new system of rural administration and local
government had a major impact on village level political
structures. Most importantly, the powers of the village
headman, now the lurah, were to some extent restricted by
the new system of kelurahan government. This is particularly evident with respect to control over land resources. As mentioned above, village councils were now
granted this authority. Nevertheless, the lurah remained
the major figure in the political arena of village society. Once elected his term in office was for life. Furthermore, as village headman he served as the chairman of
the local council, and was thereby still able to exercise
considerable influence over the distribution of land.
Finally, the direct relationship between the political
power of the lurah and his unrivaled economic position
remained intact. In lieu of salary, the lurah was
granted a large tract of village land, termed tanah
lungguh, and was also entitled to the free labor of the
local peasantry to farm his fields.

The relationship between village government and higher administrative units was also effected by the new organizational setup. The lurahs or new village headmen who replaced the bekels were no longer at the mercy of the plantation mandors. They were, however, made directly accountable to the bupati whose powers gave him the authority to remove a lurah from office and appoint his own representative in place of the choice of the local electorate. In addition, kelurahan budgets had to be approved by the bupati and all expenditures at this level needed his signature.

During this period, the lurah's dual function as both the spokesman for local interests and agent of the central government became more pronounced. No doubt, these at times conflicting roles placed great pressure on the lurah. However, as contact between the outside world and the village became more frequent, the lurah was able to convert his position as intermediator into a valuable asset.[13]

In August of 1945, Indonesia declared itself an independent republic. In the following two decades, the political arena of village society became a stage on which revolutionary drama as well as religious and class antagonisms unfolded. One major component of the many controversial themes manifested in the political discourse of these turbulent years concerned issues of centralization vs decentralization in the administration of village life. During this period, the initial changes in the political structure of village governments in the DIY were primarily shaped by the advocates of decentralization. Their primary aim was to create a third-level autonomous unit of local government. After two unsuccessful attempts to reconstruct the subdistrict level of administration (kecamatan) into a self-governing unit, the focus of the decentralization proponents shifted to the kelurahan. In the process of converting the kelurahan into an autonomous unit of local government, major changes in the political structure of village society were instituted in the DIY.

One of the first changes instituted as part of the plan to create an autonomous village government involved the amalgamation of three to four existing kelurahans into one large governing unit, also called a kelurahan. The primary aim of this change was to increase village revenues and provide a sound economic base for the proposed autonomous kelurahan government.[14] The major source of village funds had, up until now, been the kas desa. Kas desa is land owned by the village and sharecropped out to local farmers. Proceeds from these agreements, customarily 1/4 to 1/2 of the harvest, go to the village treasury. With the substantial increase in the size of kas desa holdings resulting from the amalgamation of existing kelurahans, it was hoped that the new village government would become autonomous in fact as well as on paper.

A second major change introduced during this period concerned the make-up of the village assembly, or majelis desa. Participation in the village assembly, formerly restricted to landholders, was now opened to all families residing in the village. In addition, the powers of the village assembly were dramatically expanded. From their ranks was elected a new village legislative council, the Dewan Perwakilan Rakyat Kelurahan (DPRK). The DPRK was granted extensive powers and had the authority to challenge the actions of the lurah and his staff. Unresolved disputes between the DPRK and the executive body were referred to the village assembly. If the village assembly supported the DPRK, it could force the resignation of the lurah and/or members of his staff.[15]

A final change associated with the reconstruction of rural administration during the first years of independence was the growth of political parties. The emergence of political parties was, in great part, due to the encouragement of the national government which attempted to ensure that the new legislative councils, formed at the national, provincial, and district levels, as well as at the village level, would become open forums for the expression of contrasting viewpoints. The four major national parties, the PNI, the PKI, NU, and Masjumi also played a major role in the politicization of the DIY. In addition, the Gerinda party was a potent force in the political life of the special province.

The restructuring of local government along more participatory lines involved significant changes in the political character of village society. One important effect of the new administrative structure was that the prestige and influence of the civil service in village affairs was significantly diminished. As indicated above, many powers formerly held by the bupati were now under the authority of the village legislative councils. While this change insulated kelurahan officials from the paternalistic supervision of their civil service superiors, it also opened the door for local challenges to their arbitrary rule over local matters. No longer were their life-long terms as village headmen secure, and they were forced to actively pursue and maintain a viable political base within the rural communities. Thus, the most important effect of the new arrangements for local power-sharing was that the villagers themselves were delegated a much more influential role in the government of their villages.

II

   With the advent of the "New Order" in Indonesia, many
changes in the political structure of village society
were instituted. Following the climax of rural tensions
in 1965, village legislative councils in the DIY were
stripped of their powers and eventually ceased to function. Village officials once again became directly responsible to the bupati and experiments in local autonomy
were ended. These changes have had far-reaching consequences on the political life of village society. The
amalgamation of villages (1951) referred to above significantly increased the social distance between village
officials and the main body of the community. As a result, group pressure which had served as a traditional
mechanism for influencing the decisions of village headmen became much less effective. Throughout the fifties
and early sixties, the tendency for village officials to
become estranged from their local constituency was coun-
terbalanced by the existence of legislative councils.
The elimination of these institutions has transformed the
kelurahan government into a large administrative unit
which remains relatively removed from the needs and aspi-
rations of the local populace.
   One of the major activities of village officials in
the "New Order" era is the local administration of na-
tionwide development programs. Their role in these programs is considered by many to be a determining factor in
their eventual outcome.[16] Taking into consideration the
recent changes in the village political structure as well
as the long-standing and continuing association between
the political power of village officials and their control over large tracts of village lands, there exists a
potential conflict of interest with respect to the role
of village officialdom and their impartial distribution
of development resources. Further elaboration of this
point can first be undertaken by examining some of the
more recent and long term changes in the economic organization of village society within the DIY.
   The economy of the DIY is predominantly agricultural. Of the 2.5 million people living in the province, 84
percent reside in rural areas and approximately 63 percent are directly engaged in agricultural activities.[17]
Although the vast majority of the inhabitants of the DIY
depend upon agriculture as their main source of income,
the province is a rice deficit area, and thereby suffers
from chronic and sometimes serious food shortages. Correspondingly, welfare levels in the province are shock-
ingly low. One study estimates that as much as 72 percent of the population lives below the defined poverty
line for Indonesia.[18]

While, since the turn of the century, the steady
rise in population and the severe shortage of the arable
land are two of the most important factors which have
shaped the development of economic structures in the
rural areas of the DIY, some scholars have dwelled on the
fact of what appears to be an adaptation pattern which
enables the Javanese village economy to accommodate to
these pressures; a process referred to by Boeke as
"static expansion," by Geertz as "agricultural involution," and by both authors as "shared poverty."[19] In
their view, the adverse impact of Java's population
growth has been mitigated by the almost unlimited capacity of wet-rice cultivation "to maintain levels of marginal labor productivity by always managing to work one more
man in without a serious fall in per capita income."[20]
In more specific terms, the process of involution has involved the following dynamics: the internal elaboration
of the village land tenure system; the development of a
whole series of labor absorbing improvements in cultivation methods, and the emergence of a complex network of
work-sharing arrangements.[21] On the basis of these developments, Geertz concludes that,

> under the pressure of increasing numbers and
> limited resources Javanese village society did
> not bifurcate, as did that of so many other
> "underdeveloped" nations into a group of large
> landlords and a group of oppressed near-serfs.
> Rather, it maintained a comparatively high de-
> gree of social and economic homogeneity by di-
> viding the economic pie into a steadily in-
> creasing number of minute pieces, . . .[22]

The provocative views of Geertz regarding agricultural involution and shared poverty, as well as his conclusions regarding the relatively high degree of economic
homogeneity in rural Java, have become the subject of
lengthy debate in recent years. Many critics of Geertz
agree that his remarks concerning the non-existence of a
large landlord class in rural Java are accurate if based
upon a comparison between Java and other Southeast Asian
countries such as the Philippines or Thailand. These
same critics stress, however, that if Geertz's statement
is examined on the basis of land distribution, rather
than in terms of the gross size of individual landholdings, there is little evidence to support the contention
that no significant landlord class has developed in rural
Java. Thus, while the maximum size of landholdings in
Java is generally very modest, landownership is quite uneven in its distribution. For example, in Miri, a small
hamlet located in the district of Bantul, in the DIY, 16
percent of the families own 67 percent of the sawah and
37 percent of the families own no sawah at all.[23] The

data from Miri is very typical in this regard, and indicates that within the specific context of Javanese society, there is a sound basis for talking about the emergence of a landlord class.

A conspicuous oversight in Geertz's discussion of the concepts of agricultural involution and shared poverty (and often neglected in the analyses of many of his critics as well) is any mention of the inextricable ties between village level political structures and the concomitant pattern of economic organization in rural society. The most striking interdependence between these two structures has to do with the sizeable allotments of tanah lungguh granted village officials in lieu of salary. As indicated in the previous section, the tanah lungguh grants qualify even the lowest ranking village officials as large landholders. Furthermore, in addition to these land allotments, the village headmen have control over the kas desa (community owned land) and are often in possession of substantial amounts of privately owned land. Thus, the total size of lands under their control are often enormous by Javanese standards. For example, in a study conducted in five villages, all located in Central Java, it is reported that the lurahs in each of these villages control between 12 to 17 hectares of sawah and that the total landholdings of their families range from 27 to 51 hectares.[24] These figures most likely represent an extreme case of the economic overlordship of village officials. Nonetheless, their magnitude indicates, in very dramatic terms, the importance of incorporating an analysis of political institutions in any meaningful research on village level economic structures, and serves to undo any claims concerning the relatively high degree of economic homogeneity in rural Java.

In summary, the processes described by Geertz have, no doubt, allowed the village to absorb more people. At the same time, however, there is mounting evidence that these same processes have significantly altered the economic relationships among villagers. In more recent studies of the economic structure of rural Java, it is these developments--the trend toward the internal polarization of village society--which have become the central topic of discussion. Deuster's research on economic conditions in the DIY is typical in this regard.[25] Using data from the years 1959 and 1968, Deuster demonstrates that the distribution of income among the major classes of rural society substantially widened during this period. Those who owned sufficient land experienced rises in real income of between 37 percent and 48 percent, whereas those with insufficient landholdings or no land at all suffered losses in real income of around 15 percent. In addition, Deuster points out that the ownership of rice land became markedly less equal during this period--in 1959 only 3.2 percent of the households owned 0.51 hectares and above, and in 1968, 8.9 percent did so.[26] Finally, Deuster demonstrates that the proportion of households in the lowest income categories increased during this period, from 58.4 percent to 62.9 percent.[27]

Several factors appear to play a major role in Deuster's analysis of the widening gap between the richer and poorer classes of rural society. The main hypothesis of his study is that inflation most adversely effected the lower income groups and as a result increased income inequality. In addition, it is evident from Deuster's study that the trend toward concentration of land control is a critical factor in the economic polarization of village society. Finally, it is possible to infer from his research that increased population pressure plays an important role in the emergence of a highly stratified economic structure. In order to properly understand the role of population growth in these developments, it is necessary to distinguish between the effects of increased population in relation to resource scarcity, and the relationship of population pressure in the differential access to these resources. In the first instance, increased population pressure has resulted in such changes as reduction of average landholding size, a decline in per capita income, and a shortage of employment opportunities. Such developments as the uneven distribution of landholdings are not, however, an automatic consequence of greater population pressure. To examine the emergence of a stratified economic order and the role of population growth in these developments, the focus must shift from absolute resource scarcity to control over these resources. From this perspective, increased population pressure can be examined with respect to its effects on the relative "bargaining position" of competing groups in the rural economy. In this second sense, increased population pressure has strengthened the "bargaining position" of large land owners in their relationships with the economically dependent groups of village society. This is primarily due to the fact that increased population pressure has tended to increase competition among the swollen ranks of the rural poor in their struggle to establish secure economic ties with the local "big men." With the resources under their control at a premium, local elites have been able to exact greater demands from their impoverished clients.

There are a number of other important factors closely associated with the widening gap between richer and poorer classes in rural Javanese society, factors which are not mentioned in Deuster's study, and which most notably concern a decline in the corporate identity of the village community. The rise of absentee landlordism and the use of outside labor are two of the more prominent indications of this change. However, one of the most visible manifestations of this trend is the rise of

consumerism. Beginning in the 1950s, the availability of
consumer items in rural Java has rapidly multiplied.
First bicycles, then radios, and more recently motorcycles, tape recorders, and T.V.s, have become highly
valued possessions in the village. In this context, the
new uses for which income from increased production "surplus" is allocated have had a substantial impact on the
rural economy, and can be directly related to the political and economic developments discussed above. The decline in the corporate identity of the village, and more
specifically the rise of consumerism, has grossly accentuated the differences between richer and poorer villagers and served to greatly reduce the overall size of the
"economic pie" which sustains the majority of hard
pressed villagers.

A final factor to be considered in the analysis of
existing rural economic structures is the increased importance of capital in the farm enterprise. In the past
decade, acceptance of the Green Revolution technologies
including the use of HYV's, chemical fertilizers and pesticides, has become widespread. The innovations have,
generally speaking, enabled farmers to achieve a higher
rate of return for their produce. At the same time, utilization of these new technologies has perforce required
substantial increases in the amount of capital involved
in the operations of the farm. Leaving aside the issue
of who can "afford" the new technologies, it is evident
that the capitalization of rice production in Java has
significantly affected the economic organization of village society. These innovations have encouraged the substitution of capital for labor and placed greater emphasis on the values of profit and efficiency in the management of the farm enterprise. Spelled out in different
terms, the increased importance of the profit motive in
the operation of the farm has meant that traditional labor absorbing practices within the rice economy are now
giving way to less costly and less labor intensive innovations in the organization of agricultural production.
Manifestations of this trend include the rising use of
sickles for harvesting, as well as the increased utilization of mechanical hullers for rice processing. In both
instances, these changes have improved the profits of the
landowner but at the same time reduced labor opportunities in the village.

III

The emergence of a more highly stratified society
and the attendant reinforcement of local authority structures is visibly reflected in many of the above mentioned
changes involving the organization of agricultural production, the rise of consumerism, and the deteriorating

bargaining power of impoverished clients vis-a-vis their
wealthy patrons. In great measure, many of these transformations were long in the making and the nature and
magnitude of their manifestation has, in turn, been conditioned by events and forces emanating from within a
broader and more national framework. More explicitly,
during the past decade, growing economic and social disparities within village society can be related to the
expansion of central government activities in the rural
sector. Thus, the weakened corporate character of the
village community is, in part, a consequence of increased
government involvement in local affairs. Likewise, the
capitalization of the farm enterprise has, to a degree,
been fostered by government programs to encourage the use
of Green Revolution technologies. In many instances, the
impact of these intrusions has been somewhat indirect, but
in other cases the mode of penetration has been more direct and involved a sustained organizational effort at
the local level. Indeed, the current institution building effort underway involving the BUUD movement is representative of government attempts to further enhance its
role within the rural sector. This effort is deserving
of further comment, particularly in light of what is already known about the allocation of resources and authority within village society.

In the early seventies, a new Bimas program (Improved Bimas) was introduced. The main thrust of this
program continued to be directed towards increasing rice
production, although the failure of past production efforts convinced the government that local organizations
would have to be given a larger role in the effective
administration of this new campaign. Thus, a new organizational entity, referred to as the Unit Desa (Village
Unit), was created to administer the credit and other
agricultural inputs (high-yielding seeds, fertilizer,
pesticides, etc.) now being made available in the Bimas
program. Ideally, the village unit serviced an area of
600 to 1000 hectares (two to three villages) and a population of roughly 3,000 farmers. The major components of
the village unit included: a representative of the Bank
Rakyat Indonesia (a state bank); an extension worker from
the Department of Agriculture; and a fertilizer retailer.
These three agents were to work in concert in the delivery of credit, fertilizer, and extension services, in
support of the government's efforts to increase rice production.

A final component of the village unit scheme was the
newly formed Badan Usaha Unit Desa, commonly referred to
as the BUUD. To establish this new institution, existing
village cooperatives were amalgamated into a BUUD unit or
federation at the sub-district level. The primary purpose of these new federations, the BUUDs, was to foster a
more coordinated effort in the provision of agricultural

services and other development activities at the local
level. The selection of the sub-district as the basic
unit of development for the BUUDs appears to reflect a
number of major concerns on the part of the government
regarding the position of local organizations in their
overall strategy for rural development. First, the amalgamation of existing cooperatives under the umbrella of a
single organization serves to enhance government control
over an area which in the past had been very politicized.
By defining the sub-district as the BUUD area of operation, government control over these local organizations is
assured by virtue of their close linkage to the sub-district administration. Secondly, with the sub-district as
the formally designated unit of development, it appears
that the government hopes that the BUUD will benefit
from the larger economies of scale in working with more
than one single village.

Broadly speaking, the major functions of the BUUD,
as envisaged by the government, included the strengthening of local-level administrative performance in the implementation of national development programs, and providing an opportunity, especially for small farmers, to
actively participate in the development process. The
first of these roles is directly linked to the produc-
tion-oriented aspects of government programs. The second
function more generally concerns issues related to the
well-being of the majority of rural inhabitants, and in
practice, the government has viewed this improvement in
general living standards, not so much as a separate issue
in its own right, but more in terms of a derivative by-
product directly related to the successful performance of
the first functions, i.e., the productivity goal.

Government plans for enlisting the support of vil-
lage-level agricultural cooperatives, using the BUUD as
the primary vehicle, initially called for a gradual development of their revitalized role. In the early 1970s,
only a small number of BUUDs were established, and their
activities were limited both in size and in scope. During this formative stage, low-interest government loans
were made available to many of the BUUDs for the purchase
of mechanical rice hullers, and in addition, most of the
new federations were authorized to distribute fertilizer,
and to serve as purchasing agents in the government's
efforts to maintain a floor on rice prices. In 1973,
however, this more cautious approach in institution
building was abruptly abandoned. The change in policy
was precipitated by a major shortfall in domestic rice
production in 1972, a condition which prompted the government to dramatically expand its 1973 rice procurement
targets in an effort to restore its depleted buffer
stock. Primary responsibility for the collection of
these rice procurement quotas was assigned to the BUUD
organizations, and this had some immediate and far-

reaching consequences on its growth as a viable farmer's organization. Overnight, the number of BUUDs skyrocketed. In most cases these new organizations existed on paper only, and were basically created to assist the government in its rice procurement effort. More importantly, the procurement campaign became a bureaucratic nightmare, with farmers resisting government directives to sell their rice to the BUUDs at prices below its market value. The procurement campaign was soon terminated but village support for the BUUD was severely undermined by virtue of its association with such an unpopular policy. Likewise, the rapid expansion in the number of BUUDs only served to further dilute the range of support and services the government was able to provide these fledgling organizations. Thus, today, many BUUDs remain as skeleton organizations lacking any real substantive ties to the rural economy. In some instances, these organizations have become mere appendages of the government bureaucracy or they have been absorbed into the pre-existing power structure of village society. This latter point warrants further comment, particularly with regard to some of the major functions now being performed by the BUUD.

From its inception, many BUUDs have had a reputation of being elite-controlled organizations; a distinction not undeserved and which, in great part, can be attributed to the impact of government policy. Thus, for example, many of the cooperatives amalgamated into the new federation were defunct Koperta organizations. Initiated as a government sponsored agricultural cooperative movement in the 1960s, the formation of the Koperta had generally proceeded in a very unsystematic manner, and many were simply created by government fiat, with village officials delegated as chairmen and their friends and relatives listed as members. Thus, when the new BUUD federations were formed, leadership positions frequently fell into the hands of village officials who were the local chairmen of Koperta organizations. Elite control of the new organizations has also been enhanced by the government's initial go-slow policies with regard to the development of the BUUDs. This stance not only applied to the scope of activities undertaken by the BUUD, but to its solicitation of members as well. Until very recently, most BUUDs have operated on the principles of a federation of local cooperatives rather than as full cooperatives in their own right. As such, they have had no mandate to enroll members or to engage in any other activities which involve a direct mobilizing role at the local level. Government policy in this area is beginning to change, particularly with the recent transformation of many BUUDs into KUDs (full cooperatives), but in general, the local leadership of many BUUDs show little indication that they intend to energetically pursue a policy of active community mobilization.

In the area of rice marketing there is strong evidence that local elites, rice buyers, and BUUD officials alike, have taken advantage of this program to strengthen their role in the local rice market. In this regard, one of the major functions of the BUUD is to maintain a floor on rice prices, a policy primarily designed to benefit small farmers who are often forced to sell the marketable portion of their crop (to repay outstanding debts) immediately following the harvest when prices are the lowest. For numerous reasons, however, the basic aim of this policy is frequently not achieved. First of all, the purchase of rice by BUUDs involves a considerable amount of bureaucratic red tape. Both federation officials and small farmers, who often sell only a few kilos of rice, dislike the paper work involved in this procedure and are thereby discouraged from making small sales. For this reason and others (the BUUD is not staffed to go from farm to farm purchasing small amounts of rice), many federations have entered into make-shift arrangements with local rice buyers for the purchase of their rice supply. The impact of the BUUD rice marketing activities on the operations of small farms is also minimized due to the close links between the credit needs of small farmers and the money-lending activities of the rice traders. The latter will, in many instances, acquire rights to the small farmer's produce well before the harvest by virtue of his role as a secure and reliable source of credit, and the price paid to the small farmers is often well below the floor price supposedly guaranteed by the BUUD organization. As a result, it is often the rice traders who reap the benefits of government policies to maintain a floor value on rice prices.

IV

Examination of the administrative structure and political processes associated with village society has revealed that major changes have occurred in the past decade. Of these, the most important include: the transformation of village government into a larger administrative center, which has thereby become more removed from the needs of local constituents; a weakening of those mechanisms within the local community for effectively influencing the actions of village officials; and the increased dependence of village officials on external sources of support (i.e., their critical role in the implementation of national development efforts). Recent changes in the economic organization of village society have been examined in the light of the existing make-up of the village political system, and with special regard for the fact that village officials double as large landholders. As mentioned above, these changes are characterized by the substitution of capital for labor in the farm enterprise and are manifested in such trends as the widening disparity in income distribution and the increased concentration of control over local assets. Local elites have managed, to a great degree, to free themselves from the diffuse and costly obligations of the traditional distribution system, and they appear to be maintaining this freedom by relying upon existing sources of economic, political and administrative support. The interdependence of these divergent sources of support becomes quite evident in an analysis of the BUUD organization.

The BUUD organization was primarily designed to improve the coordination of development activities within the subdistrict. Its major functions, as envisaged by the government, included the strengthening of local-level administrative performance in the implementation of national development programs, as well as providing an opportunity for small farmers to participate in the development process. To accomplish these goals, the BUUD organizations were given a major role in the rice procurement activities of the central government, provided low interest loans for the purchase of rice mills, and delegated primary responsibility for the local distribution of fertilizer.

In summary, for numerous reasons, the primary aims of the BUUD have been difficult to achieve. Its early involvement in an unpopular rice procurement campaign discouraged many farmers from becoming involved in its operations. In many instances, BUUDs have been taken over by special interest groups who have used its resources for their own particular goals (i.e., expanding their control over the local market system). To a great extent, these shortcomings can be attributed to the original design of the program. Leadership positions were frequently assigned to village officials and the scope of activities frequently benefitted the better off members within the community. These developments, however, were not just the result of superior economic power, as is implied in many analyses of the effects of the Green Revolution on village society; nor can they be attributed to deep rooted cultural factors; rather, they are the result of an assemblage of resources, both political, economic, and administrative, which frequently fall under the control of local elites.

NOTES

1. William Collier, "Size of Rice Field Operation and Adoption of High Yielding Rice Varieties" (Bogor: Agro-Economic Survey, Research Notes No. 2, 1972), p. 2.

2. D. Penny and M. Singarimbun, Population and Poverty in Rural Java: Some Economic Arithmetic from Sriharjo (Ithaca: Cornell University Press, 1973), p. 33.

3. R. Turnier, "Comments on the Special Pilot Project in Jogjakarta and Prospects of Expansion on the Villages Units" (Yogyakarta: Food and Agricultural Organization, 1971), p. 11.

4. William Staub, C. Alexander and C. Saleh, "The Market for Production Credit Among Farmers in Java," Prisma, (1976), pp. 78-87, and Nevin Bryant, "Village Migration and the Rural Economy of Central Java" (Paper presented at Conference on Indonesian Agriculture; Madison, Wisconsin, 1974).

5. Richard Franke, The Green Revolution in a Javanese Village (Ph.D. thesis, Harvard University, 1972).

6. Selosoemardjan, Social Changes in Jogjakarta (Ithaca: Cornell University Press, 1962).

7. Ibid., p. 25.

8. Clifford Geertz, The Social Context of Economic Change: An Indonesian Case Study (Cambridge: Center for International Studies, Massachusetts Institute of Technology, 1956), p. 33.

9. B. Mulherin, "The 'Bekel' in Javanese History," Review of Indonesian and Malayan Affairs 4/5, (1970-1971): 24.

10. Selosoemardjan, Social Changes in Jogjakarta, pp. 275-280.

11. Ibid., p. 273.

12. J. Furnivall, Netherlands India: A Study of Plural Economy (Cambridge: Cambridge University Press, 1939), p. 293.

13. R. Jay, Religion and Politics in Rural Central Java (New Haven: Southeast Asia Studies, Yale University, 1963), p. 45.

14. Selosoemardjan, Social Changes in Jogjakarta, p. 92.

15. Nitinegoro, Proses Demokratisering Desa Didaerah Daerah Istimewa Yogyakarta (Yogyakarta: 1968), p. 10.

16. T. Smith, "Kepala Desa: Pelopor Pembaharuan," Prisma 4, (1973): 17-30, and J. Zacharias, "Lurah dan Program Pembangunan," Cakrawala Majalah Penelitian Sosial 4, (1975): 321-343.

17. United Nations, Regional Development in Yogyakarta (Nagoya: United Nations Centre for Regional Development, 1974), p. 105.

18. Ibid., p. 95.

19. J. H. Boeke, Economics and Economic Policy of Dual Societies: as Exemplified by Indonesia (New York: Institute of Pacific Relations, 1953), and Clifford Geertz, Agricultural Involution: The Process of Ecological Change in Indonesia (Berkeley: University of California Press, 1963).

20. Geertz, Agricultural Involution, p. 80.

21. Ibid., p. 82.

22. Ibid., p. 97.

23. Penny and Singarimbun, Population and Poverty, p. 10.

24. Zacharias, "Lurah dan Program Pembangunan," p. 329.

25. P. Deuster,"Rural Consequences of Indonesian Inflation: A Case Study of the Jogyakarta Region"(Ph.D. thesis, University of Wisconsin, 1971).

26. Ibid., p. 110.

27. Ibid., p. 50.

Part VI

Migration

Introduction

One of the most striking demographic features of
Indonesia's land/man ratio is the fact that a large majority of the country's population inhabit the small island of Java, whereas the vast reaches of the outer islands remain relatively free of any great population
densities. In both the colonial and independence era,
many policy makers have been attracted to the possibility
of relieving population pressure on Java by supporting
large scale resettlement schemes and transmigration from
Java to the outer islands. Under current policy priorities in the second and third five year plans, outer island resettlement ranks very high as a major development
goal. While a sizeable budget is being allocated to support these efforts, for numerous ecological and administrative reasons, it will be difficult in the short and
medium term to fully cultivate the full potential of the
outer islands as part of a larger resettlement plan, and
in the longer term, the question still remains as to
whether push and/or pull factors can operate upon a sufficiently wide enough scale to attract a large flow of
migrants from Java to the outer islands.
The following two essays are concerned with the
various issues involved in assessing current patterns and
future possibilities for migration in the Indonesian
archipelago. The first selection is an overview of recent interprovincial and rural to urban migration, with
additional attention being devoted to analyzing the
socio-economic characteristics of migrant populations,
reasons for moving, and the relative success of migrants
in pursuing employment, education, and other self-identi-
fied goals. Existing migration data indicates that the
primary movement of people has been between Java and Sumatra, but in general, the magnitude of interprovincial
migration has been relatively small. Surprisingly, low
levels of rural to urban migration have taken place and
therefore, the rate of urban growth has not been greatly
magnified by an excessive influx of rural unemployed.

The exceptions to this statement are Jakarta and Surabaya, particularly the former, where the pace of urbanization has been greatly increased by migration from both
rural and other urban areas.

In general, when compared to other developing countries, the volume of rural to urban migration in Indonesia is still relatively limited. In part, this appears
to reflect the fact that population movement draws upon a
relatively select group of people and does not represent
a more generalized exodus of rank and file village inhabitants. Thus, a large proportion of urban directed
migration streams consist of young adults either seeking
advanced schooling or searching for their first job. In
most cases, the data indicates that many of these migrants are successful in acquiring employment and further
schooling, a condition which seems to suggest that the
rate of migration has yet to greatly exceed the capacity
of most urban areas in accommodating the needs of these
individuals. At the same time, Speare notes that about
half of all migrants end up in jobs which can be classified in the category of marginal employment, with wage
levels barely meeting subsistence needs.

The second essay addresses the prospects and plans
for expanding government efforts in the widespread resettlement of transmigrants from Java to the outer islands. The author focuses his attention upon analyzing
the paramount ecological features of the two dominant
types of outer island ecosystems (swampland and upland
areas) which are intended to function as the primary support systems for resettlement schemes. While important
ecological conditions differentiate these two systems,
they do share two features in common; both are characterized by high degrees of local variability in soil fertility, and both systems, without proper management, are
highly vulnerable to rapid environmental degradation.
Preparing these areas for a large influx of population
will, therefore, require substantial preliminary surveys
and research in developing land-use patterns and cropping
systems suitable for particular site-specific locations.

Aside from the above constraints, each of the two
ecosystems present their own set of problems and potentials in sustaining new human settlements. Major obstacles in water and pest control and in the development of
dry-season cropping regimes still need to be resolved in
swampland areas. In upland areas, the topography is not
suitable for irrigation, and therefore a major task needs
to be addressed in the design and adaptation of cropping
systems for rainfed conditions. It appears that farming
systems in these areas will require a relatively complicated mix of tree and field crops with initially long
lead times before yield levels begin to provide a profitable return.

In the final analysis, it would appear that many of the technical issues involved in the design of resource-use systems for the resettlement schemes can be overcome, but that major uncertainties still loom with respect to providing the organizational and management inputs necessary for sustaining the economic and social viability of new settlement communities. In the short and medium term, public sector institutions will have to bear the burden of providing a wide range of support services until the communities themselves are able to generate their own organizational capacities and linkages with outside trading and marketing networks. In this context, the current capacity of regional governments in the targeted resettlement areas is seriously constrained by a frequent lack of interagency coordination and major shortfalls in the number of trained personnel available for participation in project planning and implementation. Thus, further expansion of the transmigration effort will require an attendant augmentation in administrative resources. The latter task will be difficult to accomplish, as the number of trained people available to undertake the training of a larger pool of skilled manpower is relatively limited. Nevertheless, without such an investment in human and institutional resources, the expansion of the resettlement program will likely meet with some serious shortcomings.

The vision of the outer islands as a major frontier for the resettlement of inhabitants from Java's overcrowded villages continues to rank high as a goal for national development. It would seem certain that the outer islands will gradually assume a larger role as the government seeks to support a more decentralized center to periphery growth model through regional development and transmigration. It seems very uncertain, however, as to whether the volume of migration will ever reach a level which serves to relieve population pressure in Java. It also seems uncertain as to whether the outer islands will be able to absorb a rapid and large influx of new migrants without sustaining some major and adverse ecological permutations.

11
Rural and Urban Migration:
A National Overview

Alden Speare, Jr.

Population growth and economic development rarely
proceed at the same rates in all regions of a country.
In some regions the rate of economic development may be
high relative to the rate of population increase while
in other regions the reverse is true. Regional differences in opportunities give rise to internal migration.
In Indonesia there have been two major types of internal
migration. The first is migration from the densely settled islands of Java and Bali to Sumatra and other islands with lower population densities. This migration
has been in response to the growth of population in Java
and Bali beyond the limits of the land to support the
population through subsistence agriculture and the likely
opportunity of obtaining new land in the outer islands.
The second major movement of people has been from rural
areas throughout Indonesia to the cities. Much of this
movement has gone to the capital city of Jakarta. Indeed, migration from outer islands to Jakarta has offset,
to a considerable extent, the movement from Java to the
rural areas of the outer islands.
    It is important to realize that both of the above
shifts in population comprise only a part of the total
volume of migration. With increases in trade and interaction among regions which comes with development, there
tends to be an increase in back and forth movement between regions. Everett Lee has argued that the volume of
migration tends to increase with the rate of development
in a country and tends to be greater where there is
greater diversity among areas or people. He has also
pointed out that, "for every major migration stream a
counter stream develops . . . . the existence of a migration stream creates contacts between origin and destination, and the acquisition of new attributes at destination, be they skills or wealth, often makes it
possible to return to the origin on advantageous terms."[1]

In the following sections an overview will be provided on migration in Indonesia, looking first at migration between provinces, second, at the volume of migration from rural to urban areas, third, at the characteristics and motivation of migrants, and finally at the success of migrants in the city.[2]

I

Migration between provinces of Indonesia has not been particularly large by international standards. The 1971 national census reported that less than 5 percent of the people of Indonesia were living outside their province of birth (lifetime migrants) and less than 2 percent had moved across provincial boundaries within the past five years (recent migrants). Lifetime migration has accounted for a significant part of the population growth in only two provinces--Jakarta and Lampung provinces in South Sumatra. These two provinces absorbed more than half of the lifetime migrants in Indonesia. In Jakarta, about 40 percent of the population were lifetime migrants as of 1971, and in Lampung, 36 percent of the population were lifetime migrants as of the same date. Since relatively few people born in these provinces have moved to other provinces, the net-migration rates are also very high. The actual impact of migration on these two areas is greater than these figures indicate because all the children born to migrants are counted as native born. If the children of migrants were also counted as migrants, about two-thirds of the population of Jakarta and 61 percent of the population of Lampung would be migrants.

In Indonesia, as in most other countries, there is far less variation in the rates of out-migration than in the rates of in-migration. According to the 1971 census, the highest rates of out-migration were recorded for Central Java, Yogyakarta, and West Sumatra, which lost 8.2, 10.7, and 11.6 percent of their populations respectively. The losses in West and East Java were also significant in terms of number of migrants. These five provinces accounted for 4.3 million out of the 5.7 million lifetime interprovincial migrants. The out-migration from the island of Java was offset, to a large extent, by in-migration to Jakarta. While the four provinces of Java had a combined net out-migration of 3.0 million people, Jakarta had a net in-migration of about 1.7 million people. Thus, the net lifetime movement from Java as a whole was only 1.3 million people, or less than 2 percent of the 1971 population and less than the natural increase in a single year.

Sumatra gained about 1.5 million people through lifetime migration, not including the children born to migrants, and this accounted for 7.2 percent of the 1971 population. The other islands did not experience very large population movements. Kalimantan had a net in-migration of about 22,000, Sulawesi a net out-migration of 175,000 (mostly from South Sulawesi) and the other islands as a group gained 38,000 from migration.

The above measures of lifetime migration indicate the net movement of persons from the time of birth until the time of measurement. This net movement could have been due to a single move at any time during the persons' life or the result of a series of moves. Many people who move are not counted as lifetime migrants because they move only within the boundaries of a province or because they return to their place of birth. The 1971 census included a question on place of previous residence which provides a means of estimating return migration. The total number of persons with a place of previous residence outside their province of residence in 1971 was 7,219,600. This is in excess of the number of lifetime migrants, 5,703,000, because it includes not only all the lifetime migrants but also those people who have moved and then returned to their province of birth. By subtracting the number of lifetime migrants from the total number of migrants an estimate of 1,516,600 is obtained for return migrants. This means that 21 percent of the persons who were identified as migrants by the previous residence questions were return migrants. An analysis of return migration by region showed that 45 percent of the migrants from Sumatra to Java were persons who had been born in Java and were returning. If, however, these return migrants are expressed as a percentage of all lifetime migrants from Java to Sumatra, the percentage who returned is only 14 percent.

In contrast to lifetime migration, the 1971 census indicates even smaller percentages of interprovincial mobility with respect to recent migration. Recent migration can be measured by summing migrants with 0 to 4 years duration of residence in the province where they were enumerated in 1971. These sums provide raw estimates on the volume of migration during the five-year period from September 1966 to September 1971. Only two regions, Jakarta and Sumatra, had appreciable gains from net-migration. The remaining regions all experienced net losses with the exception of the other islands which contain Nusa Tenggara, Maluku and West Irian. The greatest loss due to out-migration occurred for the rest of Java and Bali (excluding Jakarta).

Moving beyond the general characteristics associated with lifetime and recent migrants and toward a greater specification of migration patterns, it needs to be noted that in Indonesia, as in most developing countries, the

largest movement of people is from rural to urban areas.
There are three types of urban areas in Indonesia, those
with official municipality status (<u>Kotamadya</u>), those
which are capitals of rural districts (<u>Ibu Kota Kabupa-
ten</u>), and other areas designated as urban by the census
because they possess urban characteristics. The municipalities of Indonesia grew by 37.2 percent between 1961
and 1971. Three percent was due to the expansion of
boundaries and to areas newly classified as municipalities between censuses. About 24 percent was due to
natural increase and the remaining 10.2 percent can be
attributed to net-migration. The total net-migration to
municipalities is estimated to have been about 1.1 million from 1961 to 1971. Most of the net-migration went
to Jakarta with a small amount going to Surabaya and
other large cities. The net-migration to Jakarta was 82
percent of the total net-migration to all 50 municipalities and the net-migration to the 5 largest cities was 99
percent of the total. Although some of the small cities
in Sumatra and Kalimantan grew rapidly from net-migration, this growth was mostly offset by losses from net
out-migration from other small cities, especially those
on Java. Thus, with the exception of Jakarta and Surabaya, the rate of urbanization in Indonesia has been very
slow.
    Data on the place of origin of migrants to different
cities are derived from a major survey of migration conducted in 1973 by the National Institute of Economic and
Social Research of the Indonesian Institute of Sciences,
(LEKNAS-LIPI).[3] Results from this survey indicate that
with the exception of Jakarta, the majority of the migrants came from the same province within which the city
was located. Three out of four migrants to Surabaya and
other cities in Java came from the same province and four
out of five migrants to cities in Sulawesi came from the
same province. Jakarta has the greatest proportion of
migrants from other islands, which is consistent with the
common finding that the larger the city, the greater the
distance from which it attracts migrants.
    Although Indonesia was 82 percent rural in 1971, not
all migrants to cities came from rural areas. Overall,
18.7 percent of the migrants came from municipalities and
37.2 percent came from urban areas. These figures indicate that the rate of movement from one city to another
is greater than the rate of movement from rural to urban
areas. The proportion originating in a municipality increased considerably with the distance of the move. The
proportions coming from municipalities did not vary
greatly by city of destination. The main exception was
Sumatra, where migrants from other islands were less likely to have come from municipalities than those from other
provinces in Sumatra. This is probably due to the fact
that much of the migration to Sumatra's cities from Java

may have been a by-product of the transmigration program. That is, migrants who moved from rural Java to rural re-settlement areas in Sumatra may then leave these areas for cities in Sumatra.

While most cities had very low or even negative rates of net-migration, many cities had a considerable volume of in- and out-migration. There appears to be a considerable flow of temporary migrants into cities-- migrants who either return to their place of origin or move on to another place after spending a few years in the city. In fact, rural studies by Hugo and LEKNAS in-dicate that there may be a much larger flow of seasonal and other short duration migrants to cities, most of whom were not counted as migrants in the census.[4]

In summary, a number of general statements can be made about migration patterns in Indonesia. First, most migrants to cities came from the same province that the city was located in, with the exception of Jakarta which drew migrants from many provinces. Interprovincial mi-gration has had a significant impact on only a few pro-vinces. The major movements have been from Java to Su-matra and from all parts of Indonesia to Jakarta, and migration and the natural increase of the migrant popu-lation have accounted for the majority of the growth of Jakarta and Lampung provinces. Because migration has come largely from areas of dense rural settlement and rapid population growth, out-migration has not resulted in a decline in population of any province, and has in fact, done no more than remove a small proportion of the natural increase from the areas of heaviest out-migration such as Central Java, Yogyakarta and West Sumatra. Sec-ond, rural to urban migration in Indonesia has proceeded at a slower pace than in most other developing countries. Most of the growth of cities has been due to natural in-crease, the excess of births over deaths, and not to mi-gration. The major exceptions have been Jakarta, Sura-baya, and a few small cities in Kalimantan and other outer islands where large projects have been developed to exploit natural resources.

II

In most developing countries migration to the city is selective of certain types of people who share a num-ber of social and economic characteristics and motives for moving to the city. Young adults are far more likely to move than older adults. Single persons are more like-ly to move than married persons and persons with higher levels of education are more likely to move than those with lower levels of education. The characteristics of migrants relate to their motives for moving, among which finding a job and obtaining education predominate. In

these respects, migration in Indonesia is very similar to
migration in other less developed countries. Thus, according to the data gathered in the 1973 LEKNAS survey,
more than one-half of the adult (over age 15) migrants
were between the ages of 15 and 24. The predominance of
young adults is greatest in the streams from rural areas
to cities. In these streams, 56 percent of the adult
males and 62 percent of the adult females were ages 15 to
24, and the proportion of persons 15 to 24 among migrants
was more than double the similar proportion for the population at the area of origin. Finally, in accordance
with their young age, fewer than one-half of the migrants
were married at the time of interview.

Migrants as a group were better educated than the
populations of the areas of origin and destination.
Overall, 59 percent of the male migrants and 41 percent
of the female migrants had completed junior high school
or a higher level of education. In comparison, only 32
percent of the males and 19 percent of the females in
urban areas had completed junior high school or a higher
level. In rural areas the percentages were much lower,
6 percent for males and 2 percent for females. There
was a considerable difference in the levels of education
between migrants from other urban areas and those from
rural areas. The majority of the migrants from urban
areas had completed junior high school whereas the majority of rural migrants had not. Nevertheless, the proportions of rural migrants who had completed junior high
school, 49 percent for males and 30 percent for females,
was considerably higher than that of the rural population
and somewhat higher than the urban population. This
means that the average migrant had an advantage over the
average urban resident in terms of education. The average migrant is, however, younger than the average urban
resident and younger persons in general have more education than older persons because of the improvements in
the school system over time. This means that at least
part of the relationship between migration and education
is due to the relation between age and education. Compared to Jakarta residents of the same age, migrants from
other urban origins were still clearly superior in education, but migrants from rural origins were not. For
example, 28 percent of male migrants from rural areas to
Jakarta had completed junior high school or a higher
level compared to 38 percent of residents with the same
age distribution.

The education of migrants differed according to the
type of city they went to. Thus, the average level of
education of rural migrants to Jakarta was lower than
that of rural migrants to other cities of Java, and the
average level of education of migrants to Surabaya was
also lower than that of migrants to Jakarta. Among males,
44 percent of the rural migrants to Jakarta had not com-

pleted elementary school compared to 30 percent for Surabaya and 23 percent for other cities of Java. For females the percentages with less than an elementary school
education were higher than those for males, but they followed a similar pattern. In this context, it may seem
surprising that the average level of education of rural
migrants to Jakarta is lower than that of other cities.
Among residents in general, the average educational level
in Jakarta is higher than that of other cities and the
nation's capital contains a disproportionate share of the
college graduates in Indonesia. The answer lies in the
fact that Jakarta is the only city in Java which experienced rapid growth during the 1968-73 period, and because
of the larger volume of migration to Jakarta, the migration was less selective. The same argument applies, to a
lesser extent, to Surabaya which had the second highest
growth rate. Essentially, the growing cities were able
to offer employment opportunities to unskilled workers
which the other cities could not offer. The smaller
cities of Java and the cities of Sumatra and Sulawesi, in
contrast, tended to serve as educational centers with
many migrants coming to these cities primarily to advance
their education.

The selectivity of migration from rural areas is
also apparent in the distribution of the economic activity of migrants before the move and in comparison to the
total rural population. A large proportion of the migrants had not worked prior to moving. Overall, 39 percent of the male migrants had been in school prior to
moving and 14 percent were classified as "other"--most
of whom were unemployed or not in the labor force. Among
female migrants, 26 percent had been students, 32 percent
had been engaged in housekeeping and 14 percent were
classified as "other". Those who had worked amounted to
46 percent of the male migrants and 27 percent of the female migrants, divided roughly equally between farm and
nonfarm work. In contrast, much higher percentages of
the total rural population were working. According to
the 1971 national census, 79 percent of the rural males
aged 15 and over and 35 percent of the females were working. The main difference is in the proportion attending
school, which is much lower for the total population.
This difference can be partly attributed to the younger
age of the migrants. In fact, since the migrants could
have moved up to five years prior to the interview and
migrants aged 15 and over at the time of the interview
were included, some of the migrants were only 10 years
old when they left the rural areas. Perhaps the most interesting results are those on the distribution between
farm and nonfarm work for those migrants who worked. For
male migrants, the figures are almost equal, whereas for
the total rural population there are almost three times
as many farmers as non-farmers. The findings for females

are similar. This means that migration from rural areas is highly selective of persons in nonfarm occupations and those who have not entered the labor force because they were in school.

Male migrants to the cities of Sumatra and Sulawesi were similar to male migrants to cities of Java with respect to previous economic activity. Female rural to urban migrants in Sumatra and Sulawesi were, however, considerably less likely to have been employed prior to working and more likely to have been engaged in housekeeping. This difference reflects the more limited role of women in Sumatra and Sulawesi and is consistent with the lower rates of labor force participation of women reported in the census for these islands. In summary, a large majority of migrants to the cities of Indonesia are young adults who are near the point of entry into the labor market. Many have not worked prior to moving, and many were in school; a condition related to the fact that they had more education, on the average, than the people who stayed behind.

Aside from sharing certain common features with respect to age, education, and occupational background, definite similarities can also be found among migrants in their reasons for moving from one area to another. In the LEKNAS survey, migrants gave three main reasons for moving: to find a job, to obtain further schooling, or to accompany other family members. Males moved most frequently for job reasons while females moved most frequently for family reasons, usually to accompany their husbands. Job related reasons accounted for nearly one-half of the moves made by men and about one-quarter of the moves by women. Job reasons were about equally divided between those who said there was no job available in the village and those who said they wanted a better job, indicating that the attraction of urban employment opportunities was as important a factor as were conditions of unemployment in rural areas. The main exception was Surabaya, where 46 percent of the male migrants and 24 percent of the female migrants said they had moved because no job was available in the village. Apparently, during the period of the study, rural conditions in East Java were worse than those in other areas of Indonesia.

Schooling was the second most important reason for moving, accounting for 37 percent of all rural to urban moves by males and 21 percent of such moves by females. The proportion who moved to attend urban schools was lowest in Jakarta and Surabaya and highest in the other cities in Java and the cities in Sumatra and Sulawesi. The relatively high proportion who moved to attend school is due to two factors. First, many rural areas have no schools beyond elementary education so that students wishing to continue their education must move to cities to do so. Secondly, many of the smaller cities which

provide high schools have not been growing and have few
opportunities to attract other migrants. Thus, students
comprise a large proportion of all migrants to these
cities. The most extreme example is Yogyakarta, which is
noted for its educational and cultural facilities but
which has had substantial net out-migration in recent
years. In Yogyakarta about three-quarters of the male
migrants came to attend school. In contrast, Jakarta and
Surabaya had much lower proportions of migrants for education reasons. This was not because they lack educational facilities, but because they also had opportunities to attract other migrants as well.

III

The above analysis indicates that most migration in
Indonesia is closely related to employment and educational issues, with the vast majority of migrants moving
to urban areas in order to obtain a better job or to secure more advanced schooling. The question arises as to
whether these individuals are successful in obtaining
these goals. Are migrants to urban areas as successful
in securing employment as urban residents? Are certain
urban occupations more accessible to migrants than other
occupations? Do migrants increase their income by moving
to urban areas, and do they earn more or less than the
average urban resident? Do income differences among
urban migrants reflect differences in their educational
background and/or differences in their place of origin?
Some preliminary answers to the above questions can
be found in the LEKNAS migration survey. The survey reveals that a majority (66 percent) of the male migrants
to cities were working at the time of interview, whereas
29 percent were going to school, with the other 5 percent
being divided among those who were engaged in other activities, were unemployed, or for whom no economic activity could be ascertained. Among female migrants, 35
percent of all rural to urban migrants were working in
the city, 40 percent were housewives and 21 percent were
students. Less than four percent of the females were
unemployed or engaged in other activities.
Most of the migrants who came seeking jobs or higher
education were successful in achieving these goals.
Among those who moved to find work or to find a better
job, 85 percent of the males and 77 percent of the females were employed at the time of interview. Rates of
employment were higher for migrants who came from rural
areas than for those who came from urban areas, indicating
that some of those from urban areas may have been seeking
skilled or professional jobs and were able to remain unemployed until they found them. Approximately six percent of the males who had moved for job related reasons

and three percent of the females who had moved for similar reasons were classified in the "other, not working"
category and it could be presumed that most of these were
unemployed. The rest were either attending school or
were engaged in housekeeping. Approximately 14 percent
of the females who had moved for job related reasons were
housewives at the time of interview. It is not known
what proportion of these were not working out of choice
and what percentage would have preferred to have a job,
but identified themselves as housewives rather than as
unemployed. An examination of the proportion of women
employed by year of arrival shows a decrease as length of
residence in the city increases. Among women who had
moved for job related reasons within the two years preceding the survey, 85 percent were working, which implies
that women were as successful as men in securing employment soon after their arrival in the city.

More than one-third of all male migrants and more
than one-fifth of all female migrants had come to the
city seeking education. At the time of the interview, 26
percent of these were attending school. However, since
some migrants had moved five years before the interview,
it is more meaningful to look only at the migrants who
moved within the last two years. Among these, 83 percent
were attending school, which indicates a high degree of
success in attaining this goal.

Comparing migrants to urban residents of the same
age, it is found that more migrants are working than urban residents of the same age.[5] This difference is
greatest among females where 36 percent of the migrants
are working compared to 20 percent of the urban resident.
Migrants are also more likely to be attending school than
urban residents. These differences are offset by lower
proportions of migrants who are seeking work, housekeeping, or migrants classified as other. While some care
must be taken in interpreting these results because of
differences in the measurement procedures between the
census and survey, the differences are large enough to
provide some grounds for concluding that migrants were
less likely to be unemployed than urban natives.

In examining the distribution of employment by different occupational categories, both the LEKNAS survey
and the 1971 census indicate that migrants held a wide
range of jobs in the cities, ranging from professions
and managers to day laborers and household servants. For
males, the differences between migrants and urban residents were not large enough to characterize certain occupations as being migrant occupations. Nevertheless, in
comparison with the total urban population, male migrants
were underrepresented in professional, managerial and
clerical jobs and overrepresented in sales and production, transportation and construction jobs. Among males,
there was little difference in the proportions engaged in

service jobs. Because urban boundaries do not always co-
incide with the dividing line between farm and non-farm
areas, approximately 10 percent of the employed males in
cities were farmers or fishermen. However, only two percent of the male migrants had agricultural jobs and the
majority of these jobs were in fishing. Thus, farming
within the boundaries of cities can be characterized as a
non-migrant occupation and it appears to be the only occupation which can be so characterized.

Female migrants are less similar to female urban
residents than male migrants are to male residents. The
most distinguishing feature of the distribution of female
migrants is the fact that 42 percent of them are employed
as household servants. In comparison, only 27 percent of
the female residents of the same age are employed in any
type of service job. Female migrants are also more likely to be employed in production jobs than female residents. Conversely, far fewer female migrants than female
residents are employed in professional, managerial,
clerical, or sales jobs.

Approximately two-fifths of the male migrants and
one-half of the female workers had jobs which could be
considered as marginal employment, i.e., peddlers, household servants, construction workers or pedicab drivers.
In addition, perhaps one-half of those engaged in sales
jobs with fixed locations, probably had only a very small
stock of goods and could, therefore, be considered to be
marginally employed. If these workers and one-half of
the other service workers are added together with one-
half of those in the "other" occupational category, the
estimate of marginally employed migrants rises to 51 percent of the male migrants and 56 percent of the female
migrants. A similar type of reasoning suggests that
about 39 percent of the employed males and 42 percent of
the employed females in the total urban population are
marginally employed. In this context, marginal employment appeared to be most common among migrants to Jakarta. Thirty percent of all male migrants to Jakarta were
peddlers and 44 percent of the female migrants were
household servants. In addition, despite the fact that
Jakarta is the nation's capital and a large percentage
of its residents are employed in government jobs, only
10 percent of the migrants of either sex were employed in
professional, managerial or clerical jobs. The proportion of migrants in professional, managerial or clerical
jobs was considerably higher for male migrants to other
cities in Java and for migrants of both sex to cities in
Sumatra and Sulawesi. This difference is probably due to
the fact that these cities are growing more slowly than
Jakarta and, therefore, are not able to offer a wide
range of jobs to migrants.

An assessment of income differences among migrants
and urban residents reveals that median incomes varied

by sex, place of origin and place of destination. According to the LEKNAS survey, male migrants had incomes which were, on the average, more than double those of females, and migrants from other urban areas had considerably higher incomes than those from rural areas. Male incomes did not vary greatly among cities in Java but they were higher in Sumatra and Sulawesi. The higher incomes in the outer islands probably reflected the higher costs of living in these areas and do not necessarily imply a higher standard of living. For example, at the time of the survey in 1973, rice sold for Rp 55 per liter in Java compared to Rp 78 in Sumatra and Sulawesi. Female incomes were roughly similar in Jakarta and Surabaya but considerably lower in other cities of Java. This difference is probably due to the fact that a much higher proportion of the females in the other cities of Java were employed in production jobs. Most of these jobs are labor intensive and pay relatively low wages. Typical female manufacturing jobs are the making of batik, sewing clothing, rolling cigarettes by hand, and foodprocessing.

For most occupations, migrants from urban places had higher incomes than the migrants from rural places, and male migrants had higher incomes than female migrants. In general, those employed in professional, administrative and clerical jobs had the highest incomes followed by salespersons working in permanent locations. Those employed as household servants and peddlers had the lowest incomes. Among females, the production and skilled transportation workers had relatively low wages, averaging only a little more than US$ 10 per month in 1973. Although comparable income data for urban residents are lacking, the rural migrants probably earned less than the average urban resident. The fact that migrants from other urban places earn substantially more than migrants from rural origins in the same broad occupation categories indicates that there is considerable variation in income among different groups. While migrants from other urban places were shown to be better educated than urban residents in general, the migrants from rural areas were not as well educated. Thus, if the income differences reflect education differences, we would expect rural migrants to have somewhat lower incomes. Furthermore, rural migrants are more concentrated in those jobs with low incomes such as household service, peddling, and female manufacturing jobs, than urban residents.

Although rural migrants may have had lower incomes than urban residents, they had higher incomes than rural residents in the areas of origin. The LEKNAS survey indicated that the median non-farm income in rural areas was Rp 3950 per month for male workers and Rp 1650 per month for female workers.[6] In comparison, male migrants from rural areas were earning about 60 percent more in the city and female migrants were earning almost twice as much.

Another measure of the success of the move is the migrant's own feeling of satisfaction with the results of the move. All migrants were asked "How would you compare your life in the city with your former village life?" In terms of material aspects, more than one-half of the migrants felt they were better off in the city, 40 percent felt they were as well off as in the village, and only about eight percent felt they were worse off in the city. In terms of "spiritual" aspects of life, most migrants felt the village was better, but it is not clear how important the spiritual aspects are to their overall evaluation of urban life.

In summary, it would appear that migrants were relatively successful in obtaining their goals for moving. Judging from the proportions attending school and working at the time of the survey interview in 1973, few migrants were unable to obtain employment or entry into school. While rural migrants tended to be concentrated in occupations which are frequently referred to as marginal, such as peddlers, pedicab drivers, household servants, and day laborers, these occupations nonetheless characterize much of the employment in Indonesian cities, and male migrants from rural areas did not differ greatly from all urban residents of the same age in the types of occupations they held. The incomes of migrants were substantially higher than those of rural residents in Indonesia, although it is not clear how much of this increase should be discounted for the higher costs associated with urban living. The fact that the proportion of migrants who felt that they were better off in the city far exceeded the proportion who felt they were worse off, suggests that the urban incomes of migrants were higher on the average than rural incomes, even when discounted for the higher costs of living in the city.

IV

The relative success of rural to urban migrants should not be taken to mean that migration is not a source of urban problems. Migrants increase the competition for jobs, housing, and other urban resources. If these resources cannot be increased fast enough to keep up with the rapidly growing urban population, then the quality of life of all urban residents will be affected. The level of living of urban migrants, while somewhat better than that of rural residents, was not particularly high. The average monthly income of male migrants was equivalent to US$ 18.14, and that of female migrants was equivalent to US$ 8.53, at the prevailing exchange rate in 1973. Since the exchange rate does not necessarily reflect the price of commodities purchased by the poor, a more meaningful comparison might be the amount of rice which could be purchased with a month's income. At an estimated average price of Rp 74 per kilogram for the cities, at the time of the survey, the average male migrant could have purchased 102 kilograms of rice and the average female migrant could have purchased 48 kilograms of rice. If one accepts the minimum standard of 30 kilograms of rice per person per month proposed by Sajogo, then the average male migrant could have provided a minimum standard of living for a family of three, and a married couple who both worked could have supported a family of five.[7] Since many migrants with families of this size or larger earned incomes below the average, many migrant families were probably living below the minimum standard of living. A recent study by LEKNAS on labor utilization estimated that more than two-thirds of the males in urban areas received incomes which were insufficient to support their families at the minimum standard proposed by Sayogo, and more than one-half of the females who were working had incomes which were insufficient to support even one person.[8] These findings suggest that urban living conditions are not improving for the majority of the urban population and are consistent with the findings reported in the chapter by King and Weldon.

The living conditions of the majority living in cities, whether rural migrants or native born city dwellers, are not likely to improve significantly in the near future. Because Indonesia is still a largely rural country and the rural population is poor and still growing, urban areas are likely to experience continued migration of poor people from rural areas. Population projections for urban and rural areas of Indonesia, which were prepared assuming that the goals of the family planning program of reducing crude birth rates by 50 percent by the year 2000 would be realized, indicate that there will be an increase in the urban population from 20 million in 1970, to 50 million in 2000, if current trends in urbanization continue.[9] However, urbanization in Indonesia has been slow compared to other developing countries. Between 1961 and 1971, the difference between urban and rural growth rates was only 1.4 percent per year compared to an average of 2.94 percent for all less developed nations, according to United Nations estimates.[10] If future urbanization in Indonesia proceeds at a rate similar to the average for less developed nations, the urban population will grow to 71 million in 2000. Such growth is likely to severely tax the cities' abilities to provide employment, housing, and other services.

The realization that the rural population will continue to grow for the rest of this century and the expected difficulty of absorbing the rural excess in the

ċities has led to increased government concern for re-
settling some of the population living in the high density
areas of Java and Bali to low density areas in the outer
islands. Suratman and Guinness report that the government is planning to increase its goal of settling 250,000
families during Repelita II to 500,000 families during
Repelita III.[11] Given an average family size of five for
transmigrant families, the goal of Repelita II, when expressed as a rate of migration and continued through the
year 2000, would yield to a net transfer of 8 million
people from Java and Bali to the outer islands. If this
migration were a substitute for rural to urban migration,
it would reduce urban growth by an amount equal to approximately 60 percent of the difference between the low
and medium projections of urban growth. If the higher
goals being planned for Repelita III could be realized,
the transfer of people to the outer islands would be
greater than the difference between the two urban projections. However, there is no reason to suspect that the
people who would move to the transmigration settlements
are the same ones who would move to the city if transmigration were not available, so that urbanization may
continue even if transmigration is successful.

There are also serious doubts about whether the government will be able to realize its transmigration goals
given the past history of transmigration programs. Gov-
ernment-induced migration schemes were initiated at the
turn of the century when the Dutch began a program of re-
settling farmers from Java in Sumatra in 1905. A full-
scale transmigration program was not undertaken, however,
until 1932, and aside from some protracted interruptions
in the 1940s, transmigration schemes continue to be supported by the Indonesian government. Thus, between 1905
and 1975, a total of 809,000 persons were resettled from
Java and Bali to the outer islands with official government assistance. Types of transmigration assistance have
varied, but usually included transportation for the family, the provision of two hectares of land at the destination and some help with housing, food, and other necessities of life until the first harvest. In addition to
these sponsored transmigrants, there were spontaneous
transmigrants who received land and whatever assistance
the local transmigration officials were willing to give,
and other migrants who settled on unused land outside the
transmigration areas. Only the sponsored transmigrants
are counted in the official statistics.

Before 1960, most of the transmigrants went to Sumatra, but since then there has been an increasing trend
towards resettlement in the other islands. Thus, between
1970 and 1975, 41 percent of the transmigrants went to
Sulawesi and Kalimantan. There has also been some increase in the volume of transmigration in recent years.
Nevertheless, to date the transmigration program has not

been very successful in transferring excess population from Java to the outer islands. The total movement of 809,000 persons is only slightly more than 1 percent of the estimated population of 86 million in Java and Bali in 1975. If allowance is made for the natural increase of transmigrants, this figure rises to about 1,135,000.[11] However, based upon data concerning return migration patterns it can be assumed that around 14 percent of the original transmigrants returned to Java or Bali, reducing thereby the above total to 976,000 or 1.1 percent of the population of Java and Bali.

In brief, while official government policy as reflected in Repelita II and the preliminary goals for Repelita III calls for further increases in transmigration, past experience would suggest that the targets will be difficult to achieve. The government is likely to continue to encounter unavoidable delays in conducting the necessary soil surveys and in obtaining clear rights to the land. Likewise, the logistics of providing the necessary services to support such a resettlement effort will require a sizeable improvement in the administrative capacities of local government agencies. Transmigration programs could probably be expanded and made more successful by focusing more attention on the selection and preparation of suitable land in the outer provinces, with less attention being devoted to the selection and financing of migrants. This shift in policy from sponsored to spontaneous migration would seem to be supported by a record of past experience with spontaneous migrants being more likely to possess the characteristics needed to make a success out of farming in the frontier settlements of the outer islands.

NOTES

1. Everett Lee, "A Theory of Migration," Demography 3, no. 1 (1966): 45-47.

2. Much of the work upon which this chapter is based was conducted while the author was a Population Council staff associate assigned to the Population Studies Center, National Institute of Economic and Social Research, Indonesia Institute of Sciences (LEKNAS-LIPI) in Jakarta, from September 1774 to July 1976. The author is grateful to the Population Studies Center for their assistance with the work and their permission to publish these materials. Some portions of the text have been drawn from a report by Suharso, Alden Speare, Jr., Han R. Redmann, and Imron Husin, Rural-Urban Migration in Indonesia (Jakarta: LEKNAS-LIPI, 1976).

3. The LEKNAS survey was conducted in 24 cities and 25 villages within 10 provinces of Indonesia. Within each city a representative sample was selected of all households containing persons, aged 15 and over, who had moved into the city within the preceding five years. A total of 17,046 migrants from these households were

interviewed. Since the survey was a household survey, those migrants who were homeless or who were living in squatter settlements, not included in the administrative system of the selected cities, were not represented.

4. See Graemo J. Hugo, "Population Mobility in West Java, Indonesia" (Ph.D. thesis, Australian National University, 1975), and Suharso et al., Rural-Urban Migration in Indonesia, pp. 92-110.

5. Although the LEKNAS survey did not include a sample of urban residents, it is possible to compare the migrants with the total urban population enumerated in the 1971 census. The data are not completely comparable because the census failed to adequately classify economic activities for about 10 percent of the adult urban population. A second difficulty in such a comparison arises from the differences in the age distribution of migrants and the total urban population. Because migrants are younger, on the average, than the resident urban population it is reasonable to expect a higher proportion of migrants to be in school. Thus, in order to control for these differences in age, there is a need to standardize the urban population on the age distribution of the migrant population. The results of this standardization does not greatly change the distribution of economic activities among the urban population. The major changes are a decrease in the proportion working, an increase in the proportion going to school, and a small increase in the proportion seeking work. These changes occur for both males and females.

6. Sajogyo, et al., Usaha Perbaikan Gizi Keluarga (Bogor: Lembaga Penelitian Sosiologi Pedesaan, 1974).

7. Han R. Redmana, Hazel V. J. Moir, and Daliyo, Labor Force and Labor Utilization in Selected Areas in Java: Results of an Experimental Survey (Jakarta: LEKNAS-LIPI, 1977).

8. Alden Speare, Jr., "Alternative Population Distribution Policies for Indonesia" (Paper presented at the annual meeting of the Population Association of America in St. Louis, April 1977).

9. United Nations, Trends and Prospects in Urban and Rural Population, 1950-2000, As Assessed in 1973-74 (New York: Population Division, 1975).

10. Suratman and Patrick Guinness, "The Changing Focus of Transmigration," Bulletin of Indonesian Economic Studies 13, no. 2 (July 1977): 102-116.

11. This figure is based on a similar calculation made by Jones for the 1932-1974 period in Gavin Jones, "Recent Developments and the Transmigration Program," in Robin Pryor, ed., Migration and Development in Southeast Asia: A Demographic Perspective (Singapore: Oxford University Press, 1978).

12
Transmigration and
Marginal Land Development

Arthur J. Hanson

Transmigration can be considered as one element in
a broad framework of critically important experiments for
marginal land utilization in Indonesia.[1] It is linked,
of course, to the pressing problems of rural crowding on
Java and Bali and is sometimes still seen as the answer
to Java's population growth problems, although such a
view can no longer be seriously entertained. Perhaps
more importantly, resettlement is increasingly being
linked to upland watershed management on Java (through
selective movement of people out of critical upland
areas) and to regional development off Java. Transmigration efforts have always been closely linked to political
winds, the more so since independence. As a consequence,
programs have been subject to rash decision-making that
sometimes bears little relevance either to area ecology,
to technical and economic feasibility, or to the social
needs of transmigrants and the local population. Limited
management skills at the local and central government
level have also held back progress in land settlement.
These problems not only frequently ruined past projects
but, as will be discussed, have plagued even some of the
most recent well-funded efforts in resettlement.
Transmigration is only one of several pathways to
an expanded agricultural base on the outer islands. Estate cash crops, large scale rice estates, and expansions
by existing smallholders are alternative approaches which
could be considered competitive for the best lands.
While future efforts in transmigration stand a better
chance of success, it is important to realize the implications of any widespread failure in the present programs.
First, it will deal a heavy blow to concepts of smallholder agriculture in new land development, since the
projects do offer a means of marshalling the most intensive levels of management available. Secondly, donor
agencies which are now very interested in prospects of
transmigration, are likely to redirect the flow of both
funding and foreign technical advisors into other options.

Resettlement projects have been defined to provide tests of transmigration under a variety of ecological situations, including fire-disturbed upland grasslands, upland forest, lowland forest, and swamp-forest, on Sumatra, Kalimantan, and Sulawesi. Of these major islands, Sumatra will clearly be the site of the most experimentation. Its provinces will be linked by a highway running along the foothills from Aceh to Lampung in the coming decade. People will be settled along it wherever there is access and suitable land. By contrast, the vast swamplands along the eastern coast are readily accessible only by boat from the coast or riverine cities, particularly Palembang. Land development options can be sharply differentiated into those suitable for peneplain areas, often on red-yellow podzolic soils, and those suitable for swampy lowlands (either with mineral or organic soils). The former can be used for a variety of upland crops. The hope for the swampy soils, of course, is rice cultivation.

These ecological differences hold for other islands as well as for Sumatra. In almost every situation there are severe soil fertility constraints, or other difficult development conditions. It should be noted, however, that many indigenous shifting or settled agricultural systems have evolved in relation to these conditions. The striking feature throughout both upland and lowland zones is the degree of local variation in ecological conditions. Areas of moderate to high fertility are interspersed between areas with soil, flood, or drainage problems. Furthermore, even in relatively fertile areas, poor management practices can lead to rapid environmental degradation and land abandonment.

To such lands the government, as recently as 1966, projected the movement of up to two million families per year onto farms of one to five hectares. The general pattern has been the promulgation of plans far in excess of either managerial or fiscal capacity, followed by rapid retrenchment to much more modest goals. Even these more modest goals were rarely met in the past. The projection for 1978 was to resettle 50,000 families, and this number is still considered to be at the pilot project level, in comparison to long-term projections of 100,000 to 250,000 families per year. Optimists, who see this level of settlement as a viable possibility, infer that transmigration agricultural development could thereby largely eliminate the need for rice and other food imports, as well as produce various cash crops for export. The range of issues facing planners involved with agricultural land development for transmigration will be examined by first discussing the prospects for outer island resettlement in swampland areas, followed by an analysis of transmigration potential in the upland areas.

II

The coastal swamplands of Indonesia are mainly
freshwater swamp forest with a mangrove fringe covering
only about 20 percent of the area. The mangrove swamps
are unsuitable for rice cultivation without very expensive reclamation and water works construction. In any
case, they are far from worthless in their natural
state--providing important forest products to local residents, and serving as an essential nursery habitat for
migratory fish and shrimp. It is the peat swamp forest
lands which are of interest for development rather than
the mangrove. These swamps are inaccessible, fragile
ecosystems, which leads one to question the rationale behind their choice for land development by transmigrants.

Where government-sponsored settlers would be wel-
come, and what they should do once they settle, have always been problems. In great measure, the answer arises
from the fact that the best lands in the upland areas are
already under use by local residents. In these areas,
traditional adat law gives land management rights to con-
tiguously spaced local units of government such as
marga.[2] Where these rights have been exercised (e.g. by
shifting cultivators) the problem of alienating land becomes more severe. Thus, in general, the upland areas in
Sumatra present a difficult situation for settlement of
land rights. In addition, the early settlements in the
upland area of Lampung have been based on the assumption
that Javanese farmers would only settle if they could
manage irrigated rice fields. Nevertheless, new irrigation systems have proved to be expensive and often unstable. Thus, it is perhaps almost inevitable that the
lowland swamps, with large tracts of forest still intact,
would become attractive for those searching for new areas
to plant the world's most important swamp grass.

The roots of coastal swampland agricultural development actually extend well past the short history of the
Republic of Indonesia, and even the period of Dutch interest in transmigration. Well-adapted planting techniques and schedules for avoiding salt or flood water
risk have been evolved over centuries of swampland rice
and coconut cultivation by Banjars in South Kalimantan
and by marga residents and Bugis in Riau, Jambi, and
South Sumatra. The Banjars took advantage of hand-dug
Dutch navigation canals, but serious government interest
and limited soil surveys into the swamplands began only
in the 1920s. The evolution of a pasang surut rice cultivation program from that point documents the enduring
attraction of these wetlands for both Dutch and Indonesian engineers.[3] It is also a history closely linked to
transmigration since 1937. From the earliest consideration of rice-field development the emphasis has been on

creating technologically more advanced adaptations of the traditional techniques of land development.

A brief chronology of swampland transmigration plans and development activities reveals five major periods of activity: (1) the pre-World War II surveys and limited settlement by transmigrants in Kalimantan; (2) planning, but very limited implementation, of a gigantic Kalimantan polder system, between 1948 and 1953; (3) the shift to more simple canal systems (no pumps or water control valves) in a 1957 Department of Public Works plan that would have opened 1.5 million hectares of tidally-influenced swamplands in Sumatra and Kalimantan over a fifteen year period; (4) the development of a plan in 1967-68 to open virtually the full 5,250,000 hectares of tidally-influenced swampland over a fifteen year time span, and a later total cut back to 500,000 hectares over the First Five Year Plan (Repelita I, 1969-1974); (5) the expansion of the Repelita I pilot projects to 1,000,000 hectares during Repelita II (1974-79), a plan then cut back to 250,000 hectares.

By the standard of meeting their original goals, none of the schemes could be considered very successful. However, it may be argued that the failures have been a result of over-optimistic projections which were, in turn, influenced by the many perturbations to Indonesian land-use planning over this forty year time span. Based on this past experience, a basic question arises concerning the future prospects for implementing an effective transmigration program in the swampland areas. Reviewing the development potential of the swamplands in the province of South Sumatra, the agronomist of an FAO Land and Water Resource Development Team presented a predominately negative view in his comments on settler activities (Bugis, local residents, and recently-arrived transmigrants);

> . . . It is inevitable that with the disappearance of the organic matter in the top layers of the soil by oxidation through too rapid drainage, yields of their rice crops will fall. Some earn supplementary cash by woodcutting and fishing and the latter should be encouraged to increase protein supplied for themselves and for the inhabitants of Palembang.
>
> The technical ability of these farmers is insufficient to master the management standards necessary for preserving the little fertility which now exists in the soil and to prevent deterioration.
>
> Education and health facilities are also insufficient and there is a danger that these and other similar settlers will face severe

hardship with little or no opportunity for
advancement. Thought must be given to the
possibility for resettlement elsewhere should
conditions deteriorate further. Civil officials must be highly active in their advisory
work here with emphasis on practical methods
for crop improvement involving little or no
expenditure. Such things as seed selection,
seed dressings, planting rice in lines, field
sanitation in weed and pest control, all cost
little actual cash but all contribute to higher income. Farmers should be encouraged to
plant off-season crops of vegetables, etc.
Off-season rice is not recommended as all irrigation water is highly saline. . .[4]

The above viewpoint is a dangerously negative one in
that it fails to appreciate differences in settler adaptations and the environmental heterogeneity of the coastal environment. Both can be used to good advantage in
designing the unconventional agricultural systems needed
for marginal lands. The swamplands of Sumatra and Kalimantan are peat lens formed on top of a marine clay. The
clay oxidizes to an acid sulphate soil if it dries out,
but is a reasonably good basal layer for rice cultivation
if kept moist. The peat layer can be used for rice if it
is less than about 1.5 meters in depth. Thicker layers
(up to 4 or 5 meters in Riau) are not fertile, nor do
they provide particularly good support for deep rooted
crops. There is also considerable local variation in
soil conditions. As a result, fertilizer and other soil
conditioning recommendations are controversial and often
show inconsistent results. But local people and Bugis
migrants, using very simple cultivation and drainage
methods, earn a substantial living. They adapt to very
localized flood and salt intrusion patterns and realize
that floods in these unique coastal habitats are not a
severe threat (in contrast to Java and to the more inland
flood-plains of Sumatra). They also spread risks by engaging in more than one type of activity.
Programs undertaken by the government employ a very
simple technology of constructing canals of up to 30
meters wide and 5 meters deep, both to drain the swamps
and to provide irrigation water from the rivers in flood
season. The system allows an exchange of water because
tidal movement results in a backup of river water for
distances up to 100 kilometers upstream (although tidal
irrigation, in general, is limited to about 30 to 50
kilometers from the sea). These canals, of course, also
allow penetration of brackish water if they are too near
estuarine conditions.
The cost element in these projects has always fig-
ured prominently, since the scale of development envi-

sioned inflates even modest unit cost figures to an enormous overall sum. Mechanized techniques for canal construction had been considered from the 1930s, with primary reliance being placed on closed canal systems requiring pumping. Current government plans eschew the use of pumps, at least for the initial stage, primarily as an economy measure. Of course, total expenditure is not a particularly sensitive guide for choice among projects if there are ecological, time, or social and economic differences likely to influence long-term use prospects, alternative uses, or the internal rate of return on investment. In comparison to other kinds of water resource development in Sumatra, the tidal rice program ranks below more conventional forms of irrigation in standard benefit-cost or internal rate of return analyses.

Regional development, and the establishment of growth poles off Java have become the predilection of Indonesian planners over the past several years. Regional development is a principal justification for transmigration programs, and regional planning the theoretically sound answer for coordinated management of natural resources, transportation, and marketing needs. Obviously, the pasang surut development effort could be considered supportive of both agricultural sectoral goals and regional development goals. Another element in regional development is the improvement of security and avoidance of disturbances in sensitive areas. The government is anxious to settle transmigrants in such areas in order to reduce opportunities for illegal activities. In the coastal zone, particularly at isolated outposts and in the network of swampland channels of rivers, there are opportunities for many kinds of smuggling. These considerations have been factors in the emphasis on coastal region development.

A final point in the analysis of why there should be such a commitment to coastal swampland-use relates to the strong role of the Department of Public Works in the plans. The historical association of this department with the various pasang surut projects is as old as the Republic. Public Works (PUTL) at present controls 40 percent of the development budget and is the best organized unit for physically implementing land or water development projects. There is no one land development agency in the country. Responsibility is generally split among at least three or four departments. Each department has favoured projects, for which it takes primary responsibility and is assisted by the other departments to the degree they can, or are willing, to participate. PUTL has taken primary responsibility for the pasang surut program as its special activity, and argued forcefully for its implementation. In total land area opened, PUTL has also been able to show results which are convincing in comparison to the efforts of other departments.

A remarkable number of studies are underway on tidal irrigation projects and there is real hope that differences of opinion will soon be resolved in determining whether investments in this area will yield substantial returns. Over the long run, assessing the success or failure of the latest swampland ricefield projects will be relatively simple if examined in the most basic terms: will the areas sustain populations and produce rice yields averaging at least 2 to 2.5 tons per hectare each year? The projects might be considered successful and worthy of replication if these goals could be met, even where there is relatively low internal rates of return (since multiple objectives are involved, and since possibilities exist for secondary activities not included in economic analyses to date).

There is now a sufficient data base to provide at least a partial answer to the above question and, by inference, to the broader one of whether agricultural development in these areas has a hope of curbing Indonesia's greater than one million ton average annual rice import. In the Delta Upang area, a transmigration site in the province of South Sumatra, rice yields have not met targets since only one crop has been grown per year when two were expected. The reasons for single-cropping are primarily related to dry season water shortage and pests. Nevertheless, yields have remained at a reasonable level five to seven years after cultivation first began. Although farmers are rice exporters from this delta region, moving to a higher output will prove to be very difficult since crop responses to fertilizers have not been good. Developing the necessary field level water control, pest control, and scheduling for a second crop, will likely take a decade of intensive field experimentation.

Regional differences in land quality will constitute a major obstacle to rapid agricultural development in other swampland areas in Sumatra. While reasonable and sustainable yields appear possible in the shallow, eutrophic peat and muck soils near the major rivers of South Sumatra, the vast area of deeper oligotrophic peats in the provinces of Riau and Jambi probably have only limited potential as rice fields.

Under an optimistic assumption that 500,000 hectares of good fields (300,000 hectares in Sumatra) could be opened over the next fifteen years, a rice surplus of perhaps 750,000 metric tons could be produced under reasonable intensive management (the average annual import level between 1970-1975 was 940,000 metric tons per year). This production level might be obtained from only about 250,000 hectares if double cropping could be established. Thus, the swampland development program could significantly influence food policy over a long time span. The impact would be much greater if the Bugis settlers and local inhabitants expand and intensify production (with or without government assistance). While the total swampland area in Sumatra and Kalimantan is perhaps in excess of ten million hectares, about five million of which are tidally-influenced, the accumulating information on soils and existing land-use patterns suggest that only a very small fraction is likely to have potential for rice cultivation. Thus, an expansion of ricefields onto at most, one million hectares, may be an eventual upper limit to development.

From a broader environmental perspective, successful swampland development involves elements other than rice production. Ecologically destructive activities are initiated with forest cutting and canal construction. If the degradation process proceeds at a rate which exceeds the combined beneficial effects of natural regenerative capacity and local management capabilities, the area is likely to be abandoned. This constitutes a major resource and environmental problem. A second possible type of problem is the impact of development on resources outside the purview of the project. For example, will the agricultural development affect estuarine fisheries? In brief, while immediate project goals may be met, there could be major side-effects.

Intuitively, the following ranking of environmentally-related objectives for successful swampland area development would seem likely: (1) persistence of settlement with specified minimum standards of living (e.g. year-round potable water supply, low incidence of transmitted diseases, adequate accommodation); (2) grain self-sufficiency and export of some commodities; (3) social stability among settler groups; (4) sustained yield of harvestable natural resource products besides the normal plant crops such as rice; (5) development of efficient and stable physical infrastructure; (6) preservation of areas of special concern according to specified use restrictions; (7) minimization of project externalities to other resources and elements of the coastal ecosystem; (8) preservation of existing cultural patterns of resource use; (9) minimization of wildlife losses. The degree to which many of these broad objectives can be met by individual transmigration projects without a strong regional planning and monitoring program is questionable. However, the area-based projects do provide a unique focus for a wide range of program activities. Theoretically, at least, the projects could become a base for creating multiple resource-use strategies and for working with both local farmers and transmigrants on the highly specialized techniques needed for their management.

III

The existing condition of upland shifting cultivation in South Sumatra has been summarized as follows:

Rainfed farming of crops other than paddy
(wetland) rice in the study area mainly consists of a form of shifting rotation around
a settlement site. A tree crop (usually rubber) is established with catch crops being
grown for the first three years. Catch crops
include upland rice (padi ladang) which is
often grown together with maize, groundnuts,
beans, chillies, cassava, sweet potato, banana,
and pineapple. Original opening of the land
involves the felling of trees and bushes, collection and burning of debris, uprooting or
burning out of stumps, second clearing, re-
burning, and finally hoeing. The land is
cleared during the dry season (June to September) in most cases by hand, using axe, parang,
and hoe. Seed selection is rudimentary (winnowing or floatation), and most seeds are local
varieties saved from the previous year's crop.
Nurseries are seldom constructed and planting
methods are primitive, planting material being
dibbled or hoed in.

Planting usually starts in September or October
according to the onset of the rains and is carried out by the farmer and his family without
external help. Use of fertilizer is rare, although better farmers use compost, urea, and
superphosphate. Hand weeding is undertaken at
least twice, with weeds being either used as
compost for bananas or left on the field. Poisonous baits and close fencing protect catch
crops against pigs, monkeys, and rats; but in-
sect pests and plant diseases are rarely controlled. Harvesting is by traditional hand
methods which are both labour and time consuming. Catch crops are inter-cropped with rubber
for about three years, after which the rubber
is allowed to grow wild. Tapping starts when
the trees are four to five years old and continues until they are about 15 years old when
the rubber and secondary growth are cleared
and burned and the whole cycle renewed. A
farmer and his family seldom cultivate more than
3 hectares per year due to restrictions because
of lack of man, animal, or machine power. The
majority of catch crops is used for home con-

sumption with sufficient planting material
being reserved for the following year's crop.
Any remaining product is sold at the local
market or to buyers from the large towns.
Prices, however, are generally low because
uniform harvest times for each product throughout the area result in glut market periods . . .[5]

This cycle of shifting cultivation can become limiting in several ways. One, of course, is when increasing
population forces people onto lands of lower fertility or
into shorter cycles of cultivation. Second, uncontrolled
burning occurs with the land opening, especially during
the occasional very dry years (one year in five). The
third set of limiting factors include rapid soil erosion
and/or decline in fertility, both often associated with
severe seed invasions. Finally, in many areas of Indonesia, the blocks of remaining upland forest are becoming
increasingly small and scattered, reducing the water
storage function of the uplands and, thereby, further
creating limits in agricultural activities.

Certainly no hope exists for irrigating most areas
of the uplands in Sumatra, although wet rice cultivation
occurs in river valley areas. Past attempts to initiate
new upland irrigation schemes in areas like Lampung have
been delayed or never completed. Current debate focuses
on cropping systems which, for the most part, must be
adapted to rainfed conditions.

Soil scientists who have surveyed the red-yellow
podzolic uplands agree on two important conclusions.
First, there is a great deal of variation in natural soil
fertility. Second, the units suitable for intensive upland crop-use tend to be fairly small. Thus, accurate
land capability analysis prior to settlement is essential. Complicated patterns involving tree crops, intensive and extensive food crop cultivation, and fodder production, are frequently recommended. In each case fairly
high doses of chemical and organic fertilizer as well as
a carefully planned annual schedule of cultivation are
considered essential. This scheduling is complicated by
the need to bring land into production over a number of
years, requiring transmigrants to alter their mix of activities each year for five to eight years from initial
land opening. As a consequence, the stream of benefits
to the farmer will not directly correlate with their activities each year. Certainly in the early years there
would be little opportunity for reducing risk by harvesting a variety of crop types, as done by existing small-
holders in the uplands.

These problems come into focus in Baturaja, a transmigration site in Sumatra, which is absorbing 4,500 families on five hectare plots as a prototype settlement for
the uplands. At least three upland transmigration models

have been proposed and could be tested at this site. Of these models, the World Bank model of staged rubber planting with mainly subsistence food cropping is perhaps the most complex in sequence of land development. Within the Province of South Sumatra alone, more than one million hectares of marginal lands are considered suitable for tree crops. Hence, the high level of interest and funding in this project is understandable. However, whether good results will be achievable, even on a pilot scale, is difficult to predict.

Possible complications at an upland site like Baturaja include both social-economic and ecological factors. Timely delivery of inputs, such as fertilizer, will be a major element in determining success, as crop growing depends very much on the gradual build-up of soil fertility. So far there has been little attention given to the possibilities of micronutrient deficiencies which appear to be a serious limiting factor at least in some swampland sites. Given Indonesia's nitrogen fertilizer surplus (mostly produced near Palembang) and the availability of limestone in the old terrace formations along the uplands of Sumatra, trials should be conducted with an eye to ensuring ecological success (i.e. sustained yields) rather than economic efficiency alone. This implies that risk be shifted from farmers to the government through subsidized inputs.

The problems of supplying seed and cattle may be less severe than for supplying fertilizer and advice on cycles of land cultivation. In Baturaja, rubber plantings will be conducted in cooperation with a government estate enterprise. This organization has access to improved trees and has expertise in appropriate planting techniques. Access to improved seed stock for food crops is not a critical constraint, although appropriate selection of what those varieties should be is. Cattle will be supplied over a long time span and cannot be guaranteed to give short-term benefits over the first five years.

Even with the most ideal inputs to improve soil and to supply good plant genetic material, the upland transmigrant farmer will still face a gauntlet of hazards which may destroy conceptually good project plans. These hazards include pest outbreaks, the likelihood of a serious dry year over the early years of tree planting, fluctuation (and low share) in market price of the basic cash crop, and difficulties in obtaining sufficient income during the early years of cultivation before trees can be tapped.

This brief description of upland transmigration areas serves to bring out several important differences with transmigration conditions in other areas. In upland areas, farmers will, in a sense, be starting with a strike against them, in that they are coming into an already degraded environment. There is no assurance of at

least a few seasons of the reasonable soil fertility
typical of land development in virgin forest areas. The
transmigrants are receiving a very large land area for a
single family on the assumption that more can be managed
than in developing an irrigated rice system. Their dependence on government assistance is much greater since
their food crops cannot bring much income in comparison
to quick-yielding lowland ricefields. Furthermore, they
face even greater hazards than lowland farmers in establishing dry season crops.

Viewed from broader human ecology perspectives, upland development could be a valuable focal point for introducing concepts of environmental management and resource conservation. Malaria control programs may become
established and the new settlements could provide good
incentives for devising a simple means of increasing domestic water supply for large areas during the limiting
dry season condition. As in the case of the swamplands,
the upland transmigrant-farms could become important
areas for introducing various forms of animal husbandry,
including fish culture. Over time they could make fuller
use of the available water resources through impoundments
and irrigation to a portion of the lands. Through such
water control activities, and by planting trees on steep
slopes, the problems of erosion and downstream sedimenta-
tion may be somewhat reduced. This goal has to be considered a very long-term secondary one, unlike the situation in Java where erosion control is a primary goal of
upland programs. A difference in this perspective is the
low priority given to terracing the uplands of South Sumatra. This level of expense is rarely justified. On
the other hand, the possibility exists for paying transmigrants to plant and maintain pine plantations as part
of reforestation efforts in Sumatra.

Earlier in the paper it was indicated that concern
over interactions with already established farmers in the
uplands was one factor which made swampland settlement
attractive. In fact, strictly from the point of view of
transmigration project implementation, these problems appear manageable. The most serious issue is conflicting
land claims. Traditional claims are generally not recorded and, in the case of shifting cultivators, are
sometimes tenuous. There is a willingness to compensate
valid claimholders, although it is difficult to know how
this works in practice. In the past, transmigrants themselves were lucky to receive official documents within a
period of several years. This situation has improved.
It is ironic, in fact, that the transmigrants are perhaps the only group to have certain hold on the land.

There are other resource conflicts, especially those
associated with grazing lands. Animals are still re-
leased onto some of these areas despite the presence of
transmigrants. A more fundamental problem is the degree

to which resettlement programs may disrupt traditional
cycles of extensive land use. If traditional settlers
are ineligible for, or cannot relate their needs to government programs, yet must compress shifting cultivation
areas or time cycles, rapid ecological degradation could
be predicted in the vicinity of transmigration settlements. Thus, equal attention to local area resident
needs is essential in upland development activities.

IV

With good management, careful site selection, reasonable levels of funding, and adequate attention to the
needs and rights of existing settlers groups, transmigration into marginal environments undoubtedly could lead to
stabilized agricultural communities. In recent years, a
financing equivalent of $5,000 to $10,000 per family has
been available for some schemes. Money then, is not
likely to be such a critical limiting factor as it has
been in the past. The elements which may have the most
important bearing on future success or failure are:
(1) the social and ecological consequences of inadequate
project planning and evaluation; (2) structural and programming problems in the existing implementing and management agencies; (3) the influence of large-scale
foreign involvement in funding and technical assistance
with projects.

Motives are important to keep in mind for any large-
scale program of land-use expansion. While in theory
transmigration is a mechanism for regional development
that should be geared to help all settler groups, it is
also a powerful mechanism to exert central government influence over territories that are still under very local
systems of control. Implicit in the transmigration
philosophy is a gradual erosion of the administrative and
regulatory powers of the marga. Competitive claims of
many sorts are inevitable. What may be most critical is
the degree to which the local leaders' reasonably well-
developed concern for multiple uses and long-term management strategies is lost as single-purpose, poorly-coordi-
nated, central government agencies exert control. Typically, local authorities abdicate (or fear to exert)
their established regulatory powers once development begins. Decisions on the forest, land, and water resources
formerly made by one leader and a local council now become lost in a morass of government agencies with varying
levels of interest and capacity to implement plans.

This situation is most evident in lands surrounding
transmigration sites where the impact of project activity, but not assistance, are felt. For example, once local control over forest-use is relinquished, forest cutting occurs without regard for boundaries of any sort

(including government concessions). Local residents and
self-sponsored settlers, like the Bugis, do require access to services, although the package inputs developed
for transmigrants are generally not of interest to them.
Certain elements of existing packages are essential, however, to avoid land abandonment. Advice on weed competition problems is one important ecological example.

Ecological and social consequences, which feed back
to project viability as instabilities of production, social order and permanence of settlement, have additional
dimensions within the boundaries of the project area. In
some marginal ecosystems, good income and nutritional
levels will be met only through exploitation of a wide
range of resources and multiple cropping. Thus, an intensive and integrated philosophy of area development
programming is required. Fisheries, forestry, erosion
control, optimal crop scheduling, and careful monitoring
of all essential factors important in land abandonment
require attention.

The promise of transmigration as a regional development mechanism is the eventual strengthening of project
planning and implementation to the point where the resources in an area can be utilized on a rational and sustained basis, and where the necessary transport and marketing of products can be assured. This level of coordinated effort has rarely taken place in the past. Certainly the necessary interdepartmental cooperation and
particularly the coordinated timing of decisions and activities has not been exemplary. Within departments the capacity to identify critical points and pathways for successful projects is highly variable. The Department of
Public Works (PUTL) is far advanced in this capacity in
comparison to other government agencies. Even within
PUTL, however, there is not a full capacity to make use
of the existing information base (e.g. land-use interpretation from remote sensing information). The pressure
for rapid results and for simultaneous involvement in
many regions, plus the persistent setting of overall
goals on an order of magnitude beyond implementation capacity, leads to a sense of mistrust on the part of other
government units that any worthwhile goals can be met
and sometimes leads to decisions that create ecological
and social disruptions.

Some of the planning and evaluation problems could
be overcome by adding well-trained staff at central, provincial, and local project levels. There is also a need
to broaden the conceptual base of the projects beyond the
simple dimensions of rudimentary physical infrastructure
for mono-crop agriculture. Clearly there are some excellent hopes for the future in these directions. The involvement of both central universities (especially Bogor
Agricultural University, the Bandung Institute of Technology and Gadjah Mada University) and provincial universi-

ties has stimulated and aided the management agencies.
The rapid strengthening of government research institutes
over the next decade will largely ensure that the necessary specialist knowledge-base now lacking will be available.

In the coming years a basis may be created for the
absolutely essential implementation of area-specific experimentation, extension, and monitoring activities. At
present, provincial level advisors and research units
cover too many situations to be effective in any one.
What is needed are test centers capable of interpreting
data from specialized social and ecological conditions
within specific geographic zones. This analysis could
then be used in the design and adaptation of government
programs. In the narrowest sense, initial efforts of
this kind are coming into existence as test farms and experimental stations on some transmigration sites. Clearly needed are more comprehensive units which might include specialists in forestry and fisheries, and social
scientists capable of developing programs with non-
transmigrants. Besides this commitment to adaptive
analysis and services, a change in the present limited
time involvement of the development project agencies is
required. The present objective is to transfer projects
to routine management after five years. Instead, there
needs to be a long-term commitment of perhaps fifteen to
twenty years during which plans would be modified as management capacity and understanding of the area's needs
increase.

Discussion of programmatic changes inevitably leads
to the question of structural changes in the complex Indonesian bureaucracy. There is no single land develop-
ment/management agency which could provide overall direction. Instead, there is heavy reliance on interdepartmental coordinating committees. In practice, not only are
functions split among agencies, but also the balance of
authority differs among projects. In the Baturaja project primary coordination lies with the Department of
Transmigration but in swampland development it lies with
PUTL. The intensity of involvement by the Department of
Agriculture often seems linked to self-initiated projects
rather than those jointly carried out with PUTL. Theoretically, the Interior Ministry and BAPPENAS could take
an active coordinating role. Clearly, however, there is
not the technical capacity in either unit, although the
Interior Ministry has apparently greatly improved the
processing of transmigrant land claims.

The Department of Public Works is gradually assuming
a more dominant role in physical planning as their superior technical skills are becoming recognized. There
will likely be less emphasis on site planning in the Department of Transmigration now that a Directorate of Land
Development in PUTL is operational. The range of activi-

ties conducted by PUTL and the receptiveness to funding
and then follow-up on a broad range of activities, ranging from regional planning, ecology and broad-based resource management analysis, to test farm activities, is
surprising to foreign advisors familiar with public works
agencies in some other countries. While these strengths
may be used to advantage in planning and project implementation, it seems unlikely that this or any other agency will be allowed to completely dominate in land settlement. Thus, a concerted effort to develop local level
coordination between departmental offices is required to
ensure continuing inputs once the transmigration project
is past the initial phase of settlement.

Regional planning offices at the provincial (Bappe-
da) and district (Bappemka) level should provide this
coordination. These newly-established units are still
weak, and they will remain so until more trained staff
are available to establish their role in the regional
planning process. The opportunity exists to train large
numbers of such staff in fields directly relevant to
transmigration land development. Indonesian universities
are just beginning to offer regional development and land
resource management programs. There will be good feed-
back of information on transmigration activities into
these programs since most of the professors also serve as
senior advisors to one or more such projects. It is essential that such training efforts be intensified. Better cooperative efforts with the many foreign agencies
and advisors involved in land development could improve
these efforts.

The financial backing for transmigration programs
comes from many donor agencies as well as the Indonesian
government. As funds have become more available, management and research tasks have increased disproportionately. As each new project is initiated, the small group of
highly skilled manpower in the private sector and universities are tempted into new obligations such that the
general performance of their institutions are reduced.
Thus, a fundamental question persists concerning the
actual capacity of existing management resources to absorb higher funding levels and further program expansion.

Undoubtedly international development agencies will
continue to focus on transmigration as a means for increasing agricultural output. It will be a temptation to
devise even larger projects which may seem to be directly
benefiting the "poorest of the poor;" (certainly transmigrants generally fall into that category). It would be
a mistake to do so without full consideration for back up
research, as well as educational and ancillary management
activities essential to making these projects successful.
There is far too little coordination among aid agencies
and only a limited perspective, even in the overview provided by World Bank in its project development documents,

(which are perhaps the best analyses available). It would seem highly desirable to have a high level Indonesian and donor agency committee, supported by a small secretariat, which could monitor overall program and budgetary needs as well as provide for information exchange.

By standard economic evaluation or by measurement of short-term impacts on agricultural production, transmigration into the marginal lands of Sumatra and Kalimantan is unlikely to be judged a very successful activity, especially given current levels of management skills for implementation. Albeit expensive, the existing projects are important experiments, even if they are not generally viewed in that perspective. The need to find ecologically-satisfactory solutions to marginal land-use will become increasingly important to Indonesia as highway networks expand and deforestation continues. Equally important will be the need to create adaptive strategies based on human ecology, marketing potential, and other socioeconomic criteria. In most situations, low cost, low technology solutions may ultimately prove superior to massive projects dependent on the large-scale transfer of people over short time periods. If modest, well-conceived projects succeed in holding people and in attracting additional settlers to habitats such as those described in this article, the way may be clear for eventual utilization of the enormous land bank considered potentially available for agricultural development off Java.

NOTES

1. For an ecological description of marginally productive lands with agricultural potential see E. C. J. Mohr, The Soils of Equatorial Regions, with Special Reference to the Netherlands East Indies (Ann Arbor: Edwards Bros., 1944); Clifford Geertz, Agricultural Involution: The Processes of Ecological Change in Indonesia (Berkeley: University of California Press, 1963); P. M. Oriessen and M. Soepraptohardjo, Soils For Agricultural Expansion in Indonesia (Bogor: Bulletin No. 1, Soil Research Institute, 1974).
2. The marga is a resource utilization unit of land and water with its forests and fishes. Use is under the control of a local council and marga chief (pesirah).
3. The term pasang surut is frequently translated as "ebb and flow" referring to the tidal back-up of river water into canals and the subsequent drainage at low tide.
4. F. B. Brown, Land and Water Resources Development in South East Sumatra (Jakarta: Food and Agricultural Organization - Government of Indonesia Agriculture Department, 1972).

Part VII

The Household Economy

Introduction

In recent years, the concern for improving the welfare levels of marginal farmers and landless labor has assumed increasing prominence in the pronouncements of many third world governments and the various international agencies involved in development financing. This is a difficult task to undertake, as little is known about the character of household economies and the patterns of labor allocation among lower income families. It is therefore, not clear where policies and programs should intervene, what problems these efforts should be addressing, and what needs should be given priority in the distribution of services to this particular target group. The government of Indonesia is currently sponsoring a number of public works programs in an effort to alleviate some of the most pressing conditions of unemployment and poverty. A number of credit programs and other services have also been designed to enhance the flow of resources to these households. In general, however, it would appear that the impact of these activities is relatively unknown. It is not clear whether these efforts are responding to the most salient problem areas or whether lower income households are even in a position to avail themselves of these newly proffered services. It would appear, however, that given the narrow resource base from which they must operate, in many instances low income households are forced to settle for short term gains and low returns to labor rather than engaging in higher risk but possibly more lucrative ventures. It is not clear how these resource constraints can be altered by outside intervention and whether more direct or indirect measures can be employed in enabling these households to improve their wage earning capacities.

The following two essays are concerned with examining some of the basic characteristics of household production and consumption for low income families in rural Java. The first essay establishes the importance of the household garden as a major income and food source for

239

those household units which have little or no access to
other agricultural land. In this context, the author
notes that major differences in garden cropping strategies are in evidence between wealthier and lower income
households. Households with access to other agricultural
land are inclined to be more entrepreneurial in the use
of their household gardens by cultivating crops which
yield higher economic returns, whereas lower income families usually engage in less risk-taking in the use of
their gardens in order to assure a stable and steady
source of food for home consumption. In addition, the
intensity of garden cultivation is generally higher among
lower income households, and thereby total output as well
as labor input in garden production is frequently higher
than what is encountered in wealthier households. When
the latter do engage in more intensive garden practices,
it usually involves the growing of more capital intensive
plants, a strategy which serves to yield higher returns
to labor than what is the case for lower income households.

While the household garden constitutes an important
component in the resource base of the low income household, it is not entirely clear how measures to enhance
its productivity could be accommodated within the resource constraints of the household economy. It would
appear that considerable work will need to be devoted to
exploring various cropping strategies which increase garden productivity without adding further burdens in risk
bearing or in the demand for additional capital and
labor.

The second essay addresses the problem of resource
use in low income households from the consumption side of
the production/consumption equation, with attention being
focused on variations in food intake and nutritional requirements. In this context, the analysis begins with
the generally accepted notion that most poor families
suffer from chronic malnutrition, a condition which in
turn fosters low work productivity and high receptivity
to disease and illness. It was soon discovered, however,
that conventional wisdom is less than adequate in explaining patterns of nutrition and human energy levels
within the sampled villages. Thus, the research revealed
no significant differences in levels of nourishment between economic classes, and while members of lower income
families might consume lower calorie intakes, there appeared to be no attendant decline in levels of worker
output. These findings would suggest that levels of food
consumption are conditioned by a wide range of social and
economic variables which seem to, at least partially, neu-
tralize the possible impact of differences in wealth and
income. It is also concluded that levels of consumption
are further mediated by variations in physiologic efficiencies: some individuals are apparently able to derive

more energy from specific levels of food intake than is the case of those who are accustomed to having a larger caloric intake.

The above findings would seem to indicate that the human organism is frequently able to effectuate modes of adaptation which allow for variations in food availability. While further study needs to be undertaken in determining whether these initial research results apply at a more generalized level in rural Java, the preliminary conclusions would suggest that the design of nutrition programs should be tailored to meeting more specified dietary problems. Thus, dietary deficiencies appear to be particularly prevalent at the two extremes of the age spectrum; i.e., the very young and the more elderly, and their needs could be addressed through education and the provision of vitamin and mineral supplements.

13
Garden Use and
Household Economy in Java

Anne L. Stoler

"In the first establishment or formation
of a village or new ground, the intended
settlers take care to provide themselves
with sufficient garden ground round their
huts for stock and to supply the ordinary
wants of their families . . . . He la-
bors to plant and rear in it those vegetables that may be most useful to his
family and those shrubs and trees which
may at once yield him their fruit and
shade; nor does he waste his efforts on
thankless soil."

Raffles, <u>History of Java</u>, 1817

Descriptions of agrarian land types in Indonesia have
tended to focus on distinctions between the intensive
wet-rice ecosystem of Inner Indonesia, and the more extensive swidden systems of the outer islands. Although
home gardens or <u>pekarangan</u> have long been recognized as a
distinctive land use type, they have not received the detailed ecological or sociological attention given to
other Indonesian agricultural systems.

This paper is a preliminary attempt to investigate
the nature and uses of home gardens in the central Javanese village of Kali Loro.[1] Using data collected through
an intensive study of household economy an effort is made
to discern how limitations in access to land influence
the pattern of resource distribution and utilization
within the village. The analysis suggests that differential access to strategic resources, as well as the nature
of the household production unit, must be considered essential factors in explaining variability in garden cultivation.

I

Studies of irrigated rice cultivation have provided the basis for the most detailed work on Javanese rural economy. In spite of this, garden land (<u>pekarangan</u>), which makes up 15 to 75 percent of the cultivable land area, may provide more than 20 percent of household income, and more than 40 percent of a household's caloric requirements. Nonetheless, participation in rice production and the distribution of sawah holdings continue to provide the simplest crude measure of rural stratification. The survival strategy of rural households, however, cannot be understood with reference to participation in rice production alone. In Kali Loro, a survey of 478 households indicated that 6 percent of households own more than half of all the sawah, 37 percent are completely landless, and another 40 percent work sawah areas too small to produce their basic rice requirements. In other words, more than 75 percent of the households have to meet some, or all of their subsistence needs through other means.

In Kali Loro, and Java in general, most villagers are engaged in a multiplicity of occupations to which they allot varying amounts of time and from which they receive varying returns to labor; among these alternate income-producing activities are agricultural wage labor, various forms of market trade, preparation of food for sale, handicraft production, poultry and livestock, and the cultivation of mixed gardens for both income and consumption. Attempts to explain participation in any one of these economic activities (such as home gardening) must take into account the total range of choices available to a household as permitted by class, household composition, and land availability.

Observers from the early nineteenth century on (such as Gelpke, Moll, DeVries, and Vink) have noted the importance of small gardens as safeguards against the scarcities imposed by crop failure, drought, and rural poverty.[2] Pelzer claims that . . . "One of the great advantages of garden culture over field culture is that there is always something ready to harvest from the former and therefore something to sell when money for daily household needs become scarce."[3] From an ecological perspective as well, home gardens are distinct from the dominant system of wet-rice cultivation. Unlike the monocropped sawah field, the tiered plantings of gardens show a tendency toward ecological imitation of forest structures, rather than transformation of the environment. Pelzer distinguishes three levels, or "storeys" of the mixed gardens; a ground floor made up of tuberous shade-tolerant plants, a middle storey of taller growing plants and small, fast-growing trees (such as banana and papaya), and an upper storey formed of tall fruit trees.[4]

Javanese home-gardens have two common ecological features. They are dominated by perennials rather than annuals, and by woody rather than herbaceous growth.[5] Secondly, they are characterized by a closed structure (provided by tall fruit and timber trees) most evident among the densely planted and gradated mixed gardens of Central Java. This closed-canopy structure functions to lessen the impact of heavy rains on the soil, reduces soil temperatures, and controls erosion and weed growth. Although the soil and water requirements of gardens are less demanding than those of sawah, both land-use types can be considered 'maintenance systems,' i.e., they provide sustained yields and cause minimal environmental degradation under continuous use. In preserving this "harvestable forest" home-gardens often lack the orderly appearance of other forms of cultivation.[6] They seem an haphazard array of scattered trees, untended plants, crawling vines, and decaying vegetation. In fact, the lack of orderly rows and clean-swept vegetation is precisely what allows pekarangan to produce its own natural fertilizers, and remain erosion-free even in critical watershed areas of poor land use. This multi-levelled "disorder" functions in part to prevent unnecessary organic wastage found under other systems of cultivation. Seen from this perspective, mixed gardens appear to be ecologically and economically viable components of rural livelihood. The fact that "variation and quantity dominate over the modern demands for uniformity and quality" is particularly adaptive to the rural Javanese setting.[7]

From a nutritional viewpoint, plant diversity is equally beneficial. Gardens provide essential sources of supplementary vegetable protein to the diet and readily available sources of Vitamin A and C. The medicinal value of roots, herbs, and leaves is common knowledge to most villagers, and the ingredients for herbal health drinks (jamu) are an essential part of the diet for any pregnant, lactating, menstruating, or ailing woman. Gardens also serve as important sources of various non-food necessities: firewood, animal fodder, building and handicraft materials.

In spite of its ubiquity, usefulness, and general ecological "soundness," gardens have been relatively neglected, both as an object of study in themselves and as a component of village economy. There are a number of reasons for this neglect. Firstly, students of Javanese society tend to focus on those aspects of village life (and particularly those economic activities) which illustrate the social dynamics of economic cooperation and conflict. Since garden land is somewhat more evenly distributed than such land types as sawah and tegal, it has not been considered sociologically as interesting as other more limited resources in Java. Moreover, garden production is, for the most part, an intrahousehold activity. Since labor inputs are generally far below those of sawah, gardens demand neither the labor-intensive cooperative efforts used in sawah cultivation, nor the complex sharecropping arrangements and patron-client ties between households designed to ensure sufficient labor and sufficient employment opportunities for both parties.

Secondly, numerous measurement difficulties arise in the calculation of home-garden production. Although gardens may provide as much as 40 percent of the caloric intake of a Javanese family or 15 percent of the cash value of total food consumption, garden produce is invariably omitted from per capita calculations of available food stuffs. Studies of rural per capita food consumption are frequently based on the ratio of production to population figures, rather than on actual consumption patterns. Thus, according to Van Veen . . .

> In typical rural areas of Indonesia, where the greater part of the population is dependent on agriculture and where subsistence farming is prevalent, an analysis of local food production and population figures can provide a valuable indicator of the local dietary pattern and its degree of nutritional adequacy.[8]

This assumption, however, involves an implicit methodological error, resting as it does upon the misleading premise that the economic pie is equally divided, and specifically that the fruits of agricultural labor are equally shared. Numerous recent studies indicate that such an assumption is unwarranted in a society as highly stratified as rural Java. Rather, a methodology for studying gardens should take into account the ways in which gardens are used by different socioeconomic groups. As indicated above, gardens are a multipurpose enterprise; they may be used as an important source of monetary income (as suggested by the studies of Gelpke and Penny and Singarimbun, already cited); as a principal source of supplementary foods; or as an additional source of staple starches. The roles which home-garden production will play in a specific household economy cannot be inferred from figures on average garden production alone. Accordingly, the methods described below were not concerned with identifying average, optimal, or ideal garden productivity, but with describing actual garden production and accounting for its different uses.

II

Although Pelzer distinguishes garden plant types according to their structural role within garden ecology,
listings of plant types compiled from 80-odd garden map-
pings in Kali Loro suggests that, for methodological purposes, cropping strategies are better explained with reference to economic criteria. While ecological factors
limit the range of plant choices, within these parameters
a number of other factors should be considered. For example, plants may be chosen for their high-caloric value
for home consumption rather than their high-cash value
for sale. Low-risk crops which bring in small profits
may be chosen over those of higher risk and higher average returns. In households engaged in other labor-intensive activities, crops with low demands for labor may be
preferred. Households dependent on garden production for
immediate consumption and income needs may opt for quick
rather than long-term investments. In brief, for methodological purposes, the importance of garden produce can
be operationalized in terms of (1) the market value of
home-grown produce consumed and sold by a household over
the agricultural year, and (2) by various qualitative
characteristics of the produce consumed and sold, e.g.,
the type of produce, regularity of yields, labor inputs,
etc.

Some general features of village as well as garden
structure determined the basic aspects of the research
strategy in Kali Loro. This village is located in the
southern part of Central Java and has a population of
about 8000. The population density (about 750 per square
kilometer) and distribution of land types is about the
average for Central Java. Sawah comprises about 35 percent of the area, residential and house-garden compounds
(pekarangan) 45 percent, and dry fields (tegal) about 20
percent. Sawah covers all land that can be irrigated,
whereas gardens are usually located above the water
source. The village, which is largely an administrative
unit, is made up of 26 hamlets (dukuh), each containing
about 80 households (330 persons). Spread over an area
of 11.7 square kilometers, the hamlets vary in size, distribution of landholdings, proximity to the markets, and
in their general topography and soil quality.

Six hamlets (with a total of 478 households) were
chosen for a general household survey from which a smaller sample was selected for more intensive studies (60
visits per household, every 6 days throughout the year)
on time allocation, consumption and income, harvesting
practices, and market activity. For the analysis below,
the sample (altogether 90 households not all of which
were visited for a full year) was reduced to 21 households. However, the distribution of landholdings and the

range of occupations in the 6 hamlet population are
largely preserved in the smaller sample.

The household survey revealed that garden production
per hectare in Kali Loro ranges between Rp 11,200 and
Rp 367,400 per hectare. Compared to other available employment opportunities, gardens provide one of the highest
returns to labor (with an average of Rp 41 per person-
hour). Nonetheless, garden cultivation occupies only
8.4 percent of the total working time of men and an insignificant amount of time for women. As noted above, to
consider averages alone can obscure important variation.
For example, households with small gardens receive the
lowest returns to labor. On the other hand, they invest
the largest amounts of labor per hectare, presumably as a
means of increasing their absolute garden incomes.
Clearly, this indicates a situation of great variation in
garden use strategies. In order to develop some hypotheses to explain this variation, it is useful to look at
the findings of some former studies on home-garden production.

The earliest and most exhaustive studies of Javanese
gardens were carried out by Ochse and Terra during the
1930s, in connection with the activities of the "Declining
Welfare" Commission. These studies were designed to investigate conditions of increasing impoverishment within
Javanese society resulting from growing population densities and onerous extractions of land and labor.[9] One of
their principal findings was that the proportion of land
allotted to gardens, together with the intensity of their
cultivation, increase as total amount of crop land per
head decreases in various agricultural regions. This
would suggest that with population growth and increasing
scarcity of land over time, the proportionate amount of
garden to rice-land increases in conjunction with the
greater intensification of garden production.

While these early studies were aware of changes in
land utilization, they did little to explain the underlying dynamics of this process. Subsequent studies by
Terra attempted to discover whether increases in size and
intensity of pekarangan were due to (1) the better financial returns of gardens, (2) the larger yields of foodstuffs, or (3) the greater need of vegetables and fruits
in regions, where as a result of population density, sawah and tegal were entirely eliminated as possible
sources of these products.[10]

Terra was concerned primarily with inter-village differences and did not question whether these variations in
land use would apply equally to all economic and social
strata within a particular village. When his hypotheses
are applied to inter-household variations some interesting conclusions emerge. The data on land-distribution
for 6 hamlets (478 households) in Kali Loro shows that a
general relationship exists between access to sawah and

access to pekarangan, although the latter is somewhat
more evenly distributed (only 10 percent of households
have no access to pekarangan through ownership, rental or
sharecropping, while 20 percent have no access to sawah).
As Terra suggested for the regional level, there also
seems a tendency within the village for households with
small amounts of sawah to control more pekarangan than
sawah, and for this tendency to be reversed among households with more than 0.2 ha of sawah.

For the purpose of explaining inter-household variations, Terra's hypotheses concerning the relative intensity of garden use are of more interest. Since garden
intensity in Terra's analysis was related not only to
garden size, but to the general scarcity of sawah per
head, it seemed reasonable to suppose that households
with limited access to sawah (i.e., to other income
sources) would increase the intensity of garden production (measured as the cash value of garden production per
hectare) as garden size decreased. Thus, as an initial
working hypothesis, it was suggested that for Kali Loro,
the intensity of garden production would be associated
with a household's relative economic welfare. To test
this hypothesis, the amount of sawah controlled was used
as a crude measure of economic welfare (an assumption
common among students of Javanese agriculture). However,
no clear pattern emerged from this proposed relationship.
Accordingly, the measurement of economic welfare was expanded to include not only sawah controlled, but also income from other employment opportunities available to the
household. (This latter variable was operationalized as
total household income minus garden production). In addition, the possibility of a more complex (i.e., curvilinear as opposed to linear) relationship was investigated. A test of this revised hypothesis showed a significant curvilinear correlation (r = .63) between garden
intensity and household income.

Since income (minus garden production) reflects not
only access to sawah but also access to other employment
opportunities, this finding supports the hypothesis that
garden intensity and access to strategic resources are
related. However, as the association is curvilinear, income increases as garden intensity decreases only up to
a certain point. A threshold is reached at approximately
0.2 ha of sawah controlled, after which garden intensity
increases as income increases. This is particularly significant since 0.2 ha represents the approximate division
between those households who can and those who cannot
provide their basic rice requirements from their own sawah. Those households self-sufficient in rice are able
to increase their garden productivity by planting capital
intensive plants or long-term investment fruit trees,
since their gardens do not represent subsistence guaran-
tees (or part of their survival strategies) so much as

sources of extra cash earnings.

The above analysis indicates that a household's economic welfare may further be measured by the amount of rice it must purchase. Households which cannot supply their rice requirements either from sawah controlled or through harvesting opportunities (the latter are also related to access to sawah), must buy additional rice in the market. In this context, the analysis showed a marked correlation (r = .64) between rice bought and the intensity of garden production. Access to sawah is often used (in this paper and elsewhere) as a crude measure of wealth. The fact that rice bought, rather than area of sawah controlled, correlates markedly with garden intensity, suggests that other available opportunities for obtaining rice wages must be taken into account in attempting to isolate the determinants of garden-use strategies.

Terra also hypothesized that as garden size decreased, intensity of garden production would increase. This was also found to be the case on an inter-household level in Kali Loro. Garden size correlates inversely with garden intensity (r = -.57), but the relationship is less marked than either of those already noted for "rice bought" or "household income." The fact that production intensity increases with smaller gardens suggests that even the smallest gardens can respond favorably to intensification efforts. In fact, labor inputs in gardens are also inversely related to garden size; per-hectare labor inputs for small gardens were on the average three times as high as those for larger gardens, with inputs of 4,700 person-hours per hectare for small gardens (less than or equal to 0.1 ha), 2,100 person-hours for those of intermediate size (0.1 ha to 0.3 ha), and 1,600 person-hours for the largest garden plots (greater than 0.3 ha).

Cassava production offers an example of the way in which a number of these factors contribute to the determination of cropping strategies. Using intensity of cassava production as the dependent variable in a step-wise multiple regression analysis, it was found that garden size accounted for 41 percent of variance (as garden size decreased, intensity of cassava production increased). Nonetheless, access to rice wages and amount of rice produced from the household's own fields accounted for another 25 percent of the variance. These findings strongly confirm that the overall economic position of the household must be considered in analyzing cropping strategies. This conclusion is also supported by data on cassava consumption. For households with less than 0.1 ha of sawah, tubers comprise 21 percent by value of the total home-grown garden-produce consumed, as opposed to only 4 percent for households above 0.2 ha. Those households below the 0.2 ha mark have less reliable sources of rice and fewer rice-harvesting opportunities, and thus minimize their consumption risks by planting sufficient

amounts of cassava. For these households with limited or
no access to rice land (the major source of calories and
proteins) cassava provides not only a supplement, but a
necessary staple in the diet. Although the non-caloric
nutritional value of cassava is extremely low, under
these conditions a cropping strategy based on intensive
cassava cultivation will yield the highest caloric returns per hectare of production. On the other hand, pro-
longed cassava production has a deleterious effect on the
soil, and unless fertilizer is used, forced continuous
planting of cassava will only reap diminishing returns
ecologically and economically.

Low-income households employ other low-risk cropping
strategies. They produce and consume more leafy vegetables in general (an excellent source of Vit. A) than
higher income households. Since spinach (bayem), the
leaves of long beans (bayung), cassava leaves (daun kete-
la), and other leaves from fruit trees (daun so) can be
harvested within two months after planting or throughout
the year, they are relatively reliable cultigens, which
serve as low-risk food sources. On the other hand, they
do not offer the high-cash returns of other less certain
or longer term crops which are more intensively cultivated by wealthier households.

Although Vitamin A has been identified by some studies as a more pressing nutritional deficiency in rural
Javanese diets than caloric and protein deficiencies, it
is interesting that in agriculturally poor areas, Vitamin
A deficiencies were found to be less common since basic
foods were in low supply and the diet was supplemented by
low-cost supplementary greens and pulses. This observation is paralleled on an inter-household level in Kali
Loro where the low-income households consume the least
amount of rice and the highest amounts of leafy vegetables per consumer-unit.

III

Ochse and Terra's study of Kutowinangun in the 1930s,
and Penny and Singerimbun's more recent work on gardens
in the coconut-sugar producing village of Sriharjo, note
a high degree of commercialization of garden production.
Both studies indicate that as much as 68 percent of garden produce was converted into cash as opposed to 28 percent (for Kutowinangun) and 44 percent (for Sriharjo) of
the rice yield.[11] The latter study further points out
that the highest proportion (75 percent) of garden output
was sold by those farmers with the smallest garden holdings.[12] In Kali Loro a different pattern emerges. The
percentage of garden produce sold varies between 26 and
31 percent, without any significant relation to garden
size. However, the fact that households with small gar-

dens and smaller absolute quantities of garden produce
sell as much as 26 percent of their total yields indicates that they retain a much smaller absolute amount of
garden produce for home consumption.

General food consumption patterns also reveal some
striking differences between households of different economic status. Households with the least amount of sawah
(less than or equal to 0.1 ha) have a 25 percent lower
total food consumption per consumer unit than that of
households with more than 0.2 ha. Rice consumption figures in particular show that poorer households consume
65 percent less rice per consumer unit than wealthier
households. Protein consumption may be taken as a further index of economic welfare. In Kali Loro the primary
and most concentrated source of protein is in the form of
fermented soybeans (tempe), a product not grown locally
but available for purchase on the market. Households
with more than 0.2 ha of sawah were found to consume 45
percent more tempe than those households with less than
0.1 ha of sawah. This evidence appears to conflict with
some recent studies of rural nutrition which found no
appreciable differences in the caloric and protein intakes of men from different economic strata. The data
from Kali Loro suggest that by examining household consumption patterns in relation to sawah controlled, critical nutritional variations can be discerned with respect
to household diets.

In summary, it is apparent that household income and
access to sawah determine to a great extent patterns of
garden use and general consumption patterns. These relationships also determine the quality and quantity of
economic activities in which a household will participate. Poorer households in Kali Loro, who generally have
the largest labor inputs and lowest returns to labor in
all activities are also engaged in the greatest diversity
of occupations. The middle-level landholding groups have
a narrower range of activities and the occupational profile of the larger landholders is even less diversified
(although the very rich tend to be diversified in a number of capital-intensive enterprises). In measuring the
relative and comparative value of these income-producing
activities it was found, as may be expected, that total
yearly household income increases with the progression
from small to large farm households. While the relative
proportion of each income source for the three sawah
groups shows that garden production contributes nearly
the same proportion of household income (between 22 and
27 percent), for the poorest households, gardens provide
the largest single source of income. For higher income
households, trade and sawah cultivation provide the major
income sources.

Since gardens provide by far the largest income
source for poor households, it must be asked why poor

villagers do not concentrate their efforts more in garden cultivation. Ochse and Terra's work suggested that in some years garden incomes would be about 50 percent higher per hectare than those of sawah.[13] One study from the turn of the century recorded garden yields almost twice as high as those of sawah, and Penny and Singarimbun note that the income from labor-intensive coconut-sugar production can yield incomes 15 percent more than that of sawah.[14] This data raises several important questions concerning the role of gardens in household economy. As pointed out by Missen, there is a qualitative difference between using a garden as a supplementary resource and living off its produce entirely.[15] To maintain a garden ecologically and economically as a single-income source would entail the use of high-risk, high-profit crops, more frequent care, and a vulnerability to market fluctuations. A diversified cash crop garden, even on a small scale, would require more continuous labor inputs than sawah and more importantly it would mean that alternate income-producing activities allowed by the scheduling of rice cultivation (in concentrated but confined time periods) would be more difficult to maintain.

If intensified cash cropping is too risky a venture for small farmers, perhaps the increased productive potential of coconut-sugar production is an alternative strategy as a means of labor-intensification by the processing of garden produce for cash sale. Both Penny and Soedarwono note that coconut-sugar production becomes increasingly important as farm size decreases.[16] The high yields from coconut-sugar (gula jawa) are procured through high-labor inputs and low-capital investments. However, farmers in Kali Loro have in recent years limited their production of gula jawa, and have opted for other activities with equally low labor returns. One explanation may be that gula jawa production demands the daily labor inputs of several household members. For households with small gardens and few coconut trees, such rigid labor demands may diminish the overall household employment opportunities. Coconut-sugar production is an inflexible activity which does not allow a household to respond to irregular opportunities for alternative and more remunerative employment. Women from households producing gula jawa are virtually the only village women with insufficient time to participate in the rice harvest. Almost none of these women are small-scale traders, since the morning cooking of sugar conflicts with marketing hours. Men must be available in the early morning and evening to tap the trees, and children must spend many hours collecting firewood and leaves for cooking the sap. Those households which have chosen this option are restricted in their employment opportunities and are among the poorest villagers in Kali Loro.

Since this study was originally carried out, pekarangan has begun to receive its due attention. A leading
Indonesian institute of ecology is presently carrying out
a study to investigate the structure and importance of
home gardens from a more rigorous ecological perspective.
Development agencies and agricultural specialists concerned with reaching the "poorest of the poor" have hit
on home-gardens as a natural target. Unfortunately, most
of their interests (and funds) have focussed on possible
garden improvements, without investigating existing patterns of garden use. While numerous other aspects of
agricultural production have been the focus of both gov-
ernment- and foreign-financed programs, only recently
have there been suggestions that mixed gardening should
receive the same funding and research attention.

Two eminent Indonesian agricultural specialists have
recently urged that a more equal distribution of pekarangan plots should be included in land reform implementation.[17] The latter suggestion seems a particularly important element in improving the access of Java's poor to
better incomes and nutrition. Mixed gardens have the potential to play an important role not only in the densely
populated areas of rural Java, but in the transmigration
and developing regions of the outer islands where shifting cultivation is giving way to more intensive permanent
forms of non-irrigated cultivation.

Javanese home gardens have survived for at least nine
centuries as economically and ecologically viable and
efficient agro-systems. Before any programs can confidently attempt to "improve" them, intensive studies are
needed to evaluate their pre-existing structure and economic importance in rural household production strategies.

NOTES

1. Kali Loro is the pseudonym for the South Central Javanese
village in which Benjamin White and myself carried out 15 months of
field research from August 1972 to December 1973. I am grateful to
Ben White for his advice and encouragement throughout the research,
and to Lawrence Hirschfeld for his help in reworking the paper and
computer analysis. My thanks also go to David Boyd, David Penny,
Suparjan, and Joan Vincent for their criticisms and suggestions.

2. See for example T. S. Raffles, The History of Java (London:
Murray, 1817), 2:81; S. Gelpke, Naar Aanleiding van Staatsblad
(Batavia: Landsdrukkery, 1878), no. 110; F. Moll, De Desavolk-
shuishouding en cijfers (Amsterdam: Algemeen Syndicaat van
Suikerfabrikanten in Nederlandsch-India, 1913); C. Hassalman,
Algemeen Overzicht van de uitkomsten van het Welvaart Onderzoek
gehouden op Java en Madoera in 1904-1905 (Gravenhage: Nijoff, 1914),

p. 22; G. Vink, De Grondslagen van het Indonesische Landbouwbedrijf (Wageningen: Veenman, 1941), pp. 154-157; and I. De. Vries, Landbouw en Welvaart in het Regentschap Pasoeroean Bijdrage tot de Kennis van de Social Economie van Java (Wageningen: Medeeling van de Afdeeling Landbouw, 1931), no. 16.

3. K. Pelzer, Pioneer Settlement in the Asiatic Tropics (New York: American Geographical Society, 1945), p. 46.

4. Ibid., p. 44.

5. G. Missen, Viewpoint on Indonesia: A Geographical Study (Melbourne: Thomas Nelson and Sons, 1972), p. 59.

6. Kampto Utomo, Masyarakat Transmigran Spontan di Daerah Wai Sekampunt (Djakarta: P. T. Penerbitan Universitas, 1957), p. 129. Although this description refers to ladang, it seems particularly apt for mixed gardens as well.

7. G. J. A. Terra, "Mixed-garden Horticulture in Java," Malayan Journal of Tropical Geography 3, (1954):35.

8. A. G. Van Veen, "Some Nutritional and Economic Considerations of Javanese Dietary Patterns," Ecology of Food and Nutrition 1, (1971):40.

9. These findings can be found in G. Terra, "De voeding der bevolking en de erfcultuur," Koloniale Studien 16, (1932); and J. J. Ochse and G. Terra, Geld en Producten-Huishouding, Volks voeding en Gezondheid in Koetowinangun (Buitenzorg: Departemen van Economische Zaken, 1934).

10. Terra, "De voeding der bevolking en de erfcultuur," p. 355.

11. Ochse and Terra, Geld en Producten-Huishouding, p. 361; and D. Penny and M. S. Singarimbun, Population and Poverty in Rural Java: Some Economic Arithmetic From Srihardjo (Ithaca: Cornell University, 1973).

12. Penny and Singarimbun, Population and Poverty in Rural Java, p. 91.

13. Ochse and Terra, Geld en Producten-Huishouding, p. 364.

14. Moll, De Desavolkshuishouding en cijfers, and Penny and Singarimbun, Population and Poverty in Rural Java, p. 35.

15. Missen, Viewpoint on Indonesia, pp. 65-66.

16. Soedarwono Harjosoediro, Beberapa Aspek Usaha Gula Kelapa di Kabupaten Banjumas (Bogor: Departemen Pertanian, 1971).

17. See Sayogyo, "Human Settlement and Land Use in Rural Areas," presented at the Workshop on National Policies in Human Settlement Cisarua, 25-27 July 1977, as well as Sjamsoe'oed Sadjad, "Bagaimana Aspirasi Migro dan Makro dapat Bertumpu," Kompas, (August 15, 1977): 7.

14
Nutrition and
the Household Economy

Wade Edmundson

In order to more effectively determine what forms of agricultural development can and should be implemented, it is first necessary to become more aware of the total nutritional complex of village life. If the objective is to set clear developmental priorities or suggest profitable paths to development in terms of rice policy or any other aspects of agricultural development, greater understanding needs to be achieved in illuminating the magnificent complexity of the Javanese village, the manifold elements of the agricultural environment, and the intricate physiologic needs of those peasant farmers who must, in the long run, develop themselves. Therefore, it is necessary to look most carefully at the biologic environment as well as the cultural and environmental endowment of the people who will or who are now undergoing the process of "development."

It is the business of the nutritional geography to examine the cultural, biologic, and environmental endowment of a population in a regional context; carefully studying the characteristics, causes, and consequences of nutrition. The following study presents a nutritional geographic overview of the relationships between land, food, and work in East Java, describing three East Javanese villages, inhabited by peoples of similar cultural backgrounds, but living in differing physical environments.[1]

I

In order to examine the relationship between land, food, and work, three villages were studied in the kabupaten of Malang in East Java. This kabupaten was selected primarily because it is basically a self-sufficient agricultural region containing a representative variety of agricultural conditions. Being located on the south side of the island, it is slightly wetter than other

areas of East Java, with a rainfall regime comparable to
the island averages in other densely populated areas.
Also, population densities are near the island averages
for densely populated areas, being higher than those of
West Java but lower than those of Central Java. Furthermore, Malang Kabupaten includes three separate agricultural and geologic regions representing the three basic
rice, corn, and cassava diets common to Java, Indonesia,
and all of Southeast Asia.

Three villages were chosen to represent each of the
major land-use types in Java: Pontjokusumo, a volcanic
slope corn village; Glanggang, an alluvial valley rice
village; and Pagak, a limestone plateau, corn, and cassava village. Bennett's prior study of population pressure, landholdings, and estimated crop production in Malang Kabupaten was used as a base for village selection.[2]
Unfortunately, the villages were each somewhat unique, for
there was no such thing as "an average village" because
between village variations were always important, and the
majority of villages tend to represent mixed forms of
land use. While it is therefore difficult to say that
any villages are typical or average, at least the three
selected villages are representative of land use types
and can thus provide insight into a wide range of village
variations.

The three study villages are quite similar in terms
of general ethnic composition and cultural background,
and in economic terms, within village variation is much
greater than between village variation. Thus, the differences between a relatively poor villager and a relatively wealthy villager in any one village are far greater than the differences between a poor villager in Pagak
and a poor villager in Glanggang or Pontjokusumo. However, the study concerns three different environmental
complexes acted upon by peoples of very similar cultures.
In this case, the site and situational differences have
had strong and almost deterministic influences in differ-
entiating land use and dietary intake, even though there
are only modest differences in overall levels of living
among the study villages.

With the above background in perspective, the first
issue which needs to be addressed is whether control of
or access to land really constitutes the basis for levels
of caloric nutrition. A profile of the three villages
using correlation matrices for land, capital, and caloric
data seems to indicate that individual landholdings do
not determine individual caloric intake. Not only is
there no correlation whatsoever between landholdings and
caloric intake, but also there seems to be little relationship between capital holdings and caloric intake. On
the other hand, the association between landholdings and
capital holdings does appear to be significant, and especially so when examined on an individual village basis.

This is as would be expected, since the productive quality of land within each study village tends to be relatively constant. Therefore, within any given village, landholdings should be a fairly good index of wealth, but neither land nor wealth seems to relate to the caloric nutrition of an individual.

There are six basic reasons why land and capital do not correlate with caloric intake. In the first place, food intake is more strongly influenced by cultural preference than economic status. In the second place, the supply of caloric staples is normally sufficient to meet at least the basic energy needs. In the third place, the poorer, landless villager often must work harder than the wealthy, landed villager and may, therefore, need more food. In the fourth place, families with large landholdings have more mouths to feed. In the fifth place, there are many alternative farm service occupations available to the landless villager. And finally, there is a system of mutual self-help within the village which provides that none should starve.

The fact that food choices are more strongly influenced by cultural preference than by economic status is an important factor in negating associations between food, land, and wealth. Culturally induced patterns of food intake are similar for all villages. Even though the staple might be rice, corn, or cassava, it is always presented in rice-size pieces and steamed as if it were rice. The wealthy, landed villagers do tend to have a more flavorful diet and they tend to eat a slightly larger proportion of culturally preferred foodstuffs, including oil, sugar, and animal protein. Still, basic meal patterns are similar for both the rich and poor and, in some cases, culturally preferred foods such as pure white rice are less nutritious than lower-status foods, such as mixtures of rice and corn.

The fact that there are few cases of quantitative caloric deficit within the villages, and the fact that the male study subjects are given food preference, also serves to negate any correlation. Although there are specific nutritional deficiency problems of varying magnitude in each village, even the poorest villagers usually have a sufficient quantity of some form of caloric staple available for consumption. The landless subjects do tend to eat more corn and cassava than the wealthy landed subjects, but their quantitative caloric intake is not limited to any significant degree. It is possible that in some of the poorest, landless families there may have been quantitative limits on food intake. However, the village families seem to realize that it is important for the hardest-working male member of the family to have enough to eat. They know that the productive male needs more food than the less productive family members; therefore, it is the worker who normally eats first, and he is

encouraged to eat all he wants of the caloric staple. He
also has first choice of the side dishes. However, if
there is an especially desirable foodstuff such as a
sweet or a meat, he is expected to restrain himself so
that all members of the family will be saved some portion
of that side dish.

Caloric intake also fails to relate to either land or
capital because in many cases the landless villager simply has to work harder than the landed villager, and because he works harder he sometimes eats a larger quantity
of food than does a landowner. It is not unusual to see
a landed villager with a significantly lower caloric intake than that of the field hand who works for him and
eats with him. In short, the wealthy landed villager has
more food available but relatively little appetite; the
poor landless villager has a great appetite but he may
not always have sufficient food available to fully satisfy this appetite.

A fourth reason for the lack of caloric correlation
is the fact that there are many alternative occupations
available within the agricultural society. The landless
individual may obtain his livelihood by sharecropping,
renting land, working as a hired hand, working in some
form of cottage industry, or working in a trade. What
outside observers sometimes fail to realize is, that even
in an agricultural society operating at a low technologic
level, there are numerous village occupations available
requiring neither land nor capital, which may provide at
least the basis for nutritional subsistence. These alternate occupations may yield very low incomes per unit
work effort, but they do provide subsistence.

There is a positive correlation coefficient of 0.50
between family landholdings and family size. This supports the clearly observed impression that within the
villages the landed wealthy families tend to be larger
than the landless and poor families. The landed and
wealthy families are usually the old, established village
families; these families often have three generations
under one roof, and they tend to be cohesive with the
married children remaining in the household. A landed or
wealthy family is also more likely to take in and care
for poor or orphaned relatives and this also serves to
equalize the per capita distribution of land and wealth
within the village.

Another factor strongly modifying the relationship
between the environmental land base and nutrient intake
relates to the social obligations of the wealthy landowner in a semi-communal society. The closeness of the
social relationships within a Javanese village still creates many obligations for the wealthy villager. The history of gotong rojang or mutual self-help, the abundance
of relatives, the small town environment, the lack of se-
crets, the mutual interdependence, and the mere geograph-

ic proximity of the villagers, enforces a degree of social concern long ago abandoned in more depersonalized,
high technology Western societies. The communalism of
village society tends to redistribute food through a complex system of social obligations. A wealthy landowner
who does not provide at least a minimum of nutritional
subsistence for near and distant relatives and close
friends will be socially ostracized. Thus, this social
service in the form of food sharing may be looked on as
an interest payment on social capital. To maintain a
position of social prominence, it is not necessary to
share all forms of your wealth. However, if you have a
surplus of food and fail to share it, allowing a fellow
villager to starve, this is a social disgrace.

II

A major premise underlying much of the research
undertaken on nutrition in developing countries concerns
the assumed relationship between levels of food intake
and levels of work output. Thus, in this context, variations in low-caloric intake would presumably account for
differences in levels of work output. In the three village samples, this postulate was tested through measurements of caloric energy intake and caloric energy output.
For all villages the average expenditure of energy for
adult males is 2446 calories per subject day. Although
these energy expenditures seem low by Western standards,
the villagers studied are more physiologically efficient
than their Western counterparts, both in terms of strength
and stamina. The villagers are smaller in stature and
lighter in weight than their Western counterparts, but
they are just as strong, if not stronger. This makes
them more physiologically efficient in that they have
more strength per unit weight than Westerners. They are
also far more physically fit and are able to perform
heavy work at sustained rates for long periods of time
without tiring.
In relation to the possible logical bias of a nutritional geographer, one of the hypotheses the study sought
to prove was that low levels of caloric intake result in
low levels of work output, thereby retarding potential
for economic development. However, the survey showed
this hypothesis to be clearly false in relation to the
Javanese study subjects. Fieldwork was based on the assumption that a given quantity of food contained a given
quantity of physiologically available calories. Based
on this belief that caloric energy tended to be a constant function of the amount and type of food being
eaten, it was assumed that individuals with low caloric
intakes would not and could not on the average, work as
hard as individuals with high caloric intakes. It was

realized, however, that there was no reason why energy intake would equal output for a given individual on a given day. Nevertheless, since there were no significant changes in weight noted in the subjects which might indicate energy storage or the utilization of stored energy reserves, and since a six-day survey is accepted as a sufficient length of time in which to obtain a valid estimate of a given individual's average rate of energy intake and output, it was assumed that average caloric energy intake would equal average energy work output, both for the group, and for the individual within the group.

In brief, the data on individual caloric energy intake and caloric energy output are somewhat startling. Average caloric intake for all subjects does agree with average caloric output, as it should in theory; however, when the six-day subject averages are examined individually, there is no association whatsoever between average intake and output for single subjects. The average daily grouped intake is 2430, as would be expected considering that, over long periods of time, utilizable caloric intakes must equal respiratory caloric outputs unless there are gross weight changes. However, when examining the correlation between the six-day averages of energy intake and output for the 54 subjects as individuals, the coefficient of correlation is found to be only 0.04. Thus, there is no correlation whatsoever between individual measures of intake and output. What this means is that a group of observers watching 54 villagers very closely for 324 days, with the specific purpose of carefully determining how hard these men were working, could detect no discernible differences in the observed work output of men with high and low caloric intakes. This is not just saying they could determine no significant differences. It is saying that they could determine not one iota of regularity in the differences between the work output of men with high caloric intakes and the work output of men with low caloric intakes. Research methodology that gave seemingly accurate results when applied to the group was invalid when applied to individuals. The only acceptable intuitive explanation for these results is that individual variability in the efficiency of caloric utilization is far greater than had been anticipated. It is highly implausible that standard research techniques are so inaccurate as to cause deviations of this magnitude. Therefore, the proposition must be considered that the lack of correlation between energy intake and output might be due, at least in part, to real individual differences in human efficiency in utilization of food intake and production of work output.

If it is assumed that methodological techniques are valid and individuals vary in their ability to utilize caloric input to produce work output, it is possible to explain both the concordance of average intake and output

for all subjects and the discordance of average intake
and output measured in relation to the individual. The
key to understanding these data lies in understanding
that caloric intakes for individuals were measured individually while caloric outputs were generalized. In measuring output, activities were measured individually, but
these individually measured activities were related to
average rates of energy expenditure. In transferring
energy output data from the group to the individual, no
allowance was made for individual variability in physiologic efficiency. Therefore, the close concordance of
overall averages for energy input and energy output may
be an indication of the overall validity of the methodological techniques in measuring the generalized averages,
and the individual variations may then be an indication
of differences in long- and short-term adaptive efficiencies,which invalidate the use of group averages in the
measurement of individual utilization of caloric energy.

If the above hypothesis is accepted, it follows that
an index of relative efficiency can be obtained by dividing the average of six days of measured work energy output for the individual by the average of six days of measured caloric energy intake for that same individual.
This index is a measure of observed units of work activity per unit of caloric intake,and the numerator is actually a qualitative assessment of how hard the subject
appeared to be working,and the denominator would be a
quantitative measure of units of caloric input. Using
these calculations of relative efficiency for the subjects under study,it becomes clear that measured work
output is independent of measured energy input. Work
output tends to be fairly close to 2400 calories per day
for all subjects whether their energy intake is high or
low, but food intake seems to be highly variable; perhaps a function of food availability. In brief, it appears that there is a wide range of human variability and
that work output is not a function of caloric intake,but
rather is closely related to varying levels of individual
physiologic efficiency, which change in response to changing levels of food availability within the structure of
reasonably constant work requirements. Obviously there
is a range of adaptation and intuitively there must be a
lower limit below which the individual can no longer increase his efficiency level. In this case, the limit
seems to be below the lowest caloric intake of any subject in the study. There may also be an upper limit beyond which adaptation is no longer necessary. Examining
the data closely, it appears that around the level of intake of 2750 calories a day the adaptive processes may
diminish and approach a constant value within a range of
normal human variability. Data are insufficient to do
more than speculate on this point; however, if caloric
value does approach a constant in societies where caloric

sufficiencies exist, and adaptations occur only in societies which are subjected to caloric stress, this might explain a number of nutritional enigmas in which other researchers measuring caloric intakes in less developed areas have noted seemingly fit individuals performing heavy workloads with measured caloric intakes far lower than those recorded in this study.[3]

The above analysis raises more questions than it answers, in that individual outputs of energy must be measured on an ergometer before speculation concerning differentials in efficiency can be further clarified. At this stage it is necessary that a research project be planned specifically to measure individual physiologic efficiencies. It is interesting to note that recently Apfelbaum, Botssarrom, and Lacatis performed a carefully controlled study using an ergometer and three types of respirometry in an attempt to measure compensated adaptive changes in physiologic efficiency. Eight subjects were required to consume a dietary supplement of 1500 calories above their normal intake and 41 subjects were restricted to a semi-starvation diet of 220 calories a day. After only 15 days of overeating the first group showed a decrease in physiologic efficiency on the order of 12 to 29 percent. The group on the semi-starvation diet at the end of the 15 days showed an increase of efficiency on the order of 12 to 17 percent.[4] This study and its replications lend some fairly solid support to the results from the three villages in East Java and the hypothesis that the efficiency of human metabolism of caloric energy is in some way a function of level of caloric intake. Thus, it would seem that in Java at least, even though sporadic famines of limited areal extent still occur, work productivity would not be increased greatly by a higher caloric input. Therefore, increase in production of carbohydrate staples should perhaps not be regarded as a direct means to development, but rather as a desirable end-product of necessary agricultural development. Obviously, programs to increase staple yields are still vital from a demographic, economic, and even a nutritional standpoint because the increases in yield may free some land for the growing of high priority protein and vitamin source food crops. However, in relation to any direct nutrient supplementation programs, caloric supplementation should have a very low priority.

III

A commonly held assumption is that malnutrition is a widespread condition within many less-developed societies. In order to examine this problem in greater detail, food survey data on average subject-nutrient in-

takes is presented and analyzed briefly along with a sub-
jective analysis of village nutrition and clinical symptoms of malnutrition observed in the villages. In addition, available data concerning seasonal variations in nutrient intake is presented, and the significance of seasonal hunger is also evaluated.

Concerning nutrient intake, each of the 54 sample
farmers had their nutrient intakes measured for six days
at six different times during the year. By considering
the averages of these six days of food intake, one ob-
tains an unusually valid estimate of how much food each
individual eats during the study year. A review of this
data in the context of Indonesian recommended dietary allowances reveals that undernutrition is not a major problem among the active male population studied in the three
villages. Average caloric intake appeared to be sufficient, although for a number of subjects minimum needs
just barely were met. Also, there was no clear clinical
evidence of protein malnutrition among any of the subjects studied. Intakes of thiamine were marginal and intakes of Vitamin A were low. Further, in evaluating village nutrient intakes it is very useful to simply de-
scribe in a general way the observational evidence of
clinical nutritional deficiencies within the villages.
Comparing the nutrient intakes of individuals with recommended nutrient allowances is really little more than an
academic exercise unless one has time to examine a multitude of qualifying factors. Furthermore, clinical nutritional deficiencies occur in individuals, not in groups,
and they are conditioned not by single factors but rather
by the synergistic interaction of a host of factors relating not only to overall level of nutrition but to generalized levels of health and sanitation as well. Therefore, it is necessary to briefly examine clinical evidence
of malnutrition not only in respect to age groups but
also in regard to overall levels of health within the
village environments.

Although malnutrition is not widespread, it still is
one important factor affecting the quality of the human
resource and the developmental potential of the villages.
The 18- to 35-year-old male study subjects were the
healthiest and best nourished of all the villagers. Like
everyone else in the villages they suffered from a high
incidence of illness due to respiratory and enteritic
diseases. Nevertheless, they were strong and fit, and
during the entire survey only two of the study subjects
(suffering from diffuse goiter) exhibited the obvious
clinical symptoms of nutritional deficiency. The teen-
agers from 13 to 18 were fully as healthy as the young
male fieldworkers, and the children over six years of age
also appeared nutritionally fit, except for the fact that
they often suffered from dermatitis. The young wives appeared to be only slightly less fit than their husbands

and exhibited nutritional deficiency syndromes, such as edema, only on rare occasions following multiple pregnancies or when suffering from severe dysentery. Likewise, the babies under two years of age, although subjected to numerous onslaughts of communicable and infectious diseases, appeared to be well-nourished except in rare cases where the supply of breast milk was insufficient.

Post-weaning children of three to six years of age presented a different nutritional picture. After the children were weaned near the end of the second year or early in the third year of their lives, they appeared not only to be malnourished, but also more susceptible to disease attack. Infantile diarrhea was a particularly grave problem for children in this age group. During the course of the study year there occurred, among the children of the 54 families studied, one death due to infantile diarrhea, and another case of severe gastroenteritis, which might have been fatal had it not been treated promptly. Almost all the children in this age group suffered from "crazy pavement" or "flakey skin" dermatitis. This condition, generally related to protein-calorie malnutrition and vitamin deficiency, may also have had something to do with the extremely high incidence of dermatitis. An important factor related to protein deficiency in this two- to six-year age group was the belief of most of the villagers that dried fish caused worms. Because of this belief, these children were denied the prime source of animal protein. In the villages, this protein-calorie-vitamin dermatitis set the stage for herpes simplex and streptococcal infections resulting in some very miserable children. The resulting skin infections could be cured with tropical applications of penicillin ointment but would quickly reappear. However, if the child was given multiple B-vitamin compounds along with the penicillin, both the infection and the dermatitis could be cured and there would be no relapse. For children of this age group in Pontjokusumo cheilosis was also common, and three cases of magenta tongue were noted during the course of the survey. This was probably indicative of riboflavin deficiency, and this condition responded promptly to multi-vitamin therapy. In Pagak, about once during each survey day, a child in this age group would be noticed with either "flag sign" or reddish depigmented hair, probably indicative of protein deficiency. In the village of Glanggang, during the course of the study, one case of kwashiorkor was noted. However, this case had a strong social as well as a nutritional etiology. Because the child's mother was divorced, she was forced to seek work in Malang as a prostitute; thus, she was unable to breast feed or properly care for her baby.

The elderly villagers over 45 years of age also seemed poorly nourished when compared to other age groups. Due to a life of hard fieldwork and lack of health care, coupled with a diet low in protective quality, the economically productive lifespan of a fieldworker appeared to be on the order of from 15 to 45 years of age. Past this age, both males and females were no longer fit for heavy fieldwork, and therefore they remained at home and their work output diminished. As work output diminished there were drastic changes in appetite and food intake further resulting in poor nutrient intake, a decrease in physical fitness, and still more rapid aging. The young study subjects were able to maintain reasonable levels of nutrition only because they worked hard and ate great quantities of food. Their mothers and fathers did little or no fieldwork, ate little, and were often malnourished and invariably thin. They often complained of shortness of breath, many had active or incipient tuberculosis, and almost all of the elderly villagers complained of "pins and needles" syndrome which they expressed as "ants eating at my feet." Bitot's spots were extremely common in this age group, and the elderly also suffered from a higher incidence of keratomalacia, due to an insufficient intake of vitamin A. In Pontjokusumo it was usually the elderly who had the most prominent long-term goiters.

In summary, overall clinical evidence of nutritional deficiencies in the villages was much lower than expected. There were severe nutritional deficiency syndromes to be seen, but when severe deficiencies did occur they were usually associated with specific cultural or medical problems. For instance, a child might suffer because his divorced mother had to work away from the village, or nutritional edema might occur following a long bout with enteritic or febrile illness. Thus, even though general states of undernutrition and protein deficiency were not common, there were many specific vitamin and mineral deficiency problems in each village. For example, goiter is a problem in highland areas, and in areas of recent volcanic mudflows throughout the island of Java. In Pontjokusumo, goiter was the outstanding nutritional deficiency syndrome. Gross grade, two, three, four, and five diffuse goiters were commonplace. A rough count of 200 adults in Pontjokusumo revealed 42 people, or roughly one in five, with visible diffuse goiters. These long-term goiters do not respond at all well to what little iodine chemical therapy was available in Indonesia; however, they might respond to preparations of thyroid extract, if such therapy were made available. The best therapeutic response noted in Pontjokusumo was that of one of the villager's own methods of treatment, which consisted simply of rubbing tincture of iodine over the surface of the goiter. Preventative therapy is desperately needed, but until iodized salt is available to the villagers of Pontjokusumo, little can be done.

In Glanggang, intake of vitamin B_1 was very low. The
study measured only the intake of raw thiamine, and it
was found that the standard Indonesian process of washing
and steaming rice can remove or destroy up to 60 percent
of the thiamine available in the raw rice. It can be estimated that actual thiamine availabilities are probably
40 percent lower than dietary measures of raw thiamine
intake. This would indicate that the average thiamine
availability for subjects in Glanggang might be as low as
0.47 milligrams, and would put the average thiamine intake well below the recommended minimum intakes theoretically necessary to maintain health. However, since none
of the subjects were suffering from beri-beri, it is
likely that the minimum set by the ICNND might not apply
to these Javanese villagers; or conversely, that the villagers may have adapted themselves to the low thiamine
intake. Nevertheless, the common complaint of subjects
in Glanggang of "pins and needles" syndrome is indicative
of low-grade thiamine deficiency.

In Pagak, the most common specific nutritional problem
was keratomalacia, a condition precipitated by a very
high incidence of conjunctivitis. The incidence rate
for conjunctivitis in Pagak during the study year appeared to approach 200 percent, or two cases per person
per year. A rough count of 200 villagers revealed 43, or
about one in five, suffering from active kertomalacia or
partial blindness due to prior bouts with keratomalacia.
Keratomalacia was first treated with tropical applications of terramycin ointment plus massive doses of
500,000 IU of vitamin A daily for 30 days. However, it
was later found that 25,000 IU of vitamin A given daily
for a period of ten days was sufficient to cause rapid
cure and partial regression. It is strange that a disease of this sort, known to be caused primarily by deficiency of vitamin A, was more common in Pagak than the
other villages. There is no doubt that vitamin A intake
was low in Pagak, as the average subject intake of 3600
IU of vitamin A per day just barely exceeded the lowest
minimum standards set by Hume and Krebs.[5] The average
daily subject intake of 3350 IU of vitamin A in Pontjokusumo was lower still, and the intake of 2610 IU of
vitamin A in Glanggang fell below the minimum recommendations. Nevertheless, keratomalacia only occurred in
Pagak and this was probably related to the slightly lower
intakes of protein.

A final comment is in order concerning malnutrition
and nutrient intake as a function of seasonal changes in
food supply. In explaining the problems connected with
conducting dietary surveys in Java, the Coolie Budget
Commission stated that the "time at which the investigation is held can greatly influence the result. This is
especially true in regard to the harvest time or meager
time."[6] In this study only a modest amount of data could

be collected concerning seasonal variation in nutrient intake and work output. However, bi-monthly data gathering rounds were set up so that Round II for October and November fell during the meager period at the end of the dry season and before the first harvests of the wet season. This is the time of the musim patjeklik, which can be translated as either the drought season or the famine season. It is clear from this data that there were small but real differences in seasonal nutrient intake. Caloric intakes, protein intakes, and thiamine intakes, as well as intakes of other nutrients were lowest during the period prior to the first harvest. However, the degree of seasonal hunger recorded was less than had been expected, and the fact that caloric intakes during Round II were six percent lower than the mean intakes did not seem to affect the work output of the villagers in any way. In brief, seasonal hunger was real but not especially significant, and in talking with villagers it would appear that significant seasonal hunger was a sporadic rather than annual occurrence. The villagers of Pontjokusumo said they suffered a musim patjeklik during the months of October and November at irregular intervals occurring about once in every five years when the second crop failed due to drought. The paddy villagers said there was no problem with a musim patjeklik in Glanggang, and the people of Pagak said they suffered from musim patjeklik at irregular intervals about once in every three years.

During the study year there was no starvation season because village harvests prior to the study year had been normal and food storage was adequate. However, the food available during the months of October and November was less fresh and less varied than that available at other times. Therefore, the slight decrease in nutrient intake prior to the harvest may be attributed primarily to the fact that food at this time is less appetizing. Other seasonal variations noted were slight decreases during the inter-harvest periods. These variations may again be due to the availability of a wider variety of appetizing foods during harvest time. The Moslem fast month of Ramadan seemed to have no significant effect on food intakes, simply because very few of the villagers fasted for more than a few days.

In summary, in terms of a set of internal priorities for nutrition improvements, this study was originally undertaken with the belief that calories, proteins, vitamins, and minerals should be stressed in that order. The evidence suggests, however, that the order should be reversed. In regard to development, caloric undernutrition was not as significant a problem as many think it to be. This is not to say that seasonal hunger and periodic famines do not pose problems in Java. If this same study had been performed in Central Java or Yogyakarta, the results might have been quite different. However, seasonal hunger is apparently a problem of limited areal extent and better approached through regionally tailored rural development programs than through island-wide programs. Therefore, it would seem that problems of periodic famine could most effectively be dealt with by the development of contingency disaster relief plans and well-trained disaster relief teams which could then be sent quickly to the specific afflicted areas. Also, it would seem that tha most economical protein enrichment programs should be tailored to areal needs and directed specifically towards the improvement and enrichment of protein intake of the post-weaning children. One program might be aimed at producing more fish, getting the fish to the protein deficient areas, and removing the tabu which presently prevents post-weaning children from getting their fair share of this prime source of protein. The problems resulting from specific vitamin and mineral deficiencies seemed to be more urgent than problems relating to protein and calorie malnutrition and should be dealt with on a priority basis. Vitamin A deficiencies and iodine deficiencies might respond best to an island-wide or even a nation-wide supplementation program. In many cases, it might be easier to produce and distribute mixed multiple vitamin supplements than it would be to change and improve cultural patterns of food consumption. If multiple vitamins containing only the minimum amounts of missing nutrients were designed, they could be produced more economically than present multiple vitamins designed to supply recommended daily vitamin requirements.

NOTES

1. In 1970 and 1971, supported by a Fulbright Research Fellowship, the author, his wife, Fakir Suroso and Rokip Effendi spent two years in East Java working together to compile 324 man days of data concerning average 24-hours nutrient intakes and work outputs for 54 adult male villagers in three villages.

2. D. Bennett, "Population Pressures in East Java (Ph.D. thesis, Syracuse University, 1957).

3. E. H. Hipsley and N. E. Kirk, Studies of Dietary Intake and the Expenditure of Energy by New Guineans (Noumea, New Caledonia: South Pacific Commission, 1965), and K. V. Bailey, "Rural Nutritional Studies in Indonesia," Tropical and Geographical Medicine 13: 216-315.

4. See M. Apfelbaum, et al., "Effect of Caloric Restriction and Excessive Caloric Intake on Energy Expenditure," American Journal of Clinical Nutrition 24: 1405-51.

5. See Interdepartmental Committee on Nutrition for National Defense, Manual for Nutrition Surveys (Bethesda: National Institute of Health, 1963): 257.

6. See Coolie Budget Commission, Living Conditions of Plantation Workers and Peasants on Java in 1939-1940 (Ithaca: Cornell Indonesian Project - Microfilm translation by R. Van Niel, 1958).

Part VIII

Resource Management

Introduction

During the past decade, major attention has shifted
to the more active cultivation of Indonesia's fishery
and forestry products. These two sectors constitute a
major share of the archipelago's renewable resource base,
and recognizing their potential contribution as major
foreign exchange earners, the government has encouraged
the channelling of both domestic and foreign investment
in coastal sea fishing and in the logging of lowland
forests. As a result of these measures, fishery production has increased and forestry production has leaped
ahead as the second most important (after oil) source of
foreign exchange earnings. Because of the vast untapped
potential in these two sectors, production should continue to rise, and with proper resource management, it
should be possible to perpetuate these yields for an in-
definite period of time. Effective resource management
can only be undertaken, however, within a policy and institutional framework which reflects a concern for a
wider range of ecological considerations and related development goals.

The following two essays are concerned with policy
and institutional issues and each author seeks to examine
the various problems which arise in a context where a
fully articulated framework has yet to be developed for
the proper management of fishery and forestry resources.
The first essay examines the artisanal fishery economies
of coastal Java, an analysis which comprehends both
brackish water ponds and sea coast fishing. Both of
these activities constitute important sources of employment and income earning activities for lower income rural
households. The author proposes that the coastal areas
of northern Java, in addition to many of the coastal
areas in the outer islands, can be characterized as a
type of ecosystem which allows for a diverse range of
economic pursuits, and if properly managed, these areas
could provide a substantial contribution in feeding and
employing Indonesia's rapidly growing labor force. Many

problems currently stand in the way of achieving these ends. This is particularly the case in the outer islands, where much more research is needed concerning local ecological characteristics before embarking upon a full scale resettlement program for the more intensive cultivation of coastal zone resources.

In the northern coastal areas of Java, the problem is somewhat different in that the resource base is already under intensive cultivation and the primary issue is one of working out arrangements which prevent resource depletion and the displacement of the more employment intensive small scale fisheries sector. In these areas the fishing grounds of small scale fishermen are being encroached upon by the recent advent of much larger and more modern trawling vessels. Likewise, the number of small scale, non-motorized fishing boats has greatly increased and as a consequence, the competition for fish has intensified in the nearby offshore fishing grounds. Many of these areas are being overfished and catch per boat has declined, a condition which is beginning to produce serious repercussions for the smaller-scale fishing unit. The growth in magnitude of this problem points to the need for regulatory measures and enforcement procedures which enable certain portions of the coastal zone to be reserved for smaller vessels in order that the employment absorptive capacity of this sector can continue to assume its proper and important role within the coastal economy.

The second essay examines the rapid growth of commercial logging in the outer islands and the variety of issues associated with the proper cultivation of this vast resource base. For numerous reasons, many of the current logging practices do not conform with existing policy guidelines in forestry management. In great measure these conditions can be attributed to deficiencies in manpower and institutional resources. The forestry service is understaffed and the current base of scientific knowledge and survey information on the concession areas is quite limited. It will take a number of years to remedy these conditions, and in the interim it is important that greater attention be devoted to the more effective administration of existing regulatory guidelines in the logging concessions in order to avoid rapid and widespread ecological harm and resource depletion.

The need for improved forestry management is particularly important in the context of the government's increased emphasis upon transmigration and the moving of inhabitants from Java for resettlement to the outer islands. Encroachment of these settlement schemes upon forested areas could result in the devastation of existing timber stands and the attendant disturbance of ecosystems in local and lowland coastal areas.

15
Aquaculture and Artisanal Fisheries

William L. Collier

Of the 80 million people living in Java, approximately 60 percent are in the coastal areas. Most of these coastal-zone inhabitants are on the northern coast where population densities range from 350 to 3,000 people per square kilometer. Since this zone is one of the most intensively worked resource units in Indonesia and is the location of most of the major cities, it is imperative that we understand how this vast population is able to find sufficient work and adequate food for survival. Based on our knowledge of Java, it may then be possible to make predictions and recommendations for specific actions in less densely populated areas in Indonesia and Asia where these population densities will be faced in the future. Although other areas may not reach these extreme population densities, their resources will also be intensively utilized to their maximum capacity.

In this paper the primary concern is with the small-scale (artisanal) fisheries located in the coastal zone which are primarily non-powered, traditional sailboat fishermen and brackish water-pond operators. From the standpoint of employment, both capture and culture fisheries are extremely important components in Java's coastal economy. A substantial number of people in Java depend on artisanal fisheries for full, part-time, or occasional employment. According to government statistics, sea-fishing along coastal Java provides work for 377,000 people and brackish water-ponds provide work for another 645,000 people. If it is assumed that they are household heads, then these one million households constitute a significant portion of Java's total population. Besides being a major source of employment, artisanal fisheries' importance is greatly increased because of its potential for intensification and extensification and its location along the coasts where population is concentrated. Consequently, it is clear that for the rural areas, fisheries are of major importance for employment and are over-shadowed only by rice, corn, and cassava production in the food sector of the economy.

I

In Java, brackish water-ponds are primarily found along the north coast, from Serang, which is west of Jakarta, to Banyuwangi at the Strait of Bali, and on the south coast of Madura. In this area there appear to be two distinct types of ponds. One area is a coastal shore-strip varying in width from a few hundred yards to occasionally one or two miles. This type stretches from near Jakarta, past Semarang in Central Java, to possibly Rembang. These ponds are almost bare of mangrove trees and other plants. Usually the size of pond ranges from perhaps one-third ha to five or six ha. However, near Jakarta, there are some much larger operations. The other type of pond area is a much wider coastal shore-strip, which is ten miles deep in certain locations. These exist primarily in the Solo and Brantas river deltas in East Java. The ponds are larger than in Central and West Java and the banks are covered with mangrove trees.

Shrimp and milkfish are the major crops which are cultured in these ponds. Most of the ponds are managed in the traditional way without the use of fertilizer, pesticides, or supplementary feeding. Production inputs into the ponds are mainly physical labor in stocking of the milkfish fry and maintaining and guarding the ponds. One expert estimated that 40 percent of the brackish water-ponds in Indonesia do not use fertilizer and do not stock their ponds with fry. The average yields for these ponds would only be 250 to 300 kg/ha/year. He further estimated that 50 percent of the ponds are stocked with purchased fry but no fertilizer is used, with yields averaging from 300 to 500 kg/ha/year. Only 10 percent of the ponds, according to his estimates, are being managed with modern techniques (applying fertilizer, protecting against pests, and stocking with fry); and the yields average between 600 to 800 kg/ha/year.[1]

Most brackish water-ponds cultivate both shrimp and milkfish together. The shrimp are usually stocked naturally rather than the operator buying post-laval shrimp for stocking. Cholik estimated that yields for this type of management were 200 to 400 kg of shrimp per ha per year. However, he states that 10,000 ha in South Sulawesi Province are suitable for intensive shrimp culture, which if properly managed, can achieve yields of 1000 kg of shrimp per ha per year.[2]

The second major coastal fishing industry in Java involves sea fisheries, a sector which has recently undergone tremendous structural change since the early 1970s. The value of sea fishery exports has leaped from only

(US)$2,821,000 in 1968, to (US)$68,185,000 in 1973.[3] Almost the entire increase in value has been due to increases in shrimp exports, which made up 94 percent of the
exports by value in 1974.[4] These production increases
can be largely attributed to the introduction of modern
fishery technology. Thus, motorized fishing boats in Indonesia increased from 1,456 in 1960 to 9,070 in 1973.
Likewise, the non-motorized fleet also increased in number at this time from 169,431 to 294,770 vessels.[5] This
increase in fishery activity has also been accompanied by
an attendant decline in catch per boat. Thus, in 1940,
the catch per boat was 4.0 tons of fish per year and the
catch per fisherman was 1.0 ton per year. In 1955, these
totals had declined to 3.13 tons of fish per boat per
year and .9 ton per fisherman per year, and by 1967, it
had decreased further to 2.6 tons per boat per year and
.8 ton per fisherman per year.[6] This decline can be partially attributed to over-exploitation and mismanagement
of fishing areas along Java's northern coast. More importantly, however, it must be noted that the effect of
the decline has not been equally distributed, for in
using modern fishing technology the catch per boat for
motorized vessels has increased, whereas traditional
sailing boats have experienced a sizeable reduction in
catch per boat.

Despite low levels of performance in the small-scale
artisanal fisheries industry there appears to be a wide
range of opportunities for increasing production within
this sector. Major production gains, especially in aquaculture, could be generated through management improvements in small-holder operations and by making available increased supplies of modern production inputs. However,
in order to properly assess the feasibility of adopting
these innovations, it is first essential to understand
the existing structure of the industry, and the constraints which will likely impede the adoption of measures to increase production.

In order to illuminate these issues in more detail,
three villages were selected for intensive study in the
northern coast of Java.[7] The three villages, named Banyutowo, Bandengan, and Rowosari, are within sixty kilometers of the city of Semarang on the northern coast of
central Java. Although the population sizes for each
village are similar, in 1974, the densities were 735 people per square kilometer in Banyutowo, 1439 in Rowosari,
and 1407 in Bandengan. The average population density
for other villages in Banyutowo's area was 1161 people
per square kilometer, and ranged from 321 to 2570. Only
two out of the 13 villages surveyed near Banutowo has
less than 1000 residents per square km, and two had more
than 2000 per square km. Those fifteen surveyed villages
near Rowosari had an average density of 1418 people per
square km; and the range was from 192 to 3298 per square

km. Again, only two villages had less than 1000, and three had more than 3000 per square km. These extremely high densities indicate the seriousness of the population problem on the north coast of Java.

The three sample villages are relatively representative of coastal villages in Java. In one study that obtained information from every village in Indonesia, the land in coastal villages in three kabupatens on the north coast was between 20 and 87 percent in rice fields, 0 to 45 percent in brackish water-ponds, and 5 to 21 percent in house gardens.[8] All three sample villages have irrigated fields (sawah) which are usually planted in rice. In Banyutowo there are 200.7 hectares in irrigated rice cultivation, 20.1 hectares in brackish water-ponds, and 39 hectares in house gardens. In Bandengan there are 82.4 hectares in rice cultivation, 79.6 hectares in brackish water-pond operations, and 10.2 hectares in house gardens. Rowosari has 82.4 hectares under rice cultivation and 31 hectares in house gardens. Although all three villages are considered to be in the coastal zone, Rowosari is situated two miles from the coast but has a river that fishermen use to gain access to the sea. One of the kampongs (section of the village) has fishermen households but there are no brackish water-ponds. In Banyutowo there are no fishermen or laborers on fishing boats.

Comparing those who have assets and those who do not, 54 percent of the household heads in Banyutowo have productive assets, and 42 percent are landless laborers; only 19 percent of the households in Rowosari have productive assets, and 60 percent are landless laborers; and 31 percent of the household heads in Bandengan have productive assets, and 46 percent are landless laborers. In Banyutowo, 52 percent of the households who own rice fields have less than .6 ha; in Rowosari 66 percent had less than .4 ha; and in Bandengan 52 percent had less than .6 ha. Only a few had more than 1 ha. Besides these amazingly small holdings, the most serious part is that only 47 percent of the household heads in Banyutowo, 19 percent in Rowosari, and 8 percent in Bandengan even own irrigated rice fields. In brief, the role of brackish water-pond operations and sea fisheries in this area, therefore, assumes great importance in providing employment and income opportunities for a relatively landless and impoverished labor force. Thus, it seems imperative that greater attention should be focussed upon acquiring a better understanding of artisanal fisheries in order to identify the future development prospects in this sector.

II

In coastal northern Java, it would appear that brackish water-pond operations hold great promise for increasing levels of production. Bardach estimates that,

> It appears technically feasible to increase aquaculture yields in the world from their present level of over five million metric tons by at least a factor of six, probably by more, within several decades, if concerted efforts are made in this direction. Biotechnical breakthroughs are not as essential here initially as are dissemination of skills and attention to basic conceptual and economic constraints.[9]

Thus, while Banyutowo and Bandengan represent villages that have low pond yields they could have exciting development prospects, if physical, social, and economic restraints can be partially alleviated. In this context, one of the most serious problems in the brackish water-pond culture of milkfish and shrimp is the shortage of fry and post-larval shrimp. Since there is not sufficient catch of fry in West and Central Java to supply these major brackish water-pond areas, most of the fry are distributed from sources along the coasts of Madura and shores in the neighborhood of Banyuwangi on the Strait of Bali. The long period of storage and transporting the fry reduces their vitality, resulting in high mortality rates of the fry in the nursery pond. The operators in Banyutowo and Bandengan give estimates of 60 to 80 percent, and even 100 percent rates of mortality. Published estimates of this rate in Java are between 70 and 80 percent mortality.[10] If only 20 to 30 percent of the fry in these ponds survive to maturity and are sold, then either the management is very poor or the quality of the fry is very bad. It is one topic which needs extensive research and improvement at the farm level because of the high cost of the fry. Only Schuster has made estimates of milkfish mortality at various stages, from catching it in the sea to the harvest of the ponds. He states that,

> At the fry stage, there is a 2 to 25 percent mortality rate during the shipment from the seacoast to the fishpond. At the fingerling stage in a six- to eight-week period, the mortality is between 50 to 70 percent. From the juvenile stage up to a maximal 500 gram weight in a period of eight to ten months, the mortality is between 20 to 30 percent. This means that for every 100 milkfish fry taken from the seacoast, only between 7 to 40 survive to reach the marketable

size of 500 grams.[11]

Recently, mortality may have been reduced by using plastic bags with oxygen supplied with it.

Stocking of post-larval shrimp in the ponds is a much different situation. Most of the pond operators rely on the tides to bring the post-larval and juvenile shrimp to their ponds, especially when the pond is being filled by sea water. Millions and millions of larvae must enter a pond to secure a normal yield. Consequently, the pond operators will frequently let water in and out to continually stock their ponds, and to catch shrimp daily. One of the pond operators in Bandengan village was informed by a relative from another area that he should switch his traditional methods of milkfish culture to an intensive polyculture of milkfish and shrimp or intensive monoculture of shrimp. In East Java and South Sulawesi, some operators do purchase shrimp and stock their ponds, but until recently, the operators in Banyutowo and Rowosari had no success in stocking their ponds with shrimp. In the past, the quality of the purchased juveniles was very poor and the mortality very high, and there is still a problem of buying enough shrimp juveniles for stocking. In brief, it appears that the intensive polyculture of fish and shrimp is a complicated management operation which must be fully understood if the operation is to be financially successful.

The high mortality rate in the culture of milkfish and shrimp for fish farmers in Bandengan and Banyutowo villages can be only partially attributed to the use of traditional production practices. Only recently (rainy season 1975) was credit available for the purchase of pesticides (Brestan-60) to eradicate the snails, and for fertilizer to improve the algae growth. The credit package also included some money to repair the dykes and water-gates, and some cash to finance adequate pond management. The effect of this improved pond technology should have been evident in the 1975 harvest, but unfortunately floods destroyed the fish crop and therefore the impact of the new technology could not be accurately measured. However, there were two fish farmers in Bandengan village who applied pesticide and fertilizer, and several others who watched them apply it, and this provides some information about their experiences and the problems associated with the use of the new technology in the ponds.

Brestan-60 was used to eradicate snails eating algae growth (kelekap) in competition with the milkfish, although in both villages snails were not a very serious problem because of their low population. Yet the use of Brestan still appeared to have some value. Before stocking, the pesticide was applied and most of the creatures in the ponds were killed, including the predators, like kakap, bloso, snakes, eels, and also shrimp. The tonang (dyke-boring eel) and crabs were also eradicated, which meant that the cost for maintaining the dykes was lower than before. Nevertheless, many pond operators felt that the use of Brestan brought about a decline in the daily catch of the shrimp. There is also a general feeling that the taste of the milkfish is not as good if the ponds are treated with Brestan. In contrast to these reports, one person claimed that the application of Brestan increased the size of the milkfish. Before Brestan was used, he stocked 2000 fingerlings, in his pond and it yielded 2 quintals at harvest, or about 100 grams in weight per fish. With Brestan in the same tambak he stocked 2500 fingerlings and the yield was 12 quintals or almost 500 grams per fish. The increased yield cannot be explained by the absence of snails or predators since he stocked with fingerlings and the mortality was low.

According to the recommended practices that accompany the available package credit program, in a one ha pond, 100 kg of Urea and 50 kg of triple-superphosphate should also be applied. In the pond of a prominent farmer the fertilizer induced a luxuriant bloom of algae growth, but this diminished quickly as the fingerlings grew larger. Successive fertilization did not duplicate the first algae bloom. In his opinion the reason was because, with every ebb-tide, water flowed in and out of the pond, carrying out the dissolved fertilizer, so that its effect was very much reduced. To dry the pond's floor completely was impossible since the water level was high due to a downpour. His experience suggests that, in order to be able to fully utilize the fertilizer, the pond should have a good water-gate able to completely stop the tide-water flow for a period of time. Also, the continued introduction of sea water brings predators with it.

Part of the money given as credit was to be used to improve existing ponds through the use of new gates and the strengthening of the dyke infrastructure, although most of the fishfarmers felt that the most pressing need was to remove unnecessary dykes which would increase the area of the pond. Improvement in pond gates is important, as most farmers use coconut-logs as timber for their gates. This is a low-cost investment, but the gates last for only 2-3 years because of the salt-water and attacks by limpets, barnacles, and shipworms. Dyke fortification is also needed against the hammering waves. If shrimp are cultured, it is especially important to deepen the pond. Improvements of this kind entail extensive moving of earth, and this takes time and requires a substantial number of laborers. Loans and other governmental assistance for this type of rehabilitation might be more important than the introduction of expensive fertilizers and pesticides.

While a wide range of measures could be adopted to improve pond production, progress in this area will like-

ly be constrained by a number of high risk factors.
Thus, annual floods, which are becoming more and more
troublesome, frequently allow an entire crop to escape,
silting up the ponds, and destroying the dykes and gates.
Pond operators in Banyutowo suffered losses because of
the floods in January 1976, and this is one reason for
their reluctance to adopt improved production practices.
Other aquacultural risks can be separated into biological
risks and physical risks. Limited knowledge about the
control of disease organisms and parasites, difficulty of
reproduction in captivity, introduction of aquatic predators through the water system, and lack of experience in
managing dense populations of aquatic animals, are the
main biological risks. Water quality, which is affected
by pollution and excessive organic matter, and storm and
flood damage, are the primary physical risks in pond culture. Because of these risks, some of which cannot be
avoided and others which are not sufficiently understood
by technical experts, it is obvious that pond operators
are confronted with many uncertainties.

Aside from further intensification and improvement of
existing pond operations, there seems to be limited opportunity for the construction of new ponds in Java.
Along the north coast of Java there are very few possible
locations for constructing ponds, mainly because mangrove areas have been severely reduced. The major exception to this is in regions near estuaries which are expanding seaward due to heavy silt loads in the rivers.
In addition, in West Java between Jakarta and Cirebon,
there are still areas that can be developed for brackish
water-ponds on the north coast. Nevertheless, a major
constraint in pond expansion is the fact that it requires
long construction periods and large capital outlays.
Construction costs near the shoreline are high because of
the continual digging and constructing of dykes against
the sea. A new pond may take as long as four years of
effort to construct before it can be used for milkfish,
and even then there is still risk of wave damage.

According to the village leader (lurah) in Banyutowo,
the first brackish water-ponds in the area were developed
in 1927 in a mangrove swamp. After this period, no new
ponds were developed because there was no siltation from
the river. Beginning in 1955, silt from the river began
forming mud deposits along the shore and they were able
to build ponds as the muddy shore advanced into the Java
Sea. The village leader in Banyutowo was given permission in the neighboring village of Bandengan to develop
six hectares of ponds in one of these newly forming shore
areas. It took five years before the dykes were stable
enough to resist storm waves. In addition, to develop
the initial pond in 1960, it took 10 men, working for 100
days at Rp 100 per man per day (in 1973 the wage increased to 150) for a two hectare pond, at a total labor

cost of Rp 100,000. The ponds were destroyed two times
in the five-year period, and it cost the same amount to
rebuild them. After the initial construction, only
shrimp could be harvested, and it was another five years
before the ponds were stocked with milkfish fry. In
brief, whatever the cost of developing new ponds, it is
clear that they are expensive to build and only the most
wealthy among village inhabitants can absorb the capital
costs entailed in such an undertaking.

III

In the three selected villages, the second major economic activity of the people is sea-fishing by use of
sailboats (perahu). Fifteen percent of the 476 heads of
households own fishing boats in Bandengan village, and
about 2 percent of the 551 households heads owned boats
in Rowosari village. No one in Banyutowo had fishing
boats and no laborers were employed in this sector. In
Bandengan, the major economic activity of 36 percent of
the household heads was working as laborer on fishing
boats, and in Rowosari, 21 percent of the household heads
were engaged as laborers on the fishing boats. In brief,
the fishing sector of the economies in Bandengan and
Rowosari employs 52 percent and 23 percent of the respec-
tive household heads.

Along the north coast of Java, a variety of boats,
both sail-powered and motor-powered, are capturing fish
using different types of gear. Sail-powered boats are
classified in three groups: small boats with a crew of
2 to 5 and using casting nets or lines; medium-sized
boats with a crew of 5 to 15 and using casting nets,
seine nets, or gill nets, and large-sized boats with a
crew of more than 15 and using traditional nets, seine
nets, or gill nets. Motor-powered boats vary from small,
outboard-powered boats with a crew of only a few people,
to inboard-powered boats of 5 to 30 gross tons with a
crew of 15 to 30 people and using purse seine or trawler
gear. Only owners of the small and medium sail-powered
fishing boats live in Bandengan and Rowosari villages,
although these people do operate in the same fishing
grounds near the coast as do the motor-powered fishing
boats which are based at the large port cities.

Indonesian policy-makers are faced with a dilemma:
how to expand fish production for the nutritional improvement of the population; how to increase shrimp exports for foreign exchange earnings; and how to modernize
the fishing fleet to take advantage of underexploited
areas. Their dilemma is, that to accomplish these three
above goals, the impact on the traditional fishing industry may cause social problems. Indonesia is not alone in
this complex situation. Christy, in one international

study of fishery arrangements, pointed out that "one particular conflict creates special difficulties in the
search for improved arrangements: the conflict between
the goal of increasing net economic returns from a fishery, and that of increasing opportunities for fisheries
employment."[13] He found that, "an increase in net economic revenues from a fully utilized fishery generally
necessitates a reduction in numbers of fishermen."[14]
Consequently, it is very difficult to achieve these two
goals at the same time.

In Java, various methods are being used to solve
these problems. Fishermen are being encouraged to buy
outboard motors to power their boats, private entrepre-
neurs have invested in motor-powered boats of 10 to 30
gross tons, and joint ventures with primarily Japanese
participation are using larger fishing vessels. Nevertheless, efforts to modernize the fleet with trawlers is
beginning to create problems for the sailboat fishermen
along the north coast. Trawling is primarily suited for
motorized fishing boats and, in contrast to other types
of fishing techniques, trawlers need a smaller crew.
Thus, what has been reported in Malaysia may now begin to
emerge in Indonesia. In Malaysia, the introduction of
trawling-gear on motor-powered boats caused unemployment
in the fishing industry. It has been reported that large
(above 60 hp) fish trawlers employed an average of 5 men,
small (below 60 hp) shrimp trawlers used 2 men, and a
purse seine boat (above 60 hp) used 20 men.[15] As the industry shifted from purse seining to trawling, fishermen
were forced out of the industry. Besides unemployment,
the other result from the introduction of modern trawling
technology was serious over-fishing in the coastal area.

In Java, increased competition for the fishery resources along the coast has been exacerbated by the present high price of shrimp in international markets and
the attempts of trawlers to satisfy this demand. According to one FAO report, in 1972, there were 100 shrimp
trawlers operating in the Cilacap area of southern Java,
and more than 200 were expected in 1973.[16] These trawlers were primarily from Sumatra, where the shrimp catches
were decreasing. It is, therefore, apparent that proper
management of the fishery resources of the north coast is
very important in order to provide maximum employment for
the people in this area.

The conflict between modern and traditional fishing
technology is a major problem in Bandengan and Rowosari.
Near the estuaries where the villages are located, the
operations of trawlers have created friction with the
local fishermen. The local fishermen accuse the powered
fishing boats of over-exploiting the fishing grounds and
damaging local fishing nets. If a new, near-shore shrimp
area is located, every boat, including the trawlers con-
verge on the spot. In the frenzy of catching the shrimp,

nets are entangled and torn, and almost always the trawlers get the biggest catch. At night these trawlers
sometimes enter the near-shore estuarine waters without
any lights and their license numbers covered. Again,
during these clandestine operations, many nets of the local fishermen are torn.

Fishermen living along the north coast of Java have
been complaining about their decreasing catch for several
years. Most blame the problem on the trawlers. Yet the
number of non-motorized fishing boats in Indonesia increased from 167,975 in 1969, to 285,700 in 1973. Relating this to the selected villages in this study, the number of small sail-powered fishing boats in Bandengan
village increased from 69 in 1971, to 182 in 1972, and to
240 boats in 1973, and with almost no increase in large-
and medium-sized boats.[17] Placing the blame on one or
the other is, therefore, very difficult, and most likely it
reflects an increased competition for the shrimp. In
addition, with the increased use of nets made of very
fine mesh, it is likely that depletion is occurring with
the catching of both immature and juvenile shrimp. The
decline in per boat catch is most dramatic for small- and
medium-sized boats. For small boats in Bandengan and
Rowosari, the average catch was 950 kg for the one-half
year in 1972, and 550 kg for the half year in 1974. For
medium boats in Bandengan, the decline was from 9,710 kg
in 1972, to 3,800 in 1974. Accompanying the decline in
per boat catch has been an attendant decrease in incomes.
Fishermen estimates of the net return to the owner-cap-
tain of the small boats in 1972 (6 months), was an average
of Rp 109,450 and in 1974 (6 months), it was 28,240. Returns for medium-sized boats also declined from Rp
161,460 in 1972, to Rp 65,580 in 1974 for the six-month
period. When the catch declines because of the sharing
system between laborers, the cost of labor also declines
proportionally. Thus, labor costs were Rp 50,810 (small
boats) and Rp 426,560 (medium boats) in the six-month
period in 1972, and Rp 18,230 and Rp 284,470 (medium
boats) in the six-month period in 1974.

Since there were no motor-powered boats owned by
residents in Bandengan and Rowosari villages, this study
was not able to include estimates of income and employment for these boats. However, other research efforts in
areas on the north coast of Java, as well as in other
regions, have included respondents who operate motor-
powered fishing boats. One of these studies was by
Supradono in Batang Kabupaten, which is located on the
north coast, not more than 100 km west of Bandengan and
Rowosari.[18] He estimates that the average net return to
the seagoing owners of the sail-powered fishing boats in
1974, was Rp 4,640 per month and the value of the catch
was Rp 17,660 per month. These estimates correspond
rather well with the figures from Bandengan and Rowosari

and point out that returns to small fishing boat operators are very low. In contrast, the returns to the
motor-powered boats in his study were substantially
greater. Using traditional gear, the motor-powered boats
caught fish worth Rp 734,120 per month in 1974, and the
sea-going owner earned a net return of Rp 198,710. Thus,
returns to this improved method of fishing were more than
40 times the returns to the traditional method, and yet
employed only three times the number of people. Larger
motor-powered boats using purse seine nets caught an estimated amount of fish worth Rp 2,925,170 per month in
1974, which provided a net return to the owner of Rp
1,405,580 per month. Employing only an average of 31 laborers in the crew, this type of boat and gear caught
more than 300-times the amount of fin fish and shrimp and
required only about 4 times the crew size as the traditional sail-powered boats. Viewed from a different angle,
a motor-powered boat using traditional gear and employing
22 crew members caught the same amount of fish as 41
sail-powered boats employing 287 people. One motor-
powered boat using purse seine gear and having a crew of
31 men caught the same amount as 165 sail-powered boats
employing 1,155 crew members.

Obviously, the above comparisons are not fair because
motor-powered boats can operate in seas that the sailboats cannot reach. However, if all three types of fishing boats are competing for the same fish and shrimp
population in the same area, there will be a displacement
of laborers by the more efficient motor boats, which are
capable of using more modern gear, especially the trawl
nets. Thus, although there are substantial groups of
people in these coastal villages who depend on fishing,
with modernization of fishery technology, the employment
opportunities in this industry appear to be shrinking.
As an example, in West Java the number of fishermen declined from 90,976 in 1968, to 56,921 in 1971, and this
was at a time when the number of fishing sailboats remained fairly constant and the number of motor-powered
fishing boats increased from 150 to 285.[19] It is not
clear what caused this decline, but part of it may be due
to the increase in motor-powered fishing boats. In Cirebon Kabupaten in West Java, the value of the fish catch
increased almost 10 times, from Rp 62 million in 1970 to
Rp 523 million in 1974. Yet, the number of fishing sailboats increased by only 11 percent and the motor-powered
fishing boats increased from 5 to 123.[20] Almost all of
the motor-powered fishing boats are from the city and
port of Cirebon. At one point in 1974, 112 motor fishing
boats were from the city of Cirebon and only two were
from the coastal villages in the kabupaten. On the other
hand, there were 19 large sailboats, 1,840 medium-sized,
and 421 small-fishing sailboats used in the coastal villages, and only 80 medium-sized and 91 small-sailfishing

boats based in the city of Cirebon.[21] This indicates
there has been a shift in the fishing fleet's base of
operations from the coastal villages to the city of Cirebon, and it appears that the major increase in the catch
was due to these motor-powered fishing boats based in the
port city. All of the motor-powered fishing boats in the
port city are trawlers, and apparently some have moved
their operations from Sumatra to the north coast of Java,
especially to the Jakarta, Cirebon, Tegal, Pekalongan,
Semarang, and Cilacap areas.[22] Because of the financial
capital needed to purchase and operate the trawlers, and
lack of credit availability, most of the fishermen in the
coastal villages cannot participate in this modernization
of the fishing fleet. Reasons for the shift to the larger ports may be that some people in these cities have
enough capital and confidence to invest in this industry.
In addition, in the larger ports there is easier access
to dockyards, landing and mooring sites, spare parts,
cold storage facilities, and buyers.

The increase in the number of trawlers is also occurring in Central Java. Between 1968 and 1973, the number
of motor-powered fishing boats increased from 121 to
269.[23] During the same period, the total fish catch increased from 30,240 tons to 35,555. However, the catch
decreased very substantially in Kendal, a kabupaten in
Central Java, where it dropped from 2,230 tons to 1,594
tons between 1973 and 1974.[24] Some officials in the
kabupaten feel that the decrease is due to the trawlers
from Semarang operating off the coast of Kendal. A recent newspaper article indicates that fish exports from
Central Java, by three exporters in Semarang, the capital
city of the province, have greatly increased. Thus, in
1974, the fish exports from Central Java yielded US
$5,584,796, but in the previous year the export revenue
was only US $374,464.[25]

The clash between modern and traditional fishery
practices on the north coast of Java brings a sense of
urgency to the task of devising techniques which would
increase production, but at the same time maintain the employment absorbing capacity of this important industry.
Apparently, there are cases where there have been suc-
cesses in modernizing the fishing fleet at a low cost.
For example in Western Samoa, the traditional fishermen
have motorized their sailboats at low cost.

Western Samoa has adopted an approach to small-
scale fisheries development in which the introduced technology appears to be both financially
and conceptually within the capabilities of the
rural fishermen. The Fisheries Division of Western Samoa estimates that the traditional Samoan
double-hulled fishing craft, the alia, can be
constructed for US $390. The 20 hp outboard

required to drive the _alia_ can be purchased
for $250 with an additional $65 required for
fishing gear.[26]

Ritterbush has also stated that "The rural fisherman's
range of operations is limited by the design and power of
their fishing craft and by their traditional fishing
methods. In the tropical temperatures of coastal areas
of Asia, between 30 and 40 percent of the catch spoils
for lack of systems to preserve and transport it."[27] In
this context, with the provision of appropriate government
assistance programs, the fishermen on the north coast of
Java who have medium-sized sailboats could afford to develop auxiliary power on their boats and perhaps some
form of small-scale cooling system for catch preservation. The fishermen of South Sulawesi already use a
single-hulled boat with double outrigger and a platform
for a small (10-20 hp) diesel motor. The cost of this
craft is approximately $500.

                            IV

    In the September 1976, issue of the _Scientific Ameri-_
can, there were twelve articles on food and agriculture
that covered topics related to providing food for the
world's future population. Unfortunately, the potential
of the world's estuaries, mangrove swamps, sago swamps,
and coastal fringes have not been included in this assessment of the world's potential. Only one of the nu-
tritionists briefly recognized the decline in the harvest
of the seas and the potential of aquaculture.[28] Since
they were writing about agriculture, perhaps this termi-
nology prevented the other authors from discussing the
role of artisanal fisheries in the food systems of the
world. If they had not been primarily concerned with the
global situation, they could have investigated the potential of food systems which are important in specific regions of the world. Thus, in this paper it is the author's view that fisheries play a significant role in the
food systems of Southeast Asia. It is likely that this
region has more artisanal fishermen, if excluding freshwater, than any other part of the globe. Potential areas
for expanding artisanal fish culture are also probably
the greatest in Southeast Asia. In his article on "The
Resources Available for Agriculture," it appears that
Roger Revelle excluded the extensive mangrove swamps of
Asia in his estimate of the potential gross cropped
areas.[29] Yet, the culture of fish in brackish water-
ponds could bring significant areas of these mangrove
swamps into production without substantial damage to the
coastal ecology. Sumatra alone has 3000 sq kilometers of
mangrove forests, both as a wide forest and as a strip

along the coast in front of the swamp forests.

The regions discussed in this paper are natural tropical coastal ecosystems of high diversity.[30] Agriculture, fishing, and aquacultural management techniques created in the temperate developed countries, usually for monoculture, have very little relevance for these very diverse ecosystems. Yet, it is this tropical coastal zone that still has underexploited and unexploited resources that can be utilized for helping to support the massive populations of the Asian countries. If the appropriate cropping patterns and coastal zone management systems are developed, then the potential can possibly be fulfilled.

The potential for increasing artisanal fishery production is particularly important in Java, where a wide range of developmental measures will need to be taken in order to generate more employment opportunities for a rapidly-increasing labor force. A review of the existing data on labor-use within Java's northern coastal economy illuminates the significance of artisanal-fishery operations as a major employment-absorbing sector. Based upon a limited number of micro-studies it appears that labor-use per hectare in brackish water-ponds ranges between 130 and 250 workdays per season, with the length of the production season varying from 6 to 9 months. In sea fisheries, small-sail fishing boats use 280 to 480 workdays per boat for a six-month period. Labor-use on medium-sized sailboats is quite varied, ranging from 300 to 1530 workdays per boat. Large sailboats have between 520 and 1780 workdays per season, and the motor-powered boats vary between 710 and 800 workdays. In contrast, for these same areas, rice production uses from 160 to 250 workdays per hectare per season, although this estimate does not include harvest labor.

Two important points can be derived from the above labor-use data. First, the three food systems (brackish water-ponds, small sailboats, and rice fields) use about the same amount of labor per unit. The ponds appear to use only somewhat less labor per unit. However, it must be noted that the average size of the ponds is much larger than the rice fields. Thus, if size of operation is used as the basis for comparison, then the brackish water-ponds clearly use 5 to 6 times more labor than rice field operations. Ranking these operations by scale, the brackish water-ponds use much more labor, followed by the small sailboats, and last would be the rice fields because of their small size. Although the facts are not yet available, an intuitive guess is, that for labor-use per investment dollar, the sailboats would be much higher than the ponds, followed by the rice fields. Comparing the two culture systems, ponds probably use more labor per investment dollar per hectare than the rice fields per hectare. Consequently, it appears that sea fishing

by small sailboats is the easiest industry for a person
with limited capital to enter. In this context, it is
important to note that Firth found in his study of Malay
fishermen that there was more opportunity for entry of
the marginal worker into fishing if he has other sources
of income.[31] Unfortunately, if current policies (and,
they appear to be changing) remain in effect which favor
the modernization of the fishing fleet along coastal
Java, the prospects for marginal and landless labor to
engage in this economic activity would seem to be quite
limited.

In terms of total investment priorities within the
artisanal sector, the evidence suggests that much could
be gained in devoting greater attention to increasing
production of brackish water-ponds. In Bandengan and
Banyutowo, milkfish yields averaged between 140 and 160 kg,
and the Indonesian Department of Fisheries estimates that
for the northern coast of Java the average yields are between 300 and 400 kg.[32] In contrast to these low yields,
a United Nations study suggests that under intensive management, yields in the tropics reach an average of 6,000
to 7,000 kg/ha.[33] Yields of this rather fantastic magnitude may be out of the reach of small-scale artisanal-
pond operators, but it does clearly suggest that a yield
of 150 kg can and must be greatly increased.

A number of development measures could be adopted to
increase per hectare yields of milkfish and shrimp in
brackish water-pond operations. Particular importance
should be attached to improving the quality and supply of
milkfish fry and post-larval shrimp to the ponds. Marketing channels and means of transport must also be improved, although less is known about this part of the industry than any other segment. While efforts are in
progress to develop a technology for spawning milkfish
and establishing hatcheries, less expensive improvements
in distribution from the catching points to the ponds
will have much greater impact on the ponds. The latter
improvement would not eliminate jobs, whereas the creation of fry hatcheries would create some labor displacement. In order to improve the capacity of the ponds and
create a demand for hired labor, credit should be provided to the operators to remove the higher parts of the
ponds and to increase their depth and to install better
functioning water gates. Public works programs by the
regional governments to improve the canals from the sea
and rivers to the ponds would also assist intensification
and provide work for the landless. These measures should
include improved drainage in the rice fields. Better
flood control, which would also require massive public
works projects, would reduce the seasonal risk in these
ponds and make investment in intensification more attractive. Finally, in order to increase income and to generate more employment, polyculture of milkfish and shrimp

needs to be emphasized, although the lack of sufficient
supply of good quality, low-cost post-larval shrimp and
the limited availability of informed extension advice
will continue to impede progress in this area. In South
Sulawesi an important development is the beginning of
monoculture or shrimp in ponds.

Some mention is in order concerning the possibility
of expanding brackish water-pond operations in the outer
islands, where significant efforts are currently underway
to open new settlement areas for transmigrants from Java.
There are potential areas for brackish water-ponds which
stretch along the east coast of Sumatra, the south coast
of Java, almost the entire length of Kalimantan, various
areas on Sulawesi, and major sections of Irian Jaya. In
Sumatra and Kalimantan, a major problem in developing
these brackish water-ponds is the type of soil in the
coastal areas. In both of these islands there are acid
sulphate soils covering 2 million hectares, which occur in
young marine deposits fringing the sea coasts of Kalimantan, Sumatra, and Irian Jaya. Organic soils (peat) occur
along the eastern coast of Sumatra, the western and
southern coasts of Kalimantan, and the southern coast of
Irian Jaya. Reclamation of the acid sulphate soils is a
delicate affair. They have poor agricultural properties,
and yields in fish ponds are low. It may be that milkfish will have low yields under these conditions, but
that shrimp culture could possibly return some satisfactory yields. The peat soils must also be carefully managed, but properly reclaimed peat makes excellent soils
for agriculture. Again, however, it is not clear if
brackish water-ponds could also be developed in these
soils. In summary, before any major development effort
is launched to expand brackish water operations in the
outer islands, feasibility studies will have to be undertaken in order to determine how much of the several million hectares of swamp can be exploited without seriously
disturbing the ecosystem of these areas. As Odum has
pointed out, "the entire estuarine ecosystem must be studied, monitored, managed, and zoned and human uses regulated in the terms of the whole. Otherwise estuaries can
only suffer the tragedy of the commons."[34]

In artisanal seacoast fishing, the main problem is
overfishing off the north coast of Java, and therefore,
new modes of resource management will be required in
maintaining the viability of this important income- and
employment-generating sector. Three alternative policies
are available for resolving the overfishing problems.
The first alternative would entail permitting only sail-
powered fishing boats to exploit the resources of the
Java Sea. This approach would serve to eliminate motor-
powered boats, but it would also be accompanied by a decline in total catch, as sail-powered boats cannot effectively reach all of the fishing grounds. A second

alternative would be to allow the motor-powered boats
free access to all the resources of the Java Sea including the coastal zone. Total catch and exports would increase but the artisanal fishermen would gradually be
eliminated and have to seek employment in other sectors
of an already excessively labor-abundant economy. A
third and more preferable alternative would be to establish fishing zones which would separate the sailboats and
motor-powered boats, with each zone being exploited to
its maximum sustainable yield. Actually, there already
have been fishing zones established by the government but
they are not adequately enforced. If inadequate regulation continues, it is likely that conflict between the
artisanal fishermen and the modernized fleet of trawlers
and purse seiners will increase and their catches will
continue to decline. One mode of stiffening the enforcement of fishing zones would be to place buoys in the
water, demarcating the zones, with motor-powered vessels
operating in the sailboat zone being liable to seizure by
local fishermen. If it was publicly announced that the
catch of any boats seized would be for the village, then
there would be a rush by the motorized fleet to comply
with the zones.

Once there is a protected zone for the small-scale
non-motor-powered fishermen, then other steps can be
taken to develop their productivity. Thus, spoilage
could be reduced through the introduction of motor-
powered purchasing ships that would buy the catch at sea
from the artisanal fishermen and quickly bring it to port
for processing. It is also possible that motor-ships
could be equipped with processing units and used to tow
the smaller sailboats to the more distant fishing grounds
in the Java Sea. Finally, artisanal fishermen could
benefit from improved nets, boat designs, and from the
increased availability of ice for use in packing fish at
sea.

In summary, this paper has examined artisanal fisheries food systems and suggested ways to develop these
systems in the framework of the traditional village economy. To support a family in Java, members work at a
great variety of jobs. By developing artisanal fisheries
on the north coast of Java, job opportunities will be
created for the landless and near-landless people. In
this way, population pressure on limited resources can be
lessened in the rural coastal villages. Other measures
will also be needed in strengthening the capacity of the
village to support its residents, and therefore artisanal
fisheries development should be only one component of a
larger effort if these villages are to survive in the
future.

NOTES

1. Fuad Cholik, "Present Status of Milkfish and Shrimp Culture in Indonesia and Its Problems with Special Reference to Those in South Sulawesi," (Macassar: Fisheries Research Institute, 1973) p. 7.
2. Ibid.
3. Eddiwan, "Economic Aspects of Fish Processing," in Proceedings, 7th Indo-Pacific Fisheries Conference, (Bangkok: Food and Agricultural Organization, 1958), p. 109.
4. "The Pattern of Fish Marketing and Its Prespects," The Indonesia Times, June 27, 1975.
5. These statistics are secured from N. Zachman, "Fisheries Development and Management in Indonesia," Journal of the Fisheries Research Board of Canada 30, no. 12, Part 2 of 2 (December 1973): 2335-2340; and Department of Fisheries, The Present Status of Fisheries in Indonesia (Jakarta: Directorate General Perikanan, 1975), p. 2.
6. Sulaiman Krisnandhi, "The Economic Development of Indonesia's Sea Fishing Industry," Bulletin of Indonesian Economic Studies 5, no. 1 (March 1969): 52.
7. An initial rice producing survey was conducted in Banyutowo and Rowosari from 1968 through 1972. Some of these 60 sampled farmers had brackish water-ponds. In 1974, another survey was conducted in the Banyutowo and Bandengan (129 sample farmers) and this involved an attempt to estimate income and employment for the year 1973 among brackish water-pond operators and fishermen. The 1974 study did not use the same sample that was used in the 1973 study, though there were several producers who were in both studies. A household census was conducted in all three villages in 1974 (total sample size of 1320), and again in the latter part of 1974, a rice, pond, and fishing study was undertaken in Bandengan (93 sample farmers). Finally, in 1974-1976, a larger study on the rice, pond, and fishing ecology of the three villages was undertaken involving a sample of 265 villagers. It is in this manner that the data on the three villages has been collected over the past seven years.
8. This information is based on village studies conducted in the Kendal, Cirebon, and Indramayu Kabupatens from the Pembangunan Masyarakat Desa's (Department of Interior) survey of all villages in Indonesia in 1971.
9. John Bardach, "Fisheries Prospects for the Future-Freshwater and Marine," in Nevin S. Scrimshaw and Mois'Se B'Ehar, eds., Nutrition and Agricultural Development (New York: Plenum, 1976), p. 379.
10. Hasanuddin Saanin, "On the Occurrence of Chanos Fry in Indonesian Waters," (Bangkok: Indo-Pacific Fisheries Council, Proceedings, 1954): 85; and W. H. Schuster, Fish Culture in Brackish Water-Ponds of Java (Bangkok: Indo-Pacific Fisheries Council, Special Publication, 1952).
11. W. H. Schuster, "Synopsis of Biological Data on Milkfish, Chanos-chanos (Forskal)," FAO Fisheries Biology Synopsis No. 4 (Rome: U.N. Food and Agricultural Organization, 1960): 17.
12. Schuster, Fish Culture in Brackish Water Ponds of Java, p. 62.

13. Francis T. Christy, Jr., Alternative Arrangements for Marine Fisheries: an Overview (RFF/PISFA, 1973), p. 26.

14. Ibid.

15. Yap Chan Ling, "Trawling: Its Impact on Employment and Resource Use on the West Coast of Peninsular Malaysia" (Paper presented at the East-West Center's Seminar on Fisheries Development, September 1976), p. 5.

16. J. A. Gulland, Some Notes on the Assessment and Management of Indonesian Fisheries (Indian Ocean Fishery Commission, FAO/UNDP, 1973), p. 10.

17. This data was secured from the Office of the Fisheries Extension Service in Kendal Kabupaten.

18. G. Supradono, "Pengaruh Tehnik-Tehnik Baru Didalam Masyarakat Nelayan," (Yogyakarta: Universitas Gadjah Mada, 1975).

19. Universitas Pajajaran, Penelitian Daerah Untuk Bahan Perencanaan Pembangunan Jawa Barat, Sektor Perikanan (Bandung: Fakultas Pertanian, 1972).

20. This data was secured from the Office of Sea Fisheries for the Cirebon Kabupaten.

21. Fisheries Extension Service, Laporan Tahunan Jawatan Perikanan Laut Jawa Barat Wilayah Kabupaten/Kotamadya Cirebon 1973/1974 (Cirebon: Sea Fisheries Office, 1975), p. 10.

22. Fisheries Extension Service, Laporan Tahunan Jawatan Perikanan Laut Propinsi Jawa Barat Wilaya Kabupaten/Kotamadya Cirebon 1972/1973 (Cirebon: Sea Fisheries Office, 1974), p. 30.

23. Fisheries Extension Service, Laporan Tahunan Dinas Perikanan Daerah Propinsi Jawa-Tengah (Semarang: Sea Fisheries Office, 1973).

24. This data was secured from the Fisheries Extension Service in Kendal Kabupaten.

25. "Tira Raya Mina Tumpuan Harapan Nelayan," Sinar Jaya, April 5, 1975.

26. Stephen Ritterbush, "Problems in Planning Small-Scale Fisheries Programs for the Pacific Islands," (International Center for Living Aquatic Resource Management, 1976), p. 6.

27. Ibid.

28. Jean Mayer, "The Dimensions of Human Hunger," Scientific American 235, no. 3 (September 1976): 45-49.

29. Roger Revelle, "The Resources Available for Agriculture," Scientific American 235, no. 3 (September 1976): 14.

30. Eugene P. Odum, Fundamentals of Ecology (Philadelphia: W. B. Saunders Co., 1953), p. 355.

31. Raymond Firth, Malay Fishermen--Their Peasant Economy (Hamden: Archon Books, 1966), p. 2.

32. Directorate General of Fisheries, "Strategy and Policy in Fisheries Development in Indonesia with Special Emphasis on the Development of the Artisanal Fisheries," (Proceedings, Indo-Pacific Fisheries Council, 1974), p. 179.

33. Report by the Secretary General, "Coastal Area Management and Development," (New York: United Nations Economic and Social Council, 1974), p. 20.

34. Odum, Fundamentals of Ecology, p. 362.

16
Lowland Forestry Management

Willem Meijer

The "New Order" rulers who assumed power in 1965, quickly discovered that forestry and forest industries can play a significant role in economic development. Indeed, during the past ten years an enormous boom developed, with Indonesian forest products now holding a position of second place behind oil as a foreign export earner. By establishing a favorable climate for foreign investment and by controlling inflation, the government has been able to attract a large volume of foreign and local capital in support of forestry development. In the wake of this capital inflow, more than half of all the available commercial lowland forests of the "Outer Islands" of Indonesia, the rather thinly populated regions outside Java, have been allocated to foreign and local timber concessions. The volume of logging in these areas is sizeable and Indonesia can now claim to be the number one exporter of non-coniferous sawlogs and veneer logs. Out of a total world trade of 45.8 million cubic meters traded during the peak year of 1974, Indonesia traded 18.0 million, followed by Malaysia 12.2, the Philippines 4.7, and the Ivory Coast 3.2.[1]

Indonesia has the largest forest resource in Asia (about 63 percent of its total area of 202.7 million hectares). The recent timber boom has caused great concern among people who are afraid that Indonesia may suffer irreparable harm as a result of the ecological stress and resource depletion associated with the logging of its tropical moist forest. In this context, the following analysis is devoted to an exploration of some of the problems currently being encountered in the management of Indonesian forest resources, with some attention also being focussed upon the issue of land use planning in the protection of forested areas.

I

The bulk of Indonesia's forest resources, 120 million hectares in total, are concentrated on the islands of Sumatra, Kalimantan, Sulawesi and West Irian. Denudation and erosion have depleted approximately 30 million hectares of this total, and current projections indicate that 48 million hectares are available for exploitation.[2] Timber concessions have been granted for over 22 million hectares of forested areas, with nearly half of this total being located in Kalimantan, where it is expected that nearly 15 million hectares of the island's forests will be conceded to commercial logging. In Kalimantan and Sumatra, most of the accessible lowland forests are already being logged, and the rate of logging is such that the entire area will likely be depleted of forests products within twenty to thirty years. Unless proper management plans are introduced, there will be a long period of regeneration before many of these areas can be reharvested for their forest products. In other cases, depleted timber concessions will simply be lost to spontaneous or organized transmigration with the land being converted to non-forest agriculture.

In great measure, the excessive rate of logging in the outer islands can be attributed to government regulations which provide an annual allowable cut based upon thirty-five year rotation. For a number of reasons, this rotational formula will not be of sufficient duration to allow for the regeneration of the lowland forests. Seedlings of dipterocarps and most other commercial trees cannot grow into loggable sizes within thirty-five years.[3] In addition, the continued practice of overcutting has meant that not enough sound, undamaged pole-sized trees are left to grow into a new crop within twenty to thirty-five years. Finally, with the increased establishment of local saw mills, it is likely that higher levels of utilization will be strived for and the heavier a forest is logged, the longer the regrowth will take; provided some dipterocarp seedlings can survive it could take from sixty to seventy years to complete the regeneration process.[4]

The current rate and magnitude of logging in Indonesia will soon pose some serious problems with respect to both the conservation of the country's forestry resources and the maintenance of the larger eco-system which serves to sustain a productive economy in forest and non-forest agriculture. Degradation of catchment areas in the cutting of protective forests has already occurred in the Lampung Province in southern Sumatra, and a new concession threatens the Lindu Lake. Other protected forests officially designated as nature reserves are being logged-over for commercial purposes. The

Kutai forest reserve in East Kalimantan, originally 300,000 hectares in area, has been partly felled. A similar fate has befallen the Way Kambas area in South Sumatra, where designated reserves have been subjected to indiscriminate logging. Likewise, in the early 1970s, concessions were given out for logging inside the Simangka reserve in south Sumatra. In many of these areas serious soil disturbance has occurred because of the use of heavy tractors and residual burning; a condition which will further delay the regenerative process.

While the exploitation of Indonesia's forests through large-scale commercial logging is increasing at an accelerated pace, the problems associated with the rapid depletion of these resources is further magnified when allowance is made for the cutting of forested areas in making way for spontaneous and sponsored transmigration schemes, and in the increasingly intensified burning of forested areas by shifting cultivators. All of these problems are dramatically illuminated in Lampung province in south Sumatra, where widespread forest devastation can be attributed to the rapid expansion of transmigration settlement schemes and the opening of forested areas to extensive commercial logging. The population of this province has increased from 1.5 million to over 3 million inhabitants in the past ten years, and a once forest-clad area of 3.2 million hectares has now been reduced to approximately 900,000 hectares of standing timber. Most of the cutting has been done by transmigrants and local shifting cultivators through slash and burn culture. These inroads have resulted in the destruction of over 2 million hectares of primary dipterocarp forest. Many of these deforested areas have either been converted to dry-land farms or left to grow over with alang-alang grass. In addition, many of the catchment areas have also been denuded, thereby reducing the prospects for introducing irrigated agriculture. In order to avoid the further destruction of the natural resource base in the province, major advances will have to be made in the introduction of land use planning, with high priority being given to the replanting of forests in catchment areas, the curtailment of cutting in remaining hydrological reserves, and the protection of soils and water supplies through the adoption of mixed tree crops in homestead gardens and orchards.

Aside from the obvious ecological hazards associated with the unplanned and unregulated depletion of Indonesia's forests, there are also other losses and costs involved in the rapid dimunition of these resources. Forests are the habitats of the orangutan, the Sumatra tiger, hornbills, anoa, babirusa, and other countless rare animals, some hardly known to science. Biologists and nature conservationists can also make a strong case for the need of preserving adequate samples of various types of tropical lowland forests, in order to safeguard the genepool of their enormous genetic diversity. More research is urgently needed to find out how large such reserves should be before the level of logging serves to depauperate Indonesia's natural ethnobotanical heritage.

An added argument for the exercise of greater caution in the logging of Indonesia's forests can be made with respect to the protection of the so-called orang asli, the aboriginal people still living in many of the interior forests. In Sulawesi some of these tribes are known as Toana; others as Tara Towa.[5] The ability of these people to live in harmony with their jungle surroundings deserves more intensive scientific study. Their uses of food plants, methods of hunting, and knowledge of poisonous and medicinal plants could be of great practical value. The existence of these and other tribes in the jungles of Sulawesi has largely been ignored by those authorities responsible for the issuing of timber licences. The mountainous regions of the Luwah peninsula are without proper surveys by forestry staff and no attempts have been made to locate native tribes in areas given out as timber concessions. According to reports from Ujung Pandang, native people living on islands near Sulawesi have been deprived of their primary jungle surroundings through wholesale logging of the forests. A similar fate threatens inhabitants of the Mentawei Islands west of Sumatra.

II

While a plan of action is urgently needed for the effective protection and proper management of Indonesia's forestry resources, it will be difficult to introduce such measures within the near future. Actions of this kind can only be initiated under government leadership, but the requisite priority of public sector interest along with the attendant required level of institutional resources is of a magnitude less than sufficient to allow for the needed reforms in the protection and regulation of Indonesia's forest resources. The obstacles which stand in the way of enforcing a rational and controlled plan of forestry development are many and various, but particular attention can be focussed upon specific and major deficiencies in policy measures, manpower development, and in the necessary generation of basic scientific data about Indonesia's forests.

In the post-1965 New Order era, the government has placed major emphasis upon the rapid development of Indonesia's natural resources. The forestry industry has been a major target in this effort and with the granting of timber concessions, major capital outlays are being

expended in logging these areas. The exploitation of
these logging concessions has largely been given over to
private firms, with much of the capital and technology
coming from foreign companies, both large and small, but
with usually passive joint venture participation with
Indonesian counterpart firms. The sudden and massive
intrusion of foreign capital in the forestry sector has
brought forth a lucrative and rewarding flow of revenue
and other financial resources to both public and private
sector institutions in Indonesia. In many cases, government agencies, long accustomed to operating on shoe-
string budgets, have been able to greatly enhance their
financial condition by virtue of their link with forestry production. In East Kalimantan, where logging activities have approached boom conditions, the provincial
government is entitled to 70 percent of the license and
royalty receipts generated by the logging concessions.
These receipts constitute a major portion of the revenue
for the provincial government and they account as well
for funds set aside for reforestation, but in East Kalimantan they are, in fact, not yet used for that purpose.
All sides, whether public or private, have benefitted
from the great surge in forestry production, and since
all have a stake in its growing prosperity, little attention has been given to the introduction of proper
management and conservation practices. Rather, all the
incentives seem to lead in the direction of relaxing
those measures which might stand in the way of sustaining and expanding commercial logging.

During the past several years some voices have been
raised against the unregulated exploitation of the country's vast timber resources, but even under the best of
conditions, where the political environment might be
supportive of enforcing such measures, the necessary
manpower base is simply not available to perform this
important but exceedingly difficult task. More explicitly, the performance of the forestry service is seriously constrained by severe shortages in number of personnel and training. Until recently, most forestry
management activities have been focussed in Java, where
a full 70 percent of the Directorate of Forestry staff
is employed. In the outer islands, the forestry service are few in number and assume only a marginal role
in forestry management. The problem is notably illus-
trated in East Kalimantan, an area where logging operations have been the most extensive. In 1973, the forestry service in this area numbered over 400 in total,
whereas nearly 3000 staff would be needed to efficient-
ly monitor an area involving 77 concessions covering a
total 7.5 million hectares.[6] Unfortunately, very little
government revenue generated by commercial forestry is
being allocated to enhance the capacities of the forestry service.

The problem of assuring proper forestry management
in a context of major deficiencies in manpower and
levels of training is further complicated by the absence of botanical research and insufficient surveys on
soil and forestry resources. Very little well documented data has been collected on detailed forest composition, the distribution of tree species, and their
specific autecology. Making good herbarium collections
of trees is no longer part of the program of foresters
carrying out forest surveys. Solid and reliable data
on the growth and yield of species are also very scanty.
Notwithstanding the availability of the magnificent
arboretum of the Bogor Botanical Garden, the diversity
of forests in Indonesia is so large that it will not be
possible to bring all the 10,000 or so species of trees
together in one central arboretum.[7] Regional research
and training centers, each specializing on its own surroundings, will be needed to undertake research of this
kind.

In the absence of an adequate data base on the
distribution of forest types, it is almost impossible to
introduce sound site-specific guidelines for proper
forestry management. Thus, while documents from the
Department of Forestry provide aggregate figures in
number of hectares of designated protective and productive forest, little reliable information is available
on the distribution of these areas by actual location.
Only 13 percent of Indonesia's total land mass has been
inventoried and specified in good but often outdated
topographical maps. Indeed, some of the forest currently allocated to timber concessions could be classified
as suitable for conversion to agriculture, and then produce a much higher output of timber per hectare than
forests which have to stay in the "tree bank." As long
as such classifications are not made and as long as no
allowance is being made for the very different botanical
comparisons between forests types in relationship to
various soil conditions and amount of stocking, there is
little justification in putting down rules for intensive
management for concessions.

In the absence of an institutional infrastructure
designed to generate baseline inventories of Indonesia's
forests, and to provide an attendant supply of trained
manpower equal to the task of managing these resources,
the government has sought to justify the rapid growth of
commercial logging on grounds that, in observing a
policy of "sustained yield" and planned reforestation,
adequate protection can be assured in the conservation
of the country's timber reserves. Upon closer examination, however, it appears that these policies hold out
little promise of enabling the government to assure adequate management of the forested areas. Thus, according
to the regulations of the Forestry Department, a policy

of sustained yield compels the private timber companies
to observe the practice of selective cutting, and it
means that trees of sixty centimeters in diameter can
only be logged for commercial purposes. However, in the
agreements with the timber companies this figure is reduced to fifty centimeters, and in actual practice, even
smaller sizes are logged. The failure to enforce the
selective cutting regulation has served to undermine the
Department's sustained yield period of thirty-five years.
Overcutting by area is so extensive that at current
rates of logging, forest concessions can be logged in
much less than thirty-five years, and this time can be
reduced to a five or ten year period in the case of hydrological reserves and natural reserves. Striking
evidence of these contraventions of official policy can
be found in Lampung province in south Sumatra, where in
some areas, nothing is left of designated production
forest.

Since the effective implementation of a sustained
yield policy is greatly hindered by a lack of site
specific information on density and composition of timber stands, as a second best strategy, regional authorities frequently rely upon logging companies for information on the production capacity of their concessions.
This practice may lead to over-estimates of actual yield
capacity and, in turn, to overlogging and a reduction in
the sustained yield period. Manning cites evidence
where the level of intensive logging has reduced the
productive life cycle of a concession to a five year
period.[8]

While a policy of sustained yield seems to be enduring more in theory than in practice, some regeneration
of logged-over forests is planned through the introduction of plantation trees. While a policy of reforestation might appear to compensate for some of the laxity
in not observing the principle of sustained yield, in
actual fact, little planting efforts have been underway
during the recent past, and it is likely that even with a
possible increase in replacement through plantation
trees, many over-logged areas will never be returned to
a level of high productivity. Furthermore, a number of
serious questions can be raised concerning the government's belief that logged-over natural forests can be
easily replaced by plantation trees. For the most part,
it is planned that these forests will be converted to
plantations and planted with some kind of fast-growing
pine species. Nevertheless, replacing natural dipterocarp forests with artificial monoculture plantations
adds tremendously to the further erosion of Indonesia's
plant genetic resources. Because of their apparent
utility for paper and pulp, pine trees are given preference to the use of native broadleaf species in reforestation projects, a condition which ignores the more

diversified needs of the local timber market. This
problem can be quite visibly discerned in the area of
South Sulawesi, where an excessive emphasis upon the
growing of pines in reforestation projects has served to
reduce the supply of all purpose utility timbers for the
local market. Because of their very poor structure, pine
trees do not fulfil local needs for housing construction.
For construction timber, illegal tree fellings are rampant in the remaining natural forest above the pine
forests. In addition, undergrowth on the pine plantation is almost non-existent and as a consequence, their
value as water catchments is very low.

The displacement of the natural forests through
monoculture plantations is not unique to Indonesia. In
Brazil and other Latin American countries, the wide array
of tree resources of the natural forests have been narrowed down by foresters with monocultures of pine and
eucalyptus. In the Indonesian context, the root of the
problem is the great lack of botanical dendrological expertise among tropical foresters. Most Indonesian institutions are ill-equipped to collect data on tree
flora and increased exploitation of the forests has
caused an even greater decrease in the botanical exploration of forests and trees.

III

While a number of policy and institutional factors
will continue to circumscribe the prospect for undertaking effective action in the management of Indonesia's
forests, these constraints need not eliminate the imperative for assessing opportunities and priorities in the
conservation of these natural resources. For example,
although densely populated, on Java there is still a lot
of waste land available for forestry development.
Agathis, Rasamala, Puspa, and a score of other trees
could be more extensively planted in these areas. Existing coniferous plantations in East and Central Java
(16,000 hectares) could produce considerable amounts of
wood for pulp and paper production. Finally, the great
demand for firewood and for wood as building material
can be satisfied when more wood processing plants are
built in Java instead of in the thinly populated outer
provinces.

While some advances in the proper management of
forestry resources can be made in Java, these increments
are quite marginal when compared to the abundant opportunities for forestry and land development in the vast
and sparsely settled areas of the outer islands. Given
the increasing pace of forestry exploitation in these
islands and the projected development of large transmigration schemes in Sumatra and Kalimantan, it becomes all

the more urgent that immediate steps be taken in the design of land-use plans which provide for the adequate
protection of Indonesia's forestry resources. These
actions should also assure that the forest industry is
effectively integrated and sustained in the larger economies of the new settlement areas. The full magnitude
of this planning and management task becomes all the
more formidable when seen in the context of Indonesia's
population growth over the next several decades. Thus,
by year 2000, the archipelago's population will be approaching a figure of around 250 million inhabitants. If
it is assumed that the output of unmilled rice will rise
from 2.2 tons per hectare to 3.5 tons per hectare, then
in order to reach a reasonable nutrition standard by
year 2000, vast new areas will have to be brought into
agricultural use outside Java.

The range of alternatives with respect to the expansion of agricultural production in areas where new
settlements will be introduced can be quite varied, and
will obviously need to be tailored in accordance with
the specific ecological conditions prevailing at the
identified sites. In this context, where major emphasis
will need to be placed upon forestry development and
conservation, much can be learned from Java as an example
of a durable and environmentally sound agro-ecosystem.
Only when such a model can be adapted to the outer islands will it be possible for the larger islands of Sumatra, Kalimantan and Sulawesi to feed a large number of
people and at the same time provide room for nature reserves, wildlife areas, and a permanent forest estate
with a sustained yield harvest. This will entail the
adoption of a mixed agricultural regimen of irrigated
rice fields surrounded by homestead gardens and smallholder tree crops for local use and for export. This
type of cropping pattern will be applicable along the
delta of the great Mahakam River in Kalimantan and along
rivers in Sumatra. It will need to be modified in the
different environments among peat lands and poor sandy
soils along the south coasts of Kalimantan. Nevertheless, given enough hydrological and soil surveys, the best
localities can be found in the undeveloped or partly
developed river basin areas where great potential exists
for the creation of stabilized agriculture with irrigated
rice fields surrounded by permanent forest estates and
agricultural tree crops. Extensive preparation and planning will need to be undertaken in the proper management
and development of these settlement schemes.

While new and long-range planning is needed in
making way for the rapid expansion of agricultural production and the establishment of new settlement schemes
in the outer islands, the problem of assuring that these
developments do not seriously encroach upon areas reserved for forestry production and protection is a

formidable task, and nothing less than a major investment will be required in building an institutional network to undertake the necessary research and training
functions. Manpower training and modern forestry research in the Malaya peninsula, Sarawak, and Sabah, during
the last thirty years, has built such an infrastructure,
but in Indonesia such a base hardly exists at this time.

The first and most compelling need is the upgrading
and expansion in the number of personnel within the
forestry service. The establishment of regional research
and training centers, with each institute specializing
in its own localized surroundings will be needed to
undertake this task. Studies on better timber utilization and research on forest regeneration are seriously
hindered by lack of good field training and the absence
of local research centers outside Java. These centers
will need to undertake basic work in forestry management,
dendrological studies, silviculture and nature conservation practices. In order to adequately perform these
educational roles, the institutes will need to engage in
a wide range of research and data gathering tasks. In
particular, major emphasis will need to be placed upon:
(1) ecological studies of tree species useful for affor-
estation, (2) forest bio-metric studies, (3) the use of
aerial photographs in forest mapping, volume determination and land capability studies, and (4) forest hydrological water and soil conservation studies in relation
to rural development projects.

Even under the best of conditions where the necessary commitment and funds would be immediately forthcoming from public sector sources, it will take another
decade or more before sufficient manpower and knowledge
is available to adequately manage Indonesia's forestry
sector. In the meantime, however, government initiatives
must be taken in a number of areas where further undue
delays could bring about irreparable harm in the depletion of existing forestry resources. Most pressing is
the need to consolidate the existing national parks and
nature reserves in order to prevent the complete disap-
pearance of unique types of lowland forests with their
special eco-systems and intricate plant and animal life.
Areas accessible to centers of population and communication, water catchment areas, and locations with great
ecological variation should be given priority as protected zones. In this regard, specific and immediate
conservation measures are needed for the Leuser area
(North Sumatra), the Barisan Range (West Sumatra), the
Kutei nature reserve (East Kalimantan), the Meratus
mountains (Southeast Kalimantan) and Mere Betiri (East
Java). Along with the identification and protection of
reserve areas, a concommitant effort is needed in undertaking a basic resource inventory of areas assigned for
commercial logging. Intensive training and research is

needed in all of the major concession areas for Indonesian foresters in matters relating to the regeneration of these forests prior to and after logging. Forest regeneration is the major factor in effectuating a policy of sustained yield in the concession areas. Nevertheless, there is little experience in this field in Indonesia, particularly in areas outside Java. The current agreements with the commercial logging firms are based on the Indonesian selective system whereby a lower girth limit of 50 centimeters in diameter is imposed in the cutting area. Major studies in growth and yield rates are needed to assess whether differences in geological conditions and forest types should entail some variation in recommended cutting and regenerative practices. Current survey samplings on potential timber yields are of low intensity, and for some places, not more than mere occular estimates. Thus, it is reported by government sources that dipterocarp forests in Kalimantan contain between 45-60 cubic meters per hectare, although the average output in this area is currently 80 cubic meters. It is likely that most other areas have lower volumes of commercial trees, but more accurate estimates in yield potential will need to be compiled through high intensity surveys.[9]

The current lack of manpower and of expertise in forestry management within the public sector means that the government must shift the burden of assuring adequate forestry regeneration directly upon the concessionaires themselves. Such an effort will compel the timber companies to develop long-term plans for the harvesting and regeneration of their concession areas. Sample plots will need to be set aside to monitor growth and distribution of species before and after logging. The adequacy of these plans will depend upon assuring the accuracy of the identified trees, the statistical reliability of the sample plot, and the proper use of aerial photographs. Once this preliminary survey is completed, a basic work-plan can be formulated and the concessions can then be appropriately sub-divided into permanent long-term harvest areas, short-term harvest areas suitable for plantations, shifting and permanent cultivation areas to be developed for agricultural and timber tree crops, and finally, virgin jungle reserves, and areas for water catchment and arboretum.

The problems of forestry development in Indonesia have many dimensions. The economic engine of timber production is fed by the growing demand of the developing countries with high living standards for industrial woods. Indonesia, with one of the lowest average annual per capita incomes of any country in the world can supply these raw materials at relatively low cost. Nevertheless, if present trends continue, within five to ten years timber logging will be pushed further inland and

there will be little room left in Indonesia for permanent
productive forestry. The archipelago still has the
largest forest stand in Asia, and it would be a major
calamity if these resources would be squandered within
the crucial period that the earth will have to transfer
from non-renewable to renewable natural resources.

NOTES

1. United Nations, FAO Yearbook of Forest Products, 1974
(Rome: Food and Agricultural Organization, 1975), pp. 3-16.

2. Inspectorate General Forestry, Konsep Master Plan Kehutan
(Bogor: Planning Division, 1970).

3. Dipterocarps are a family of timber trees dominant in moist
lowland forests of Sri Lanka, Vietnam, Thailand, Indonesia, Malaysia,
and the Philippines.

4. See Willem Meijer, Indonesian Forests and Land Use Planning
(Lexington: University of Kentucky Bookstore, 1975); J. E. D. Fox,
"Natural Regeneration of the Dipterocarp Forests" (Ph.D. thesis,
University of Wales, 1972); and J. E. D. Fox, "Constraints on the
Natural Regeneration of Tropical Moist Forest," Forest Ecology and
Management 1, (1976): 37-65.

5. See Robin Hanbury-Tenison, A Pattern of Peoples: A Journey
among Tribes of Indonesia's Outer Islands (New York: Scribner, 1975).

6. Meijer, Indonesian Forests and Land Use Planning, pp. 33-88.

7. See J. T. Williams, C. H. Lamoureux, and N. Wulijarni-
Soetjito, eds., South East Asia Plant Genetic Resources (Bogor:
Symposium at Bogor, March 20-22, 1975).

8. Chris Manning, "The Timber Boom with Special Reference to
East to East Kalimantan," Bulletin of Indonesian Economic Studies 8,
no. 3, (November 1971): 41.

9. Gatot Subagio, "Production Forest," in Kuswata Kartawinata
and Rubini Atmawidjaja, Coordinated Study of Lowland Forests of Indonesia (Bogor: Biotrop, 1977), pp. 55-65.

Index

DATE DUE

6.15 '82

19 '86